The Soul at Work:

Listen ✦✦
Respond ✦✦
Let Go

Embracing
Complexity Science
for Business Success

Roger Lewin
and
Birute Regine

Simon & Schuster

SIMON & SCHUSTER
Rockefeller Center
1230 Avenue of the Americas
New York, NY 10020
Copyright © 2000 by Roger Lewin and Birute Regine
All rights reserved, including the right of reproduction
in whole or in part in any form.
SIMON & SCHUSTER and colophon are registered trademarks
of Simon & Schuster, Inc.

Designed by DEIRDRE C. AMTHOR

Manufactured in the United States of America

10 9 8 7 6 5 4 3 2 1

Library of Congress Cataloging-in-Publication Data
Lewin, Roger.
    The soul at work : listen, respond, let go / Roger Lewin
and Birute Regine.
        p. cm.
    "Using complexity science for business success."
    1. Organizational behavior—Case studies. 2. Success in
business—Case studies. I. Regine, Birute. II. Title.
HD58.7.L477 2000
658—dc21   99-16253
                                                  CIP

ISBN 0-684-84384-6

Acknowledgments

We'd like to thank all the people we had the privilege of meeting and talking to while we researched this book. We are especially grateful to the people in the organizations we worked with: we deeply appreciate their openness with us and, given their busy schedules, their generosity in spending time with us. Although many of the people we spoke to have not been mentioned by name, their thoughts are present in the narratives we wrote, and they certainly helped shape the final work.

There have been many who influenced our thinking as we developed a new model of the workplace, but we would like to especially acknowledge the work done on understanding relationships at the Harvard Project on Development of Girls and Psychology of Women and at the Stone Center at Wellesley College.

We'd like to acknowledge Barbara Rifkind for her insight and wise advice for improving the book; Sheryl Erickson for her support in this work; and Linda Rusch and Linda Brimm for taking time to read the manuscript and offering helpful suggestions. We were fortunate to enjoy stimulating discussions with Cindy and Bill Adams. And we benefitted from encouragement and support from Ernst & Young's Center for Business Innovation, and particularly its director, Chris Meyer. Stuart Kauffman nurtured the notion that there was a book to be written on complexity science and business, even though, like us, he did not know what direction it might take. Special thanks are due to Curt Lindberg, who has been both an inspiration and friend on this ongoing journey of understanding complexity in human terms.

We feel fortunate to have the guidance and support of our editor, Fred Hills. And we are grateful to Sharon Friedman for initially taking on this project, and for the ongoing encouragement of our agent Ralph Vicinanza.

Finally, we are most fortunate to have family and friends who cheered us on along the way.

for our mothers, who worked hard,
which allowed us to do this work
and for our children and the next generation,
who are finding their work

Contents

I am because we are
—African aphorism

Chapter 1

Relationships: The New Bottom Line in Business

Man will occasionally stumble over the truth, but usually manages to pick himself up, walk over or around it, and carry on.

Winston Churchill

We took the daytime flight from Boston to London's Heathrow Airport and arrived about 9:00 P.M., which allowed for a quick taxi ride to one of our favorite Greek restaurants, Anemos, on Charlotte Street in London's Soho district. It was near closing time and only a few tables were occupied. Nevertheless, vibrant Greek music filled the room, which was all decked out in murals of images of Greece both ancient and modern. We had barely begun to eat when Kypros Pesekanos, the manager, emerged from the kitchen carrying a stack of dinner plates. It was time for a tradition that has been going on in Anemos for twenty-five years: Pesekanos began to toss the plates onto the small dance floor, white fragments scattering everywhere. Beaming, and bearing a paunch that proclaimed a lifelong dedication to being a trencherman, Pesekanos was quickly into the spirit of the thing. Crash! Crash! Crash!

The plate throwing at Anemos is a continuation of an old tradition from the homeland, which, Pesekanos explained to us, was a means of letting off steam at bars called Pouzouki (a bouzouki is an instrument like a lute). "You'd get away from the demands of work and family life for a while, drink ouzo, throw some plates to get rid of frustrations and annoyances. And then you're ready to dance—in the rubble," Pesekanos explained.

Urged on by Pesekanos, we joined a group of half a dozen people in vigorous plate tossing, and danced amidst the mosaic of white shards. For us it was a wonderful way of throwing off the crimps of our transatlantic flight.

Afterward, we joined our fellow revelers around a big table and we began to talk. They were from Denmark, and in the textile business. They were traveling through Europe, checking on sources of fabrics they were using for their designs. "Business has changed for us," they told us. "How so?" we inquired. "Now what's most important is paying attention to the people you do business with," they explained. "Business is not just commerce anymore; it's about developing relationships. Honesty and connection is what we look for, in our employees and in our suppliers. You can see it in the eyes. What we're building is a community; this is our leverage for business success."

What our dancing companions were saying reverberated deeply with us. We had been talking to various businesses in the United States and in Britain, and we were hearing a similar phenomenon occurring among them. A shift is taking place in the world of business, where valuing people and relationships is not just a good or espoused idea, but a conscious management action that has a positive outcome on the economic bottom line. We were hearing that by genuinely caring about people in the workplace, the economic bottom line often benefits as well.

This encounter at Anemos was in the fall of 1997. We were about a year into our study, which involved talking with people in a dozen companies, of different sizes and different business sectors. Some we interviewed several times, for a longitudinal perspective; and often we did a cross section of interviews, from CEO to secretary. We were interested in companies that were following principles from the new science of complexity in running their business. All we had to begin with was an understanding that businesses are complex adaptive systems, and the principles that underlie such systems. Some of the companies we talked to were using complexity principles explicitly to guide how they operated; others reached this place intuitively. It didn't matter which was the case for our work. We found these organizations mostly by word of mouth.

We will delve into complexity science in more detail in later chapters, but suffice it to say here that the new science is the latest attempt to understand the structure and dynamics of complex systems in the natural world, including human social systems such as business organizations. Complexity science views such systems as being like living organisms, which adapt and evolve, rather than being like machines, which has been the traditional perspective. Companies whose management is guided by principles of complexity science are organizationally flat, have fewer levels of hierarchy, and promote open and plentiful communication and diversity. Complexity science argues that these properties enhance businesses' capacity for adaptability, thus giving them a cutting edge in these fast-changing times. The companies we chose for our study therefore shared the properties of being organizationally flat and having rich, open communication. But initially we had no idea what our study would find in the realm of organizational dynamics, of management style, and people's way of working.

What we began to hear about consistently was a new way of doing business—from Babel's family paint and decorating stores of thirty-five people, to St. Luke's advertising agency of a hundred, to Monsanto Company of 22,000. For these organizations, people had become the new bottom line, not simply for humanistic reasons, but as a way to promote adaptability and business success. In today's business environment of rapid change, a collective effort, a recognized need for others, becomes the means of survival and success.

Reflecting on the plate-throwing evening, we realized that this old tradition was a timely analogy for what we were hearing as being the current climate in these companies: breaking of old ways of doing things, seeking a new freedom, and trying to have fun while doing it. Pesekanos had told us that Anemos means "wind," which was apt, too, because a wind of change is blowing through the business world, bringing with it a new hope and a potential for a deep human resonance within organizations, which we all seek deep in our hearts. But it also brings anxiety, uncertainty, and fear, because it is predicated on far less control and far less predictability than is assumed in traditional management practice. Bending with these winds, business practice is becoming more like an improvisational dance on the broken plates of change.

A World in the Throes of Change

The business world is in the throes of revolutionary change, a time when business leaders are frantically preoccupied with change itself. Modern management theory borders on being obsessed with change of one sort or other—how to generate it, how to respond to it, how to avoid being overcome by it. The reason is not hard to find. Pick up any newspaper, magazine, or business book and there it is: chaos reigns. At the cusp of the twenty-first century, we are experiencing structural shifts in our economy brought about by the revolutions in computation and communication technologies. But, as Intel's Andy Grove indicates, change is not exactly a welcome guest in business: "With all the rhetoric about change, the fact is that we managers hate change, especially when it involves us."[1]

The change is not only real, but it is also accelerating, driven by rapid technological innovation, the globalization of business, and, not the least of it, the arrival of the Internet and the new domain of Internet commerce. A new kind of economy is emerging—call it the information economy, the connected economy, call it what you will. The world of business is transforming, a shift that rivals the onset of the Industrial Revolution in its impact on society and the way commerce is transacted. With this shift, managers are finding many of their background assumptions and time-honored business models inadequate to help them understand what is going on, let alone how to deal with it. Where managers once operated with a machine model of their world, which was predicated on linear thinking, control, and predictability, they now find themselves struggling with something more organic and nonlinear, where limited control and a restricted ability to predict are the order of the day. No wonder most managers and executive professionals are uneasy, and eagerly seek new ways of coping. One thing is certain in all this, however: you can't figure out what to do in the future by looking at how you did things in the past.

Business Theories, Business Theories, and More Business Theories

These turbulent times are reflected in the proliferation of new business books on change—there's seemingly hundreds of them. Managers have never been short of advice for new ways of working, of course. The history of the (currently) $17-billion-a-year management consulting business (in the United States alone) is a litany of new techniques that successively offer relief from the "old" and, by implication, wrongheaded management style. "Management theorists have a passion for permanent revolution that would have made Leon Trotsky or Mao Zedong green with envy,"[2] write John Micklethwait and Adrian Wooldridge in their book *The Witch Doctors,* the title being a none-too-subtle commentary on the authors' perceived validity of some of the theories. The list is long and includes management by objectives, management by walking around, total quality management, and the biggest of the more recent offerings, reengineering. There have been more than twenty such nostrums in the past few decades, and the pace of their birth and subsequent demise is picking up alarmingly, which, say Micklethwait and Wooldridge, smacks of a certain "faddishness."[3]

Managers are ambivalent about management theories: they want tools to help them manage, but have become skeptical that, as the pace of the birth of successive theories picks up in the way it has, they will barely have time to master the present one before it will be replaced by the next. Managers clearly display an admirable degree of open-mindedness in being willing to take on new ideas, but business fads can be crazy-making as well. Front-line workers, on the other hand, are less ambivalent, as the popularity of Scott Adams's *Dilbert* cartoon attests. An article in *The Economist* says of Adams that "whereas most business writers write for the one in ten people who are interested in management theory, he writes for the nine of ten who hate it."[4]

We will argue in this book that managers, consultants, entrepreneurs, executives, other business professionals, indeed, anyone who works, can take some comfort in the fact that they are not alone in riding a bucking bronco of change that demands a different understanding of the world. Science, too, is in the midst of an important intellectual shift, a true Kuhnian paradigm shift that parallels what is happening in business, or, more accurately, is the vanguard of that change.[5] Where once the natural world was viewed as linear and mechanistic, where simple cause-and-effect solutions were expected to explain the complex phenomena of nature, scientists now realize that much of their world is nonlinear and organic, characterized by uncertainty and unpredictability. As in science, managers are discovering that their world is not linear but rather predominantly nonlinear, not mechanistic but rather organic and complex. It's amazing how far we have been able to take the linear model for understanding the world, both in science and in business. But in the new economy, the limitations of the mechanistic model are becoming starkly apparent. A new way of thinking is required.

Enter Complexity Science

The realization that much of the world dances to nonlinear tunes has given birth to the new science of complexity, whose midwife was the power of modern computation, which for the first time allows complex processes to be studied. The science is still in its infancy, and is multifaceted, reflecting different avenues of study. The avenue most relevant to understanding organizational dynamics within companies and the web of economic activity among them is the study of complex adaptive systems. Simply defined, complex adaptive systems are composed of a diversity of agents that interact with each other, mutually affect each other, and in so doing generate novel behavior for the system as a whole, such as in evolution, ecosystems, and the human mind. But the pattern of behavior we see in these systems is not constant, because when a system's environment changes, so does the behavior of its agents, and, as a result, so does the behavior of the system as a whole. In other words, the system is constantly *adapting* to the conditions around it. Over time, the system *evolves* through ceaseless adaptation.

Complexity scientists are learning about these dynamics of complex systems principally through computer models, but also through observation of the natural world. "That's all fine and dandy for scientists and academicians," one executive commented when we made this point, "but what's it got to do with me and my problems?" The point is that business organizations are *also* complex adaptive systems. This means that what complexity scientists are learning about natural systems has the potential to illuminate the fundamental dynamics of business organizations, too. Companies in a fast-changing business environment need to be able to produce constant innovation, need to be constantly adapting, and be in a state of continual evolution, if they are to survive.

"Oh no, not another fad," one manager said. There is always that danger, of course. But if complexity scientists are right in arguing that if complex adaptive systems of all kinds—in the natural world and the world of business—share fundamental properties and processes, then the science offers something that most management theories do not. The argument here is that most management theories are not really theories at all, but merely techniques for managing in a certain way. Complexity science is still nascent as a theory but it has determined certain fundamental processes and characteristics of complex adaptive systems. In other words, when we speak of businesses as complex adaptive systems we are not speaking of a metaphor or a technique; rather, we are saying that by understanding the characteristics of complex adaptive systems in general, we can find a way to understand and work with the deep nature of organizations.

"Right," said one consultant. "So what do I know that's different about empowerment, participatory management, and learning organizations by understanding complex adaptive systems that I didn't know before?" This new science, we found in our work, leads to a new theory of business that places people and relationships—how people interact with each other, the kinds of relationships they form—into dramatic relief. In a linear world, things may exist independently of each other, and when they interact, they do so in simple, predictable ways. In a nonlinear, dynamic world, everything exists only in relationship to everything else, and the interactions among agents in the system lead to complex, unpredictable outcomes. In this world, interactions, or relationships, among its agents are the organizing principle.

Complexity science in the business realm therefore focuses on relationships: relationships between individuals and among teams; relationships to other companies in their business environment, or economic web; and, ultimately, relationship to the natural environment. And because the dynamics of complex adaptive systems are complex and largely unpredictable, accepting businesses as being such systems requires a different mind-set: managers and executives cannot *control* their organizations to the degree that the mechanistic perspective implies; but they can *influence* where their company is going, and how it evolves.

Complexity science is already finding its way into the business literature, as some managers and consultants embrace complexity and the uncertainty it entails. Articles with titles such as "Between Chaos and Order: What Complexity Theory Can Teach Business" and "From Process Management to Complexity Management" are already beginning to fill the pages of management journals. Conferences, such as Embracing Complexity: Exploring the Application of Complex Adaptive Systems to Business, the Big Five company Ernst & Young's foray into the new science, now in its third year, are drawing big audiences. And two prominent business journalists—Tom Petzinger of the *Wall Street Journal* and Simon Caulkin of Britain's *Observer* newspaper—declared in 1998 that complexity science had finally appeared on the radar screen of business. All this reflects the pervasive hunger among managers for help in managing in the new economy, and the hope that complexity science apparently offers. There is, however, a long way to go, and a lot yet to discover about complexity.

Walking into a Question Mark

In our study we wanted to discover people's working experience in companies that operate by the principles of complexity, and how they see themselves as part of a larger economic web; and through this to understand what is most important in how such businesses work, what helps and what hinders the emergence of creativity and adaptability, the path to successful change. And perhaps also to reach a new model for describing organizational dynamics.

We embarked on the venture with no agenda of what specifically we would find in terms of organizational dynamics. How could we? Neither of us is a manager or executive: one of us (Roger) is a science writer, whose experience with complexity theory is through writing a book on the topic, *Complexity: Life at the Edge of Chaos;* the other (Birute) is a developmental psychologist, whose work has been addressing the complexity of relational dynamics within human systems, such as couples and families. We are not being defensive when we say that we feel that our status as outsiders is a strength, because, having not been steeped in management theories, we had no preconceptions or assumptions as to how things should be. And, following the lines of complexity thinking, diverse perspectives are the source of potentially new and creative insights. As our agent, Sharon Friedman, said to us, "You walked into a big question mark." She was right.

The original working title for the book was *Complexonomics,* not a word we particularly liked much, but it reflected the context in which complexity science was being talked about at the time: in operational problems, such as scheduling; in strategy; and in organizational dynamics. Of the three, organizational dynamics was the least developed. As Ernst & Young's Chris Meyer said of this domain at the first Embracing Complexity conference in 1996, "We have only the vaguest sense of what we are trying to achieve with complexity organizationally."

In our book proposal, organizational dynamics merited just three paragraphs, saying something like "relationships could prove to be important in the overall context." We encountered more than a little resistance to even this minimal speculation, a signal, we believe, of the pervasive skepticism in business that relationships may be important, despite what Peter Drucker has been writing for half a century in terms of businesses as social communities. Even our beloved editor, Fred Hills, was initially distinctly dismissive of this facet of the proposal. (He has since become our greatest champion in this respect, we should add.)

As things turned out, relationships became the central theme of the book, led there by what we heard, not by where we wanted to go. We could have stayed with our original plan, and explored complexity science in the operational, strategic, and organizational dynamics realms of business in the companies we talked to. But we soon found that relationships were at the forefront of most people's concerns, and in their strategies for success. Seeing that organizational dynamics was the least developed realm of complexity science in business, and hearing people's desire for something new there, we were therefore ineluctably drawn into it, into the realm of relationships, to the exclusion of other issues.

We are not talking about relationships in terms of networking and the like. Rather we are talking about genuine relationships based on authenticity and care. We knew from complexity science that interactions among agents of a system are the source of novelty, creativity, and adaptability. And we therefore expected that companies guided by the science would in some manner attend to interactions among people in them. But this could have simply manifested itself in a concern for prolific communication. Open and prolific communication was indeed what we found in these companies, but universally it was in the context of genuine care. Those people we spoke to who had worked in companies other than their present ones told us that, in their experience, this is uncommon in the business world.

We can restate this in the language of complexity science as follows: In complex adaptive systems, agents interact, and when they have a mutual effect on one another something novel emerges. Anything that enhances these interactions will enhance the creativity and adaptability of the system. In human organizations this translates into agents as *people,* and interactions with mutual effect as being *relationships* that are grounded in a sense of mutuality: people share a mutual respect, and have a mutual influence and impact on each other. From this emerged genuine care. Care is not a thing but an action—to be care-full—to care about your work, to care for fellow workers, to care for the organization, to care about the community. We saw that genuine care enhanced the relationships in these companies, with CEOs engendering trust and loyalty in their people, and the people being more willing to contribute to the needs of the company. In the context of complexity science, care, which enhances relationships, in turn enhances companies' creativity and adaptability.

We can see, therefore, that management practice guided by complexity science leads us to a very human orientation, and this was a surprise, counterintuitive. Of course, there have been many human-centered approaches in management before, among the more notable being political scientist Mary Parker Follett's work done in the 1920s and 1930s in the United States, in which there has been a recent resurgence of interest. For more than half a century, there has been a constant battle between human-oriented management and scientific or mechanistic management, with the latter prevailing. But it is only now, and for the first time, that there is a science behind this way of thinking that gives a legitimacy to the whole realm of human-centered management. With complexity science, we have human-oriented management practice emerging from science, a novelty.

What About People?

We attended many conferences on complexity science in business, which typically focused on computer algorithms that made difficult operational problems tractable. Time after time, at the end of the day we would hear people say, "This all has great potential and it *will* be important in business, we know that. But what about me? What about people?"

Yes, what about people? "Business is about people" has been bandied around for some time, and yet rarely addressed with any human depth. Consequently, the feeling of not being valued is pervasive in the business world, and a few writers recognize the fact. "Too many people feel insecure, threatened, and unappreciated in their jobs,"[6] writes Tom Morris, a philosopher and business consultant. "Overall job satisfaction and corporate morale in most places may be at an all time low."[7] Peter Senge, director of the Center for Organizational Learning at MIT's Sloan School of Management and author of *The Fifth Discipline,* notes that the prevailing mechanistic model of business encourages managers to see people as machines, not as people. "We deeply resent being made machinelike, in order to fit into the machine," he says.[8] Henry Ford once said, "How come when I want a pair of hands, I get a human being as well?" A manager in today's knowledge-based economy might paraphrase this: "How come when I want a mind, I get a heart as well?"

And how come there commonly continues to exist a denial in the business mind, a stark omission of the importance of people and valuing them for not only the revenues they bring in, but simply as human beings? How come we refuse to see the obvious—that when people are treated as replaceable parts, as objects to control, are taught to be compliant, are used as fuel for the existing system—that inevitably you are going to have an organization that is fraught with frustration, anger, and isolation, which ultimately is detrimental to the business?

Some managers recognize the lack of humanity in their organizations, and are frustrated with the perceived impossibility of doing anything about it, anything *genuine* that is. Alan Briskin, author and business consultant, quotes a manager in a large conglomerate as follows: "We're so busy moving people around, trying to meet our deadlines, trying to influence people to believe in what we're doing, that we just don't want to really look into anybody's eyes and see they have souls. We should start with the premise that we have souls. But souls are difficult to manage. And even if we talked about people having souls, it would probably be from a corporate viewpoint."[9] The manager's last point is that making "soul" into some kind of company slogan would be worse than not recognizing the existence of workers' souls in the first place. But more to the point, trying to influence people to believe in what they are doing, without seeing who the person is, wanting them to be something for you rather than recognizing them for who they are, is an act of imposition, not engagement. To be blunt, it's dehumanizing. And people will resist when they're not included in the process and have things imposed on them.

Even Michael Hammer, one of the developers of reengineering, eventually came to realize that management is not just about organizational structures or process teams. In an interview in the *Wall Street Journal,* he admitted that in his enthusiasm to make companies more efficient and profitable he forgot about people. "I wasn't smart enough about that," he conceded. "I was reflecting my engineering background and was insufficiently appreciative of the human dimension. I've learned that's critical."[10] Trust is critical if organizations are to excel, as the European business consultant Charles Handy argues forcefully in his recent book *The Hungry Spirit.* And trust was one of the major casualties in the rush to downsize in the name of reengineering. More than 70 percent of U.S. companies are struggling with low morale and lack of trust, principally as a result of the trauma of downsizing, according to a 1997 Wharton School survey.[11] The same is true in Europe.

"In the living company, the essence of the underlying contract is mutual trust," says Arie de Geus, a former senior executive of Royal Dutch/Shell. "Before they will give more, people need to know that the community is interested in them as individuals."[12] An important reason why some companies fail, he says, is that "managers focus exclusively on producing goods and services and forget that the organization is a community of human beings that is in business—any business—to stay alive."[13] It is common sense that if people are treated as machines, not as people, they are unlikely to give loyalty and trust—they will not give of their best. And yet, unfortunately, to use Voltaire's phrase, "common sense is not so common."

Many companies that are anything but human-oriented in their management practices survive and even thrive, of course—for a time. "If you've drained the tank of human goodwill and motivation, you can continue to coast downhill for a while, even at a pretty rapid clip," observes Tom Morris, "but heaven help you if you encounter any big bumps in the road or the competition forces you into an uphill struggle."[14] Senge is even more emphatic about the matter. "As we enter the twenty-first century, it is timely, perhaps even critical, that we recall what human beings have understood for a very long time," he says: "that working together can indeed be a deep source of life meaning. Anything less is just a job."[15]

It *is* possible for people to be valued for themselves in the workplace, not just their function; for people's souls to be nurtured and allowed to emerge where they work. In short, it *is* possible for work to be more than just a job, that work can be fulfilling and a life-enhancing experience, with all its trials, tribulations, and thrills. This is precisely what we observed for the most part in the companies we talked to.

To the manager who says, "This all sounds soft and unbusinesslike," beware: these companies are all very successful in traditional bottom-line terms, not *despite* being human-oriented, but rather, as many of the CEOs we talked with argue, *because* of it. To the executive who says, "Okay, that sounds easy, I'll try it," beware: it's not easy; it's hard, perhaps the hardest of all management practices. And to the manager who says, "That sounds all well and good, but I can't afford to spend time on relationships," beware: you are not getting the best out of your company. In fact, it's more a question whether you can afford *not* to. It doesn't have to be either/or, a dichotomy between money and people. In fact, it can't be. Our world is too complex.

Structure of the Book

We present our work in three parts. In the first part, "The World of Complexity Science," we introduce the ideas from the new science in the context of complex adaptive systems, specifically as they relate to the world of business. We give a little history of management theory, principally to show why something new is needed in the new economy, and to see why complexity science might be that something new, which can expand rather than simply replace existing business models.

In the second part, "The World of Complexity Experience," we present stories of organizations that we talked to, to be read with the principles of complexity in mind. Although each story is qualitatively different, each exhibits a common way of working, that is, striving toward greater adaptability by attending to their organizations as complex adaptive systems.

These stories are not case studies in the traditional sense, but rather they are narratives of people's experiences within these organizations. We chose this form because narratives can contain the complexity of people's experience, can provide a vehicle for readers to connect with their passion, to their struggles, to the kinds of challenges that you, too, may struggle with and identify with. We are not trying to establish formal and empirical proof; rather we seek resonance and verisimilitude as the source of validation, rather than validity. As New York University's Jerome Bruner, a psychologist, states when discussing two modes of thought, and two distinct ways of ordering experience and constructing reality: "Arguments convince one of the truth, stories of their lifelikeness."[16] He also states that "narratives deal with the vicissitudes of life."[17] This is clearly evident in the organizations' stories that we tell.

You will see that these stories are uniquely their own, reflecting the character of each organization—from stories written totally in people's own voices, to others as journeys we tell. The form of each story emerged from our interaction with the organization. We hope that as you see these other work lives, at least some of you will be validated in your beliefs and say, "I'm not crazy; that's what I want, that's what I think is right, too." And as these stories interact collectively in your mind, perhaps you will begin to see patterns emerge from them.

Part Three, "The World of Relationships," pulls together the organizations' stories and discusses common patterns of behavior we found among them. These patterns of behavior lend themselves as a guide for how CEOs, managers, executive professionals, teams, and front-line people can begin to embrace complexity in their workplace—that is, working in a constructive way with the processes of complex adaptive systems.

This is not a linear and simplistic "seven steps to success," how-to section, however. Embracing complexity in business is more about a practice, a different way of *being,* that influences a different way of *doing.* It is based in the day-to-day *practices* of the workplace. We call them practices because they are behaviors to strive toward. The word "practices" recognizes that as humans we will often fall back into old ways of being and doing, but, once recognized, you can begin again. What's important is not the falling, but rather the getting up. In this sense, we offer it more as a guidebook than a step-by-step manual.

Our conclusion, "Care-nections and the Soul at Work," points to future horizons and challenges for a different way of working.

The Soul at Work

The title of the book, *The Soul at Work,* derives from an interview with Patrick Burns at the Industrial Society, a management consulting company in London, one of the stories we present in this book. He was telling us about a three-day company retreat, a very emotional event, where the entire workforce had collectively come to see their purpose, of which they had lost sight. "Although we think we know all about management and that we ourselves have all been doing it, that we're experts, we're actually not," he said. "We're only just rediscovering the world of the soul at work." When we heard the phrase, we immediately recognized that, in fact, we were in the privileged position of being witness to many souls at work in the organizations we talked to. It seemed fitting for the title to emerge this way.

What *is* the soul at work? In complex adaptive systems, how we interact and the kinds of relationships we form has everything to do with what kind of culture emerges, has everything to do with the emergence of creativity, productivity, and innovation. When more interactions are care-full rather than care-less in an organization, a community of care and connection develops, creating a space for the soul at work to emerge.

"The soul at work" is a double entendre: it is at once the individual's soul being allowed to be present in the workplace; and it is the emergence of a collective soul of the organization.

We witnessed the individual soul at work—where many people, once disheartened at work, evolved to being engaged in meaningful work. When the individual soul is engaged, people naturally want to add value, are willing to go the distance and devote time to endeavors they feel, regardless of how small, are worthwhile. Many people feel lost in their organizations, feel *apart from* them rather than *a part of* them. Many see themselves in a system in which they have little or no influence. Too often we heard front-line people, when reflecting on former places of work, say, "Nobody ever asked me what I thought, and it was hardly a possibility that they would act on it if they did." The business mind that becomes myopic, singularly valuing the financial bottom line and techniques to boost it, ultimately dehumanizes the organization, and, self-protectively, people disconnect from their soul so as not to be exploited. People suffer and their organizations suffer.

Actually, most people want to be part of their organization; they want to know the organization's purpose; they want to make a difference. When the individual soul is connected to the organization, people become connected to something deeper—the desire to contribute to a larger purpose, to feel they are part of a greater whole, a web of connection. When this context develops, people begin to openly acknowledge the need for others, to see their interdependence, and their desire to belong—their tribal instinct awakens.

The soul at work is also a collective soul. We listened to the collective soul at work—the transformation of the protean spirit of the organization in all its shades and hues—from trauma, to hope, to infinite possibilities. The collective soul at work is a journey of aligning individual abilities and values with the collective, shared purpose, an unfolding identity that is constructed and reconstructed continually by the people who are part of the system. And it is this collective soul at work that is most capable of intelligent, humane action that benefits the whole.

How, then, to engage the soul at work? There are no simple solutions. But it begins with altering our perspective. It is to pay as much attention to how we treat people—co-workers, subordinates, customers—as we now typically pay attention to structures, strategies, and statistics. That is, attending to the interactions within the system creates the potential for more human connections and thus a more robust system, just as complexity science predicts.

To engage the soul is to see people as people, not as employees. It is to assume an intention of goodwill on their part, and that it is better to err in trusting too much than not enough. It is in recognizing a job well done, not just with money but also with a genuine appreciation. It is to remember that people are inventive. It is to believe in them, not just the numbers. This perspective affects the quality of the interactions in the system, creating positive rather than negative feedback loops; that is, creating trust and commitment, not suspicion and disconnection. It is these feedback loops that can transform the system.

To engage the soul at work is to focus not only on a plan of action but also to be alert to unfolding and unexpected directions and outcomes that are inherent in complex systems. As James Gleick, author of the book *Chaos: Making a New Science,* writes: "Put your faith in the process—not your estimate of the final outcome."[18]

To engage the soul at work is to realize that talking to people, listening to them, responding to them is not a waste of time. Rather, this is creating a context where people are more willing to change and to adapt, which in turn makes the organization more adaptable. This human-centered context allows people to further the aims of the organization while retaining their personal integrity and gaining greater personal fulfillment.

For the skeptics and the cynics: suspend your disbelief, soften your vision, and consider that you may be settling for less than you really want and can actually have. Consider that perhaps you don't ask for enough. There *is* a better way to live and work. It clearly is more desirable in human terms. And it is also an economic necessity in business terms. What it takes is an open mind and courage.

PART ONE

The World of
Complexity Science

Chapter 2

The Vernal Pool

The real act of discovery consists not in finding new lands, but in seeing with new eyes.

Marcel Proust

Michael Pollan lives in the Connecticut countryside, amid rolling hills and lush woodland, classic New England terrain. Six years ago he thought to enhance the bucolic nature of the view from his studio window by having a strategically placed pond excavated. "I thought that a tranquil view of water would have a calming effect on my workday," he explains. So exuberant and delighted was Pollan when the project was complete that he wrote an effusive article about his creation in the *New York Times*. "I gushed, stupidly, about its wonders, how it had so miraculously filled, first with water, then with life," he recalls in a second article in the *Times,* published early in 1998;[1] "a few months' time had transformed a gaping wound in the earth into a thriving habitat giddy with life." Then, with a level of hubris he would soon come to regret, Pollan claimed that his pond was "proof that humans like me can actually improve on nature—can change the land in ways that increase not only the beauty but also the sheer quantity and diversity of life in a place."

Within a few days of the first article's publication, the water level in Pollan's pond began to drop. And drop. And drop. Until, by August, it was no more. The frogs had to "pack up and leave, a file of startled refugees making their way across the road to the neighbor's pond." Then, just as surprisingly and dramatically as it had emptied, the pond began to fill again in the fall, beginning a cycle that has repeated itself every year since then. "As reliably as it empties in summer, the pond steadily and mysteriously fills every autumn, rain or shine," says the bewildered Pollan. Instead of the aquatic idyll of his dreams, Pollan felt he had created a failed pond.

What to do? Pollan roamed New England for seminars on problem ponds, but gained nothing but sympathy for his plight. No concrete advice. He invited pond experts—excavators, engineers, hydrologists—to inspect the failed pond and offer insight. Their collective wisdom "would fit into a small paragraph," Pollan laments. "It is easier to imagine the weather on Venus than to conceptualize the behavior of ground water just a few feet beneath the crust we walk on every day." Some solutions to the problem pond were proffered, however, including spreading bags of powdered clay along the banks, or sealing it with the kind of clay used to line toxic waste dumps. Every potential remedy was not only expensive, but also not at all guaranteed to work. Even filling the pond with water from his well, or filling it in with earth, thus giving up on a failed venture, would cost thousands of dollars.

Finally, Pollan telephoned yet another local contractor, Pat Hackett, who, says Pollan, "displayed an understanding of my leaky pond that was uncanny, when you consider that he has never laid eyes on it." Pollan simply explained the pond's location, and that was sufficient for the sagacious contractor to understand what the failed pond's problem was, and what to do about it: nothing. "You're on a slope of glacial till there," Hackett began to explain. "There's a tremendous amount of ground water coming down the hillside, heading toward the Housatonic [River], and my guess is that it's riding above a ledge of rock. That's what's filling your pond. It's also what's emptying it after the snow melt, because glacial till won't hold water moving like that." Nothing would make the pond a permanent feature, water-level-wise, no matter how strong a lining was installed, because of the great hydrostatic pressure of the flow of water through the earth, Hackett explained. Pollan's pond wasn't so much a pond, after all, more a "window on a seasonal underground river," as Pollan puts it. There's a name for an ephemeral pond such as this, Hackett told the disconsolate Pollan; it's a vernal pool. "Interesting habitat," observed Hackett. "You might want to look at it that way."

Because vernal pools hold water for just part of the year (usually in the spring, hence the name) and are dry for the rest of the time, fish cannot become established. This is good news for frogs, because tadpoles can thrive without the danger of becoming some fish's supper. At a time in history when frog populations are in danger, a vernal pool is a force for ecological good. And because the pool fluctuates between being full and being empty, the ecosystem is more diverse than if it were permanently wet. After spending some time reading about vernal pools, about their interesting and important role in the ecosystem, Pollan came to see his creation not as a failed pond, as he had previously, but for what it really is, a vernal pool. "That made all the difference," he says. Pollan had come to see his world through new eyes, and was content.

Management Lessons from Nature

What are the lessons of this story? Several, in the context of complexity science in biological systems and its relevance to business systems. First, Pollan's plan had been to create a pond by digging a hole on his land. He got something that was *like* a pond, but it was actually something more complex than that—a vernal pool. In other words, it is often difficult to create something even as simple as a pond in a controlled way in a complex ecosystem, and you should expect some surprises.

Complexity science—and hard experience—teaches us that the same is true of planning in business: because businesses are complex adaptive systems, nested in large complex adaptive systems (the economy), you should always expect surprises, no matter how carefully you plan, or how simple the goal. Indeed, you should not even *attempt* to plan too precisely, because inevitably a linear approach will fail in some respect or other as the business environment constantly changes. Colin Crook, a former senior executive with Citicorp, recognizes the limitations of rigid planning in the new, complexity-driven economy in an article in *American Programmer:* "We must abandon the formal, static, linear planning process," he writes. "In the new nonlinear world, no predictions remain valid for too long."[2]

The second lesson has to do with the assembly of the species to form an ecological community. In his first article, Pollan had written rapturously about the diversity of species that came together to form the pond's community: animals, plants, and insects vibrantly interacting in a rich network that formed a complete, cohesive ecosystem. Pollan could not have planned which species would become actors in the pond's community; nobody could. All he could do—all he had to do—was to create the conditions in which the assembly of a new ecological community was possible: namely, dig a hole in the ground in a suitable location.

Again, the same is true in business. It is the manager's job to create the conditions that will nurture creativity, not to try too assiduously to direct that creativity, otherwise you are more likely to stifle rather than enhance it. This is the point that the strategy consultant Gary Hamel made in an article in early 1998. "Once we start thinking of strategy as an emergent phenomenon, you realize that we have often attacked the wrong end of the problem. Strategists and senior executives have too often worked on 'the strategy,' rather than on the preconditions that could give rise to strategy innovation. . . . Order *without* careful crafting—I'd like to suggest that this is the goal of strategizing."[3]

Third, Pollan initially looked on his pond as a failure, something that he had to fix. But when he was able to see with new eyes, and accept the pond for what it was, a vernal pool, he no longer felt he had a failure that required fixing, but something that had value in itself. In business, managers often view chaos, or things not going as predicted, as undesirable, a signal that the organization is out of control and needs to be fixed. When managers accept that periods of chaos are natural—even desirable—in business, then they will come to see chaos with different eyes. Specifically, periods of chaos can be embraced as a portal to change, which may be enhanced through respectful and limited influence, not as an aberration that needs to be avoided. We can embrace chaos as a process of creative destruction, a time for fundamental change, to reorganize, to rearrange. "The challenge lies in our ability to make sense of the rapidly changing context in which we are doing business," comments John Seely Brown, director of Xerox Corporation's Palo Alto Research Center. "We need to find new ways of doing things. . . . To do things differently, we must learn to see things differently . . . it is a matter of survival in the new world of business."[4]

Finally, through these unfolding metaphors between biology and the world of business, the story of the vernal pool gives us a deep connection with nature, and that has value in itself. Each of us is born with a profound, innate affinity for nature, which the Harvard biologist Edward O. Wilson calls biophilia. Nurtured in some while quelled in others, biophilia nevertheless lurks deep within each of us. And the business world of the future will need to pay more attention to our connection with nature, if future economies are to be sustainable.

We know that in nature, species in an ecological community interact within a rich network of connections, forming the local ecosystem which has system-level properties. Similarly, companies operate within a rich network of interactions, forming the local economy on a local scale and the global economy on a global scale. Businesses are not only just *like* natural ecosystems, but also share some fundamental properties, specifically nonlinear processes, because both are complex adaptive systems. In other words, economies are not just *like* biological systems; they follow the same deep laws. These laws will not play out in *exactly* the same way in economies as they do in biology, largely because in economies conscious decisions are made by people, whereas in biology there is no intent in the same way. But if we can improve our understanding of these laws in nature, we will gain valuable insights into the workings of companies and the economy of which they are a part.

A Revolution in the World of Science

The machine model of business was founded on Newtonian mechanics—simple-to-understand, action-and-reaction systems, easy to control, predictable—which the American engineer Frederick Winslow Taylor established in his book *The Principles of Scientific Management,* published in 1911. Influenced by the prevailing science of the time, particularly in physics, Taylor's *Principles* revolutionized American industry, and became the bedrock of rules of mechanistic management. Within a few years of the publication of Taylor's book, however, physicists' view of the universe changed dramatically with the development of Einstein's theory of relativity and the rise of quantum mechanics. As a result, uncertainty replaced predictability as the quintessence of the universe. These were—and remain for most mortals—fairly arcane byways of science, however, and were certainly not sufficiently pertinent for managers to throw up their hands and change the way they did things, rejecting certainty and embracing uncertainty. In any case, leaders and managers could take comfort in the fact that most of science remained mechanistic in a way, that is, through seeking to understand nature by taking systems apart, studying the component parts, and concluding how the system works as a whole.

Reductionism, as this approach is known, has been very powerful. Most of what we know about our world and the universe is the fruit of this reductionistic endeavor. The level of detail with which we can describe the human body, for instance, in terms of its molecular and cell biology borders on the incredible. And within a few years, very early in the twenty-first century, the entire genetic code of *Homo sapiens*—written as single "letters," three billion of them strung in a string—will have been deciphered. But biologists are barely closer than they were three decades ago to understanding how the single fertilized egg, which we all begin as, becomes a mature human being. This process of embryological development, as it is known, is still a deep mystery. The reason is that it is not a simple, mechanistic process; it is highly complex, and involves rich networks of interactions, from which the human form emerges, from which all biological form emerges.[5]

Complex, Not Complicated

The rationale of reductionism is that even very complex systems are comprehensible, given sufficient information about their components, and that the description will be very complicated. In the terms of mathematics, such a description would require many lines of equations. But let's make it more concrete. At the United Airlines terminal in Boston, there's a machine that engages the rapt attention of children of all ages. It's a machine of levers, springs, pulleys, and so on, around which balls travel, going through hoops, bouncing off beams, running down chutes—an endless cycle of the unexpected. Except, of course, it is much the same every time. In the United States, such a contraption is known as a Rube Goldberg machine, and in the United Kingdom as a Heath Robinson contraption. These machines are complicated, just as a watch is complicated, and as an internal combustion engine is complicated, and would require lengthy, detailed description if you were to explain them verbally or draw up a blueprint. But they are not complex, at least not in the way that embryological development is complex and in the way that scientists are coming to recognize that most of our world is complex.

As we've said, most of what we know about our world has been gleaned through reductionism, or linear thinking. The orbiting of the planets and shots in a game of pool are systems that can be understood by linear analysis. But in recent decades, science has come to appreciate that linear systems represent only a small fraction of the world. Ecosystems—from life in a pond to the entire biosphere—are not simple, linear systems, but instead are complex, nonlinear, and highly interactive in the way they operate. The same is true of human social systems. And of companies and economies.

Most of the systems in the world, then, are nonlinear and complex, not in the sense of complicated, but in the sense that the interactions of the components in the system generate something that is more than the sum of the parts, or qualitatively different from the sum of the parts; and that something is constantly changing. This process is known as *emergence*. In nature, for instance, an ant colony is a complex adaptive system. Individual ants interact in a few simple ways, following simple rules of behavior—such as "danger, come quickly," "food, follow me," and "I am a nest mate, not an alien"[6]—and from this emerges a complex nest architecture, a complex social dynamic, and even properties such as temperature and humidity control of the colony. None of these emergent features can be predicted by knowing how the individual ants interact. In ecosystems, what emerges from the interaction of its component species are properties of the system that make it behave like a superorganism, resisting invasion by alien species, for instance. We'll give an example of this in a later chapter, and show how the same is true in the context of the business world. The human brain is also a complex adaptive system, in which simple neurons interact in exceedingly simple ways, and yet from this emerges highly complex properties, such as creativity and consciousness. In human social systems, an important emergent property is civilization, with its religious and political institutions.

More than anything else, emergence captures the quintessence of complex adaptive systems. John Holland, a complexity science pioneer at the University of Michigan, describes emergence as "much coming from little," which gives the phenomenon an aura of mystery and paradox. Indeed, in the early decades of this century, some biologists described many complex aspects of nature as being emergent, that is, as arising from processes that were not well understood. When the age of reductionism dawned, the word "emergence" was shunned as being a sign of fuzzy thinking, as having a mystical, unscientific air to it, as being an appeal to forces almost supernatural. Since the birth of complexity science, however, emergence has been resurrected as a genuine phenomenon, not something mystical but a central property of complex adaptive systems that can and will have deep scientific explanation in terms of the processes that underlie it.[7]

Most complex systems in the world not only display emergence, but also learn from their experience of their worlds, and so, as we said earlier, are known as complex *adaptive* systems, because in a creative way they respond to their environment, adapt, and often become more complex in the process, as they continue to evolve.

It's worth making a point here about language and the way it reflects our deep assumptions about the world, which we heard from Alan Beyerchen, a historian at Ohio State University.[8] We use words to describe how we perceive much of the world is, and then add a negative prefix to describe exceptions. Real and unreal, for example, natural and unnatural. But most of the words we use to describe the dynamics of the world are in fact the exceptions, not the rule: namely, "linear," "stable," and "equilibrium." In fact, 95 percent of the world is nonlinear, unstable, and far from equilibrium. To describe 95 percent of the world as "not" something is contrary in the extreme. It reflects a lot about our psyche, and the way we have assumed things to be, not as they really are.

Complex Adaptive Systems Operate by a Few Simple Rules

Nonlinear behavior is therefore a characteristic of complex adaptive systems, and, as the great proportion of modern mathematics is based on linear analysis, it is inadequate to analyze such systems. In fact, as yet there is very little established mathematics that is appropriate. As a result, complexity scientists have for the most part relied on computer simulations of complex adaptive systems—in effect, algorithms that interact and evolve in the machine—to study the properties of such systems. There was long the belief in science that complex order in the world was generated by complex processes. Contrary to this belief, however, complexity scientists have discovered that complex systems are usually generated from a few simple rules for the behavior of the individual components in the system, as described above.

There's a classic and oft-cited example in the complexity literature, but it is no less evocative for being repeated yet again here. No one who has watched flocks of birds swirl through the sky can fail to be impressed by the precise coordination of the flock *as a whole,* as hundreds of birds swoop and turn in unison. The feat of coordinating the motion of hundreds of individuals in so precarious an environment seems complex and daunting, and looks as if someone (chief bird) must be imposing central control. In fact, in one of the earliest models developed by complexity theorists, Craig Reynolds discovered that the complex behavior of the flock emerges from a few simple rules of individual behavior. Wryly, he called his computer simulation "boids."

In Reynolds's model, each boid obeys just three rules: 1) fly in the direction of other boids; 2) try to match the velocity of neighboring boids; 3) avoid bumping into things. The simulation begins with the boids placed randomly in space, but very quickly the individuals form themselves into a flock that behaves just like real birds, wheeling and turning together, and avoiding obstacles in their path. The point is that the complex behavior of the system as a whole—the coordinated motion of the flock—emerges from a few simple rules of interaction among individuals, not from a single leader. This has been called *distributed control*, in contrast with *central control*, which is what many CEOs usually try to achieve when they follow a mechanistic model of management.

Much of complexity theory therefore focuses on the nature of interactions among individual "agents" in a complex adaptive system, and monitors their effects. As important, however, is the system's response to external change, when interesting patterns are seen to emerge. For instance, systems in which interactions are numerous become turbulent when prodded by external change, because change in one part of the system cascades through many other parts, and back again. And again. In contrast, systems in which interactions are few hardly respond at all, because change in one part of the system can remain isolated from the rest of it. In the first case, the system is described as *chaotic*, and in the second, *static*. Neither state, if maintained for long periods of time, is particularly well adapted to respond to change. Obviously, a company that stays for a long time in a chaotic or static state is likely to face a difficult future, because it will fail to adapt to a changing business environment.

Complex Adaptive Systems Find the Zone of Creative Adaptability

One of the key discoveries of complexity science, however, is that computer models of complex adaptive systems often evolve themselves to a critical point poised between being chaotic and static states, where their emergent response is measured, richly creative, and adaptive. And unpredictable. There are strong indications that the same is true in nature.[9] This poised state has been blessed with the unfortunate term, *the edge of chaos*. Order emerges at the edge of chaos—this is the phenomenon of self-organization, or spontaneous organization. The order that arises is not imposed by central design; it derives from distributed influence through the interactions of the system's agents. It is hard—and often impossible—to predict in detail what emergent order will look like, but it is certain that order will emerge.[10]

The complexity models also show that the emergent order will be richer, more creative and adaptable, if there is a diversity of agents in the system, agents with different characteristics and different behaviors. The message for business leaders is obvious: value diversity if you value creativity and adaptability. And nurture distributed control—that is, true empowerment—and people will self-organize around problems that need to be solved.

Emergent order at the edge of chaos describes very well the dynamics of populations of organisms and ecosystems in the world of nature—and, under the right management style, it describes the behavior of companies. A company is a system made up of "agents" that interact, and from these interactions among individuals and among teams emerge the company's creativity, culture, and collective purpose. We recognize that, to a manager, the edge of chaos might not sound like a very desirable place to be, even though it *is* in the context of complex adaptive systems. A more congenial term, we suggest, is *zone of creative adaptability*. Companies that operate in the zone of creative adaptability will experience perpetual novelty,[11] constant surprise, as new patterns of behavior ceaselessly emerge. Although, traditionally, managers have disliked surprise—because, for instance, it might mean that their business plan has gone awry—they should in fact welcome it and see it as an opportunity. Surprise is the currency of adaptable change, as the business environment constantly shifts and predictability is difficult.

The most important lesson of complexity science, therefore, is that complex adaptive systems generate emergent, creative order and adapt to changes in their environment, through simple interactions among their agents. In turn, the emergent order influences the behavior of individuals in the system, in a feedback loop. For instance, culture is an emergent property of the behavior of individuals in the society; and culture—religious and political belief systems, for example—influences the way people behave. Similarly in business, the culture that emerges in a company will influence people's behavior. There is a constant interplay between people's behavior and the culture that emerges, a dynamic feedback loop.

Small Changes Can Lead to Large Effects, Often Fast

Edward Lorenz, of the Massachusetts Institute of Technology and a pioneer of chaos theory, coined the term *the butterfly effect* to describe a certain type of behavior of complex systems, and it is now a classic citation in the complexity literature. A butterfly flapping its wings in Brazil can set in motion escalating meteorological processes that lead to a tornado in Texas, said Lorenz. A small change at one point in time in a system can lead to larger changes later on, and these in their turn trigger still bigger changes, a dynamic of escalating effects. This is contrary to the mechanistic world, in which small changes will lead to small effects, and large effects can only be caused by large changes. The next time the butterfly flaps its wings, however, no such escalation occurs, because the slightest difference in initial conditions, and subsequent states, greatly affects the outcome.

An example from U.S. history of "small changes may lead to large effects" is Rosa Lee Parks's refusal to move from the front of the bus in Montgomery, Alabama, in 1955, which at the time was reserved for whites, to the back of the bus, which is where black people were supposed to be. That small act was an important trigger to the civil rights movement that overturned a social system. In business, the "small changes" property of complex systems has important implications for how managers achieve change: Experiment. Experiment. Experiment. The practice of constantly exploring small possibilities in the business environment, rather than trying to achieve a major goal with a major leap, is likely to be more productive and adaptive in the long run. Although many of the experiments will lead nowhere, some will produce big surprises, perhaps new and major business opportunities or a radical new way of organizing around the present business. In fast-changing business environments, where future products and markets are hard to predict, ceaseless experimentation, rather than deep planning, is the most adaptive way to proceed. This is precisely what Microsoft does, for instance, through constantly exploring new business ventures.

The phenomenon of small changes leading to large effects is linked to a further property of complex adaptive systems. Namely, that when change comes, it can happen fast. These phenomena are partly the result of the connectedness within the system, so that change in one part of the system may cascade through the rest of it because of the configuration of interactions at that moment. It's not hard to see the relevance to the world of commerce, such as the crash of the U.S. stock market in 1987, and the ripple effect of the Asian financial crisis that began in 1997.

Connectedness is important in this process, but so, too, is critical mass, in terms of available resources, ideas, or people's willingness to go in a particular, previously resisted, direction. Complex systems are continually fluctuating, as agents constantly interact, and as the system responds to and explores its environment. Gradually, however, a certain pattern that emerges may be more and more favored, and then, suddenly, the whole system converges on that pattern. A critical mass builds and builds, and when it is reached, change comes quickly.

Organizations experience this phenomenon all the time when, for instance, a team struggles to find a solution to a particular problem. Team members argue back and forth about what is needed, ways to proceed, and for a while the whole process seems chaotic. But in fact, small pieces of the solution are being slowly assembled, even if they are not recognized as such at the time. And then, suddenly, there may be a collective "Aha!" and the solution emerges very much fully formed, and typically not anything that anyone could have predicted. We experience the same thing as individuals, when we struggle with a problem in our heads. Insight is typically an "Aha!" phenomenon, not a step-by-step assembly of parts of the solution. Our brains are complex adaptive systems, not machines.

The Attraction of Attractors

Complexity scientists have a term for a favored state in a complex adaptive system: *attractor.* It can be a little misleading, because it seems to imply that the attractor pulls the components of the system toward it, like a whirlpool sucking in a hapless boat that strays too close. But in fact, the attractor is the product of the system itself, an expression of its dynamics at any particular time. In a company, collective vision is an attractor, as is, say, a propensity for innovation.

We can try to think of this in visual terms. Imagine a football field, where the long side represents an increasing willingness to take risks, in an east-west direction; and the short side is a measure of increasing playfulness, in a south-north direction. If, in a company that is highly innovative, you ask people to stand on the football field at a spot that best expresses their degrees of risk taking and playfulness, you are likely to find that the northeast corner of the field is crowded while the southwest corner is only sparsely populated. The congregation of people in the northeast corner (high risk/high playfulness) is an expression of an important attractor for that company at that time, not because people are pulled there but because it is how they want to work. If, now, the economy goes into a nosedive, and risk taking is viewed as dangerous, because failure might put the company out of business, people might drift more toward the southwest corner of the field, because they have become more conservative and fearful. Low risk/reduced playfulness is a new attractor for the company in a new business environment.

A complex adaptive system—a computer model, for instance—that finds itself in a particular attractor might continue to persist there for a long time, if it is a powerful one. The system has to be vigorously perturbed if it is to be wrested from it, and into another one. The same is true in business. A company's culture, or way of working, can become so deeply ingrained that it is extremely hard to have people collectively work in a different way. There is a comfort and security in old, collective habits. CEOs often face the challenge of transforming their organization, of shifting the company from an undesirable way of work to a more desired one. Thinking of such a transformation with the concept of attractors shows why this is often hard to do.

Complexity Science in a Broader Context

The science of complexity is the latest attempt to describe the source of complex order in the world. In this sense, it builds on earlier attempts, and did not arise fully formed out of nothing. For example, when speaking of complexity science to people, we were often asked, "How does this relate to systems theory?" and "What is its relationship to chaos theory?" These are good questions. The answer is that they are part of a continuum in the struggle to explain order in nature, with systems theory[12] (or, rather, body of theories) being an intellectual precursor to chaos theory,[13] and chaos theory an intellectual precursor to complexity science. The journey has been one of a deeper and deeper understanding of the complexity of the processes involved and what they create.

There are a series of contrasts between systems theory and complexity science, but two of them are key: nonlinearity and emergence. Systems theory deals with nonlinearity, but it doesn't include the concept of "small changes can lead to large effects." This *is* part of chaos theory, of course, because that is where the phenomenon was first recognized. The key insight of chaos theory was that chaotic (but not random) systems could be described by simple equations, or rules. But the theory deals only with complex systems in the chaotic state, whereas complexity science recognizes that such systems can exist in three states: chaotic, stable, and the zone of creative adaptability that exists in between. Chaos theory is therefore now a subset of complexity science.

The property that distinguishes complexity science from both systems theory and chaos theory is the emergence of order in the zone between the stable and chaotic states of complex systems. Moreover, complexity science recognizes that complex systems are capable of adaptation and evolution, which were also not important aspects of systems theory and chaos theory, because the phenomena are linked with emergence. As we noted earlier, complexity science became possible only with the advent of modern, powerful computers, which systems and chaos theorists did not have available to them.

Deep Metaphor, Not Superficial Analogy

Metaphors are powerful tools that can instantly conjure powerful images in our minds, creating a rich picture of one thing as informed by what we know of another, and they have been popular in the business literature.[14] For instance, many businesspeople find military metaphors appealing, with managers liking to see themselves as generals at the head of an army. Witness the success of business books such as Wess Roberts's *Leadership Secrets of Attila the Hun*. However, the world of business is not a military battle, although it might be *like* it in some ways. Taken too far, military metaphors are misleading. Similarly, one business consultant, armed with ten years' experience as a game warden in a South African game park, is talking to what Britain's *Financial Times* describes as "rapt audiences" about his seven-point strategy for a successful business: focus, stalk, pounce, kill, hoist, eat, rest. "The pounce of the leopard is likened to exceeding the expectations of the customer," explains the article, "the kill, to the closing of a sale."[15] And so on.

Graphic, even compelling, though these images may be, they have more to do with male hormones and ego than they do with reaching a more penetrating understanding of the business world. Likening a leopard kill to a sale is therefore a superficial analogy, not rich, instructive metaphor. Businesses are not leopards, period. And you cannot learn anything about the dynamics of businesses by looking at the carnivorous nature of leopards. Nevertheless, certain biological metaphors have deeper cogency in business. We often heard from managers and consultants that biological metaphors made difficult problems more readily comprehensible. This is surprising, because metaphors typically invoke something familiar in order to illuminate something unfamiliar. In this case, it's the other way around. Images of biology, with which many businesspeople are unfamiliar, are being invoked to illuminate something familiar, the world of business. We would suggest that this reflects in part the lingering biophilia in each of us, so that we readily resonate with images from nature.

But it goes further than that, because it focuses on the issue of metaphor and analogy in the business context, and which is the more pertinent and useful. Drawing parallels between a leopard's pounce and closing in on a sale is a superficial analogy, because businesses are not carnivorous animals. Drawing parallels between ecosystems (such as a vernal pool) and businesses, by contrast, is deep metaphor, because both are complex adaptive systems, and, although there will be some differences, they do share certain fundamental properties. Although it might not pump the adrenaline in the same way, we can learn more about businesses by learning about the genesis of a vernal pool than by thinking of ourselves as leopards on the prowl or as being a machine.

Chapter 3

Management in Wonderland

Curiouser and curiouser . . . .

Lewis Carroll, *Alice in Wonderland*

For many people, golf is a Zen-like, almost mystical game, where success has much to do with mental preparation. But when club hits ball, it is a quintessential linear process, the embodiment of a Newtonian mechanistic world, as the ball arcs from the tee toward the green. In principle, the perfectly struck shot will arc perfectly into the hole. If you play golf, don't you wish it was always like that? In practice, of course, that rarely happens. But the good golfer will usually land the ball on the green, or at least in the direction of the green. Action and reaction, equal and opposite, linear, predictable, controllable (depending on your skill!). This is very much how many managers see the world of business, or at least fervently wish it would conform to that comforting mechanistic model.

In reality, the world of business is much more like Alice's experience in Wonderland, when she played croquet under the direction of the Red Queen. When the Queen ordered the players and participants to "Get to your places," uttered "in a voice of thunder," we read in *Alice's Adventures in Wonderland,* everyone began "running about in all directions, tumbling up against each other." After a few minutes, everyone settled down, and the game began, a very strange game indeed. Alice was bewildered by what she confronted: a croquet ground that was all ridges and furrows; the balls were live hedgehogs; the mallets were live flamingoes; and soldiers formed the hoops, by bending over, touching the ground.

Alice's first difficulty was in handling her flamingo. "She succeeded in getting its body tucked away, comfortably enough, under her arm . . . but generally, just as she got its neck nicely straightened out, and was going to give the hedgehog a blow with its head, it *would* twist itself around . . . and when she got its head down, and was going to begin again, it was very provoking to find that the hedgehog had unrolled itself, and was in the act of crawling away." Alice's problems didn't end there, however. She found that wherever she wanted to send the hedgehog, a ridge or a furrow was in the way. And the soldiers kept on standing up and walking away. "Alice soon came to the conclusion that it was a very difficult game indeed." Nonlinear, little predictability, limited control, just as it is in the world of business. The game of business doesn't have inanimate objects, like golf, but living beings and an ever-changing environment, as in Alice's croquet game. Welcome to Management in Wonderland, a complex, organic world of uncertainty, surprise, and wonder. Except, of course, that it is reality, not fantasy.

The Roots of Scientific Management

In 1992, the *Harvard Business Review* carried an article titled "Is Management Still a Science?" The author, David Freedman, answered the question thus: "Management may indeed be a science—but not the science most managers think."[1] In other words, the way scientists perceive the world has changed dramatically in recent decades, but many managers still hew to an outdated, scientific mind-set, one that is now on the intellectual scrap heap.

As we said earlier, scientific management was essentially invented by Frederick Winslow Taylor, who grew up in a privileged home in Philadelphia, and was educated in Europe and the United States. He also invented carbon steel machine tools. His great work, *The Principles of Scientific Management,* became a classic in management literature, and its thesis has had an enormous influence on management practice, and continues to do so in many ways. As we noted earlier, Taylor's thoughts were heavily influenced by prevailing scientific thought, particularly from physics. The two most important scientific ideas were Newton's laws of motion and the new science of thermodynamics, which together allowed scientists to calculate how a machine could operate with maximum efficiency. This was Newton's clockwork universe on a smaller scale, but just as mechanistic. Taylor took this collective, mechanistic paradigm of science and imported it into the world of work, where he became obsessed with efficiency as applied to organizations. There was a tremendous waste of human effort in the workplace, Taylor bemoaned, and, he said, "the fundamental cause of this waste of human effort was unscientific management."[2]

Taylor's solution was to do what modern scientists term *reductionistic analysis:* that is, analyze the system down to its component parts and find out how each operates. For scientists, this would lead to a complete understanding of the system as a whole, or so it used to be argued. For Taylor, it would be to reorganize the way people work, to find the "one best method" to lead to greatest efficiency. "The best management is a true science," Taylor wrote, "resting upon clearly defined laws, rules, and principles as a foundation."[3] The system defined by these laws, he said, was comprehensible, predictable, and controllable. "In the past the man has been first; in the future the system must be first."[4] Workers, he said, were to be viewed as "passive units of production," and the system, or the workplace, was like a machine. The job of the manager was to ensure that the machine ran smoothly. The workers, while offered financial incentives for faster work, were merely cogs in the machine. It was all steep hierarchy and narrowly defined job functions for the workers.

Henry Ford embraced Taylor's scientific management theory, and the assembly line of Model Ts began to roll with ever greater efficiency. Taylorism was responsible for tremendous increases in productivity in the workplace, and effectively created modern Industrial Age management. Although it has undergone many changes, Taylorism still remains the dominant management theory today, with the machine model of business as its core.

A More Human-Oriented Management Philosophy Emerges

Not surprisingly, the distinctly mechanistic thesis of scientific management provoked a reaction in those who objected to the dehumanizing tenor of Taylorism. One of the earliest voices to create a human relations school of thinking, as it came to be known, was Mary Parker Follett, a political scientist born in Boston. Beginning with lectures and published articles in the late 1920s, Parker Follett established a more humanistic approach to management that, while sharing some goals with scientific management—namely, improving cooperation in the workplace and increasing productivity—was concerned with more human-oriented problems such as "the monotony of work, absenteeism, turnover, conflict, unrest, wrong attitudes, and low morale."[5] The differences in idealism and fundamental conception of the workplace of scientific and human relations management could hardly have been sharper. Although human relations management flourished in Europe for a while, particularly in Britain, where it was aided by strong trade unions, it fared less well in the United States. Taylorism now predominates in management practice, if not always in management literature, in both continents, and is even gaining in strength, particularly in the United States.

To Jeffrey Pfeffer, of the Stanford Graduate School of Business, this is distinctly puzzling. "Something very strange is occurring in organizational management," he writes in his book *The Human Equation.* The book is, among other things, a compendium of data that show that human-oriented management practice consistently increases the economic performance of companies that follow it when compared with companies in the same economic sector that do not. "But even as these research results pile up, trends in actual management practice are, in many instances, moving in the direction *opposite* to what this growing body of evidence prescribes."[6] Pfeffer is currently seeking an explanation for this apparently contradictory behavior.

We offer a speculation based on behavior in another sphere of human activity, the rise and fall of civilizations. There is a common phenomenon in the histories of past civilizations: namely, as a civilization nears collapse, as they all do at some point, collective stress and apprehension is expressed in a surge of monument building, which historians see as a desperate attempt to retain control.[7] In the modern business environment, it may be that the rising enthusiasm for embracing a Tayloresque style of management in the face of evidence that encourages the opposite is a collective expression of apprehension at the prospect of the rising tide of uncertainty and chaos that is washing over the business world. In other words, it might be a desperate effort to retain control by turning ever more fervently to what is familiar rather than seeking new, unfamiliar, and uncertain ways of managing. Another speculation is that businessmen—and it *is* men who occupy 95 percent of senior management positions, despite representing less than half the workforce as a whole—are so uncomfortable with the humanness of human relations management that they retreat into the "safer" mechanistic realm of scientific management, despite the force of the data that indicate that the alternative approach leads to a more robust bottom line.

Enter Peter Drucker

When Peter Drucker wrote *The Future of Industrial Man* in 1942, he began a five-decades-long line of argument that sought to weave together the best of scientific and human relations management. (His approach has been labeled "structural analysis."[8]) In recognition of the seminal influence of Parker Follett in the human relations realm, Drucker recently described her as "the prophet of management."[9] Seeds of much of modern management theory—such as organizational flattening and empowerment of workers that Parker Follett talked about—were sown in the modern management world by Drucker, who views businesses as social organizations as well as economic machines. Early on he realized that the glue that holds companies together is a shared vision of the future—and that it was for the CEO to generate that vision. And it was Drucker who coined the term "knowledge worker," which has become emblematic of the basic currency of the new economy.

While most managers would say they embrace the more humanistic aspects of Drucker's writings, lip service is rife. America's CEOs would not be sacking their workers with one hand, while awarding themselves huge pay raises with the other, if they understood Drucker's social concept of business.

The Sloan Model of the Firm

Until recently, the dominant organizational structure in business—particularly in big business—was in the mold of Alfred Sloan, who became president of General Motors in 1923. Just as Ford had formed workers into an efficient, reliable, mechanistic system, so Sloan transformed management in the same way. His great achievement was to invent the multidivisional firm, in which companies are divided into separate units that enjoy a degree of operating autonomy, but report to a headquarters that is in charge of long-term strategy. Despite the semi-autonomy of divisions, management in the Sloanist company is decidedly command and control. Initially a paragon of efficiency, encapsulated in the success of General Motors in earlier years, with the passing of time this business model became less and less limber, more bureaucratically constrained, and a haven for managers concerned more with their immediate rewards than the health of their company. Sloanism, as this model is dubbed, is on the way out, for several reasons, and not just because of Tom Peters's Technicolor diatribes about the banalities of gigantism and ossified corporate arteries. "What do you get when you merge one huge, dumb company with no ideas with another huge, dumb company with no ideas?" we heard him ask at a recent conference, as commentary on a recently announced mega-merger. "You get one *humongous,* dumb company with no ideas!"[10]

Other reasons for the demise of Sloanism include the success of team-based operations in Japan in the 1980s, the triumph of nimble, innovative companies that characterize Silicon Valley, and reengineering, which literally ripped apart the functional divisions that were the infrastructure of the Sloan company, and replaced them with flexible, cross-functional teams linked by plentiful channels of communication. The companies that are most admired in today's economy, such as Hewlett-Packard and Intel, are organizationally flat, where decision making really has been handed back to front-line workers, and where, in the case of Intel at least, the CEO, Andy Grove, occupies the same kind of nine-foot-by-eight-foot cubicle that everyone else does. Post-Sloanist companies have limited structure, and an important part of what holds them together is their culture, not a way of being that is imposed but something that emerges when workers and managers are aligned in their purpose and trust of each other.

Tom Peters, the Harbinger
of Chaos and Anarchy

Beyond his incantations against Sloanist gigantism and innovation-inhibiting Taylorism, Tom Peters is the harbinger of chaos and anarchy. Inadvertently, but pertinently anyway, his book *Thriving on Chaos* was published on October 19, 1987, the day the Dow Jones average plummeted 508 points. "Of course I didn't know it was coming," he writes in a later edition. "But the book is concerned with precisely such turmoil. In many ways, the crash certified ours as the age of uncertainty."[11] Peters has never been accused of being understated, nor is he in any imminent danger of being so. "Put a torch to your bureaucracy, throw out the rule book, do crazy things, have fun!" is essentially his message when he walks among his audience, staring intently at one individual and then another, daring each and every one of them to join the revolution. "Throw out your schedules. . . . Who needs middle managers anyhow? . . . Dare to be wrong, make mistakes," and on and on.

Peters is absolutely right when he says that we are entering an age when the business environment is characterized more by chaos than by stability, and where play is an important way to productive learning. But, it is important to remember, even the craziest organizations need *some* structure and *some* stability if they are to survive. Complexity science implies that CEOs and managers must give up control—or, rather, the illusion of control—when they are trying to lead their organization to some goal. But they *do* need to create the environment in which creativity can emerge. Some structure *is* necessary, if a company is to avoid slipping into anarchy and out of business. The message of complexity science is *not* just sit back and wait for good things to emerge. The degree and nature of control that CEOs establish in their companies has everything to do with what emerges. Too little control is just as misguided a business strategy as too much.

Nevertheless, Peters is definitely closer to the pulse of the real world than most management theorists are because, if the world is not quite as crazy as he seems to imply, it is definitely moving in that direction. Dee Hock, the founder of Visa, describes the shift as nothing less than revolutionary. "It is my personal belief . . . that we are at the very point in time when a 400-year-old age is dying and another is struggling to be born," he says; "a shifting of culture, science, society, and institutions enormously greater than the world has ever experienced."[12] Colin Crook, formerly of Citicorp, says much the same. "Businesses, individuals, and entire societies are now confronted with a world characterized by unprecedented change," he argues. "This is occurring in a time frame unimaginable 10 years ago. . . . This is the world of the 21st century."[13] Globalization and the connectedness of the new economy are propelling this new world of change.

Despite the urgings of Peters and a few other like-minded people, such as Dee Hock, to embrace the business world as a place of unpredictable complexity, the prevailing business model is, as we've said above, still very much Tayloresque, very much predicated on planning and control, very much mechanistic. This has at least two important implications. First, it affects the way people are perceived, are treated, and how they view themselves, as we argued in the previous chapter. Second, it represents a disjunct with the way the world really is.

Complexity Science Leads to a Novel Form of Management

A complexity science approach to management is relevant to modern business in a very direct way, for the following reasons. First, it views organizations not as machines but as complex adaptive systems, which is much more organic, and is much more in tune with the dynamics of the new economy. It therefore offers an opportunity for executive professionals and front-line people to work together in a different, more effective, adaptive, and creative manner, leading to business success. Second, as is revealed in the stories we tell of people in the organizations we talked with, this form of management also engenders a very human-oriented management practice and a workplace culture that strives toward genuine humanity and care, a place with the possibility of personal fulfillment in addition to business success.

In his book *Models of Management,* Mauro Guillén, of the Sloan School of Management at the Massachusetts Institute of Technology, lists seventeen ideological and practical features of Tayloresque scientific management and human relations management, such as favored techniques, authority structures, and predominant social relationships. From our observations of these same seventeen features in companies managed along complexity science principles, complexity-guided management falls squarely in the human relations column, and scores zero in the realm of Taylorism. So, as we will see, the science of complexity leads to a human-oriented management practice, one in which valuing people for themselves does not have to be defended as simply "being nice," but is based on a scientific understanding of the workplace.

Managers are in a position rather similar to that of natural scientists before complexity science was developed. They think they understand the relationships between cause and effect in their organizations, but, in fact, most don't. They view their organizations as machines, not as living systems, which in reality they resemble in deep, fundamental ways. Most managers, at any rate. Some—such as those whose stories form the bulk of this book, and many others that are not part of it—have discovered that letting go of absolute control and nurturing the conditions for constructive self-organization can lead to astonishing creativity and adaptability, a robust financial bottom line, and a caring organizational culture.

Businesses As Complex Adaptive Systems

The recognition that businesses are complex adaptive systems allows us to draw on what is known about such systems—in computer simulations and in nature—so that we can learn about the fundamental dynamics of businesses and the economic webs of which they are a part. Common to the dynamics within and among businesses is the emergence of (mostly) unpredictable patterns from the interactions that occur there, because of the connectedness of the systems. For those who have the courage—and it takes courage—complexity science offers a new way of doing and being in the workplace of the connected economy: in short, a new management theory.

Most management theories attempt to transform businesses into something new, as we saw with the Sloan model and with reengineering, which dismantled Sloanism. Complexity science is different. It says, let us recognize that businesses are complex adaptive systems—and always have been. You don't have to bring complexity to the world of business: it is already there. The issue is, what kind of management practice is likely to nurture underlying processes in companies so that they will naturally be as adaptive and creative as they can be? We saw that computer-based complex adaptive systems can be tuned to a static state, a chaotic state, or to a zone of creativity, and this happens in nature, too. A command-and-control, or mechanistic, style of management tends to shackle companies close to the static state, because it dampens interactions among its components, which impedes the emergent creativity from the level of front-line people. This model of management worked well enough in the Industrial Age economy, but is much less effective in the connected economy of the Information Age. It is time for something new, not in terms of making businesses something they were not previously, but in terms of seeing businesses for what they are, and finding ways of enhancing the potential creativity of businesses as complex adaptive systems.

Having said that, however, we should acknowledge that mechanistic management is sometimes appropriate, when goals are clear and there is little uncertainty in the prevailing business environment. As Shona Brown and Kathleen Eisenhardt comment in their book *Competing on the Edge,* "It is not that traditional strategies are wrong but rather that they are just not enough in industries with intense, high-velocity change."[14] Complexity science therefore does not *replace* mechanistic management. Rather it *encompasses* it in a larger context, which includes seeking the uncertainties and paradoxes of the zone of creative adaptability. And, as we said, it even welcomes periods of chaos as not only natural but sometimes desirable. For instance, when old ways have to be abandoned and new paths found, chaos is the road to follow—briefly—because it allows the exploration of many possibilities in a surprisingly innovative way, and leads to an opportunity for the company to reorganize itself in a more productive form. Andy Grove, CEO of Intel, recognizes this when he says: "The old order won't give way to the new without a phase of experimentation and chaos in between."[15] For a manager to push his or her company into chaos for a while sounds counterintuitive, even foolhardy, but it is the way to escape old attractors and find new, more suitable ones. In the following section, you will read several examples of CEOs who did exactly this, and quite deliberately so.

So, just as natural complex adaptive systems fluctuate among the three states, depending on the prevailing environment and the nature of interactions among their agents, so, too, will a company fluctuate among the three states. Fluctuation is to be welcomed in complex adaptive systems, because it is the wellspring of the capacity to adapt to changing environments.

For instance, although most of us are unaware of the fact, paradoxically the heart rate of healthy people is constantly fluctuating in small degrees, while a heart rate that falls into a constant, stable rhythm is often the prelude to heart failure. Fluctuations tune the heart to be ready for different demands put on it, while a constant, unchanging rate is tuned for one response only, and cannot cope with other demands.[16] In many ways the Information Age is also a world of paradox for businesspeople, with unforeseen changes in the business environment putting many different demands on the organization's ability to respond. The successful leaders of the future will be those who are sensitive to the fluctuations between states—static, chaotic, adaptive—and know which is pertinent, and then to operate appropriately.

What is appropriate management in those states that are not mechanistic? And what does a company whose management practice is guided by complexity science principles *look* like, *feel* like? You will tap into answers to these questions in some depth through the realm of experience in the stories we tell of the companies we worked with. But at its root, complexity science points to the following few simple guidelines for working with organizations as complex adaptive systems, which we heard in the companies we talked to, and you might want to bear in mind as you read their stories:

- *When agents interact and mutually affect each other in a system, this is the source of emergence.*

In business this translates to the important and often denied need to attend to relationships characterized by mutuality among people, among teams, and among companies in order for novelty to emerge.

- *Agents' behaviors in a system are governed by a few simple rules.*

In businesses, rules become practices because people aren't perfect. The practices that guided these organizations were shared values, and small in number.

- *Small changes can lead to large effects, taking the system to a new attractor.*

Multiple experimentation on small scales is the most productive way to lead to change, rather than trying to leap too quickly to a perceived desired goal on a large scale.

- *Emergence is certain, but there is no certainty as to what it will be.*

Create conditions for constructive emergence rather than trying to plan a strategic goal in detail. This includes nurturing the formation of teams and creativity within teams, and *evolving* solutions to problems, not *designing* them. Further, hierarchic, central control should give way to distributed influence, and a flat organizational structure.

- *The greater the diversity of agents in a system, the richer the emergent patterns.*

Seek a diversity of people, their cultures, their expertise, their ages, their personalities, their gender, so that when people interact in teams, for example, creativity has the potential of being enhanced.

Complexity Science Points to a New Style of Management

Some of these practices are already present in some current management paradigms, particularly in the Drucker model of business for instance, with its emphasis on businesses as communities. But complexity science brings them all together under an umbrella of a scientific understanding of the deep nature of business organizations. Management guided by the principles of complexity science therefore constitutes a style that is very human-oriented in that it recognizes that relationships are the bottom line of business, and that creativity, culture, and productivity emerge from these interactions. For the first time there is a science of fundamental organizational dynamics that gives a foundation for a human-oriented management practice. It's a new style in that it says, place more emphasis than you have previously on the micro level of things in your company, because this is a creative conduit for influencing many aspects of the macro level concerns, such as strategy and the economic bottom line. It's a new style in that it encourages the emergence of a culture that is more open and caring. It's a new style in that it does not readily lend itself to being turned into "fix-it" packages that are the stuff of much management consultancy, because it requires genuine connection with co-workers; you can't fake it and expect to get results. It recognizes that the intelligence and sources of solutions to business problems are distributed throughout the organization, and are not confined largely to the top; and gives guidance for tapping into that intelligence.

The complexity-guided style of management is hard to do, very hard, especially for managers who seek safety in a command and control practice. It is hard even for those who embrace its principles, because the everyday urgency of business can make time spent interacting and nurturing relationships seem like a waste of time, a distraction from tough business realities. It is hard because it requires constant attention, constant vigilance of one's own behavior and the behavior of others.

We suspect that many managers will resist this style of management, because it is so much at odds with much of prevailing business practice, especially in relation to the issue of control; and also because of its requirement for an authentic human-centered presence in the workplace that some managers find difficult. This style of management is not for everyone. Witness the reaction of one manager who was attending a seminar by Ralph Stacey, a British business school professor, who is among the few people to address the human side of complexity science in business. Stacey was urging his audience to embrace uncertainty, give up tight control, and allow for unpredictability, when someone in the audience wailed, "You have just set management back fifteen or twenty years!"

This sentiment is a call to have your backs to the future, to prepare for the past, again. The future belongs to managers who can embrace complexity science, yes in operational and strategic realms, but most particularly in the realm of organizational dynamics that we are addressing in this book, the realm of nurturing people so that they can achieve and contribute beyond what they—and their managers—could ever have imagined; so that the organization can achieve far more than *anyone* could ever have imagined.

Chapter 4

The Consequences of Connections

Nature is always hinting at us. It hints over and over again. And suddenly we take the hint.

Robert Frost

Accepting that a company is a complex adaptive system, and shaping management practice appropriately, is just one step in a larger challenge for businesspeople seeking to survive in the new economy. The second step is to recognize that every company is embedded in a larger complex adaptive system, the economic sector in which it operates. Every company, no matter its economic sector, is a player in an economic web of connections that is changing traditional modes of doing business. One consequence of being part of a network of other companies—some of which are competitors, some collaborators, and some complementors—is that new rules of interaction are required that go beyond those that prevailed in the simple win-lose competitive situation. Another is that the modern business environment is less predictable and less controllable than has typically been assumed, and business leaders have to come to terms with the fact that the fate of their companies is not solely in their own hands. (Complementors are companies that sell products or services that are complementary to your own. For example, Intel and Microsoft are complementors.)

The rules of the business game have changed; indeed, the game itself has changed, as Adam Brandenburger, of Harvard Business School, and Barry Nalebuff, of Yale School of Management, have argued. "Business language is full of expressions borrowed from the military and from sports. Some of them are dangerously misleading," they wrote in a 1995 article in the *Harvard Busi-*

ness Review. "Unlike war and sports, business is not about winning and losing. Nor is it about how well you play the game. Companies can succeed spectacularly without requiring others to fail. And they can fail miserably no matter how well they play if they make the mistake of playing the wrong game."[1] Or if they find themselves in a hostile playing field.

For example, no one questioned that the NeXT workstation, the brainchild of Apple Computer co-founder Steve Jobs, was technologically superb. Powered by chips from Motorola, the hyper-chic-looking machine was easy to use, had multimedia capabilities, and was far more advanced in many ways than its competition. And yet, when Jobs launched his brilliant creation in the late 1980s, it became merely a curiosity cherished by a few devotees rather than achieving deep penetration in a lucrative market. Despite its technological superiority, NeXT was a commercial failure.

Similarly, Digital Equipment Corporation developed its Alpha chip half a dozen years ago, and correctly boasted that it was the fastest microprocessor in the world, outpacing its nearest rival by more than a factor of three. But there were few buyers. The Alpha remained ahead in the race for speed for a long time, being twice as fast as the Intel Corporation's popular Pentium chip. But, despite a mammoth marketing effort by Digital executives during 1997, the Alpha is *still* an also-ran in terms of market share (1 percent as opposed to Intel's dominating 92 percent).

What do these tales of commercial woe have to do with the failure of, say, an exotic, superbly adapted seed-eating bird to become established in the highland forests of Hawaii? Everything, because in both cases we are dealing with system-level effects, and the behaviors of such systems are unpredictable and often counterintuitive.

Companies Are Enmeshed in Business Ecosystems

The notion of using ecosystems as a metaphor for business systems, while once considered bizarre by most managers, is now becoming more common, as the network character of the new economy is becoming ever more apparent. For instance, Lew Platt, CEO of Hewlett-Packard, has become an enthusiastic supporter of these ideas, as has Andy Grove, CEO of Intel. In some of the stories we tell, you will see ecosystem thinking, on different scales. As the new perspective is still in its infancy, however, most of the explicit references to the idea in the business literature are to be found by observers of business, such as academics and consultants.

For example, in an article on the fast-paced world of high-technology companies published in 1996 in the *Harvard Business Review,* the Santa Fe Institute economist Brian Arthur used the term ecosystem (or its derivatives) seven times. Similarly, one of the best-selling business books in the United States during recent years is titled *The Death of Competition,* with the subtitle, *Leadership and Strategy in the Age of Business Ecosystems.* "Leaders who learn to understand . . . ecology and evolution will find themselves equipped with a new model for devising strategy, and critical new options for shaping the future of their companies," writes its author, James Moore, a business consultant in Cambridge, Massachusetts.[2] Even the oh-so-conservative *Wall Street Journal* recently carried an article by John Baden, of the Foundation for Research on Economics and the Environment, with the following revolutionary statement: "When we understand that the economy is an ecosystem—not a machine isolated and insulated from the environment—we grasp fundamental truths about what makes the economy work."[3]

Something is changing in the world of business, as managers are coming to recognize that companies interact with each other like species interact in ecosystems, a powerful biological metaphor. This recognition has two important implications. First, as we've said, CEOs will have to get used to thinking of their companies as being more like living organisms in communities than mechanical machines, which changes the nature of their organizational dynamics and their economics. And second, CEOs have much less control, not only over the day-to-day life but also of the long-term fate of their companies than they have liked to believe.

Parallel Changes in Thinking in Ecology and Business

There are striking parallels in a shift that is going on in business and the study of ecology, in the way leading practitioners describe their disparate worlds. First, as we've indicated, it is a shift from viewing the world as simple, predictable, and settling to equilibrium; to acknowledging that it is complex, unpredictable, and far from equilibrium. Second, it is a shift from head-to-head competition as being viewed as the key force shaping the business/ecological community, to recognizing that each is a complex dynamical system in which competition is just one of many factors that influence the life of the community. Other factors in ecosystems, such as predation and population fluctuation, combine with competition to generate unpredictable emergent patterns in the community.

The Eco-Bowl

First, what do we mean by worlds at equilibrium and worlds far from equilibrium? A visual model will help. Imagine you have a metal bowl, and you toss a ball into it so that the ball rolls around the sides. Eventually the ball will come to rest at the bottom of the bowl. The system has now reached equilibrium. Imagine, now, that the bowl becomes distorted, so that the ball is once again propelled into motion. Once again the ball will eventually come to rest; the system has been disturbed from one equilibrium, only to find a new equilibrium. In the business world, you could imagine a company turning out a product in a stable market. Then, a new competitor might come on the scene, or new technology forces a shift in the nature of the product desired by the market. The company makes the appropriate adjustments, and once again settles into stable production mode. This is the equilibrium model of the economy, and, indeed, it is sometimes like that.

In the new economy, however, the equilibrium model will become a rarity, as companies are immersed in a ceaselessly changing business environment. Here the bowl is made of something like rubber, and it is constantly changing shape so that the ball never stops moving. The system rarely comes to rest, as it responds to perpetual shifts in its environment, and, further, responds to the fluctuating dynamics of the system itself, as is seen in simulations of complex adaptive systems and is observed in nature.

In ecology, the traditional view was encapsulated in the comforting phrase, "The Balance of Nature," in which ecosystems were seen to rest at equilibrium until they were disturbed, and then they found a new equilibrium. Just as in economics, the shape of the eco-bowl is constantly changing, causing constant fluctuations in species' populations in ecosystems, the result not just of external changes but of internal dynamics, too. "Ecologists didn't deny that complex dynamics exist in nature," says Stuart Pimm, an ecologist at the University of Tennessee in Knoxville, "but they explained them as the result of genuinely unpredictable factors in the external world, such as fluctuations in climate. More and more of us are beginning to realize that these behaviors are emergent properties of the internal dynamics of the system itself."[4]

One such emergent property is the above-mentioned ability of an established ecosystem to exclude a would-be invading species, despite its being competitively superior to its potential rival within the community. The network of connections in a mature ecosystem, of which the would-be invader's rival is an established part, protects the incumbent species from outside competition. "The potential invader has to be very much more competitively superior, if it is to surmount this system-level effect," says Pimm. He has seen this system-level effect many times in ecosystems simulated in the computer, and in real habitats in Hawaii.

For example, "More species of birds and plants have been introduced into Hawaii than anywhere in the world," explains Pimm. "But there are two separate ecological worlds. There's the highland region, which is still pristine, with native plants and birds having formed a tight network of connections over a long period of time. Relatively few species have successfully invaded here. And there's the lowland region, in which human settlement has disrupted established communities and made them vulnerable to invasion, because the ecosystem network is poorly formed." Pimm's statement about the requirements of a successful would-be invader in ecosystems is echoed with eerie similarity in Brian Arthur's 1996 *Harvard Business Review* article, when he comments on the commercial failure of NeXT: "A new product has to be two or three times better in some dimension—price, speed, convenience—to dislodge a locked-in rival."[5] Again, a network of connections in the form of often informal alliances between key companies, such as Microsoft, Hewlett-Packard, and Intel, repelled the would-be invader, Jobs's NeXT workstation. The same technological ecosystem excluded Digital's Alpha chip from gaining a foothold.

Food Webs and Economic Webs

Another important, unpredictable, emergent property in ecosystems is food webs, which describe the patterns of interaction among the species within the community—these involve primary producers, herbivores, carnivores, parasites, and so on, or who eats whom. Not so long ago, ecologists believed that there was an infinity of food web patterns, because of the many possible combinations within a community of even modest size, say fifteen species. Not so. Food webs, ecologists have learned, have just a few major characteristics, such as the length of the food chains (a progression of who eats whom, from the bottom of the food web to the top), and the ratio of predator species to prey species. You see these common patterns wherever you look. Because of the complex network of interdependence that these deceptively simple patterns represent, it is extremely difficult to predict the outcome of simple changes within the community, such as the introduction of a new species. Sometimes the community may be affected very little, while at other times it might cause cascades of local extinction. The outcome is unpredictable.

The intellectual shift in ecology, therefore, is one of a deeper understanding of how the real world works: it is a whole lot more complex than was once realized. In the business world, by contrast, the shift is of both perception *and* reality, as the connectedness of the new economy burgeons. The equivalent of food webs in the business world are economic webs, which describe patterns by which companies do business with other companies, and how. Economic webs have always existed in society, of course. But in today's fast-moving, high-technology economy, their patterns are much more complex than they once were, and the patterns change more rapidly, too, as companies break old alliances and form new ones in their quest to survive and thrive. The maneuvers of Microsoft and Netscape in their separate struggles to dominate the Internet are a good example. And yet web thinking—or ecosystem thinking—is only now beginning to emerge in the business environment.

"The way to think about economic webs is in terms of niches around some kind of activity," says Stuart Kauffman, a complexity science pioneer and co-founder of BIOS, a consultancy company that is bringing complexity-related solutions to business problems.[6] "In the days before the automobile, transport centered on the horse-drawn carriage, which required wheelwrights, blacksmiths, saddleries, wayside inns, and so on." This was the horse-drawn carriage ecosystem. "When automobiles arrived, a whole new ecosystem coevolved, requiring paved roads, gas stations, motels, and so on, which replaced the previous ecosystem." If, as a wheelwright, for instance, you were unable to transform yourself in the face of this change, perhaps to make wine barrels or rustic furniture instead, then you would go extinct, as your niche—making wooden wheels for carriages—shrank to virtually nothing. The process of coevolution is producing even more complex economic webs in the world of high technology, with software, hardware, and Internet companies interacting to produce a complex economic web.

Constantly Changing Adaptive Landscapes

The coevolution of businesses can also be thought of in terms of what complexity scientists call adaptive landscapes, a concept borrowed from evolutionary biology.[7] This is best described by example. Imagine a species of antelope, with a fast running speed, broad diet, and high ability to extract nutrients from its food. These properties endow on the species a certain biological fitness, or ability to survive and thrive in relation to its competitors and predators. The adaptive landscape concept asks us to imagine an abstract landscape that maps the potential fitness of the antelope, given these and other properties. The place on the landscape where fast running speed, broad diet, and efficient digestion are highly beneficial will be represented by a high peak, and suboptimal combinations are smaller peaks or even valleys. If the antelope has adapted well to its environment, it will occupy the highest peak, metaphorically speaking.

There will usually be several peaks of different heights on an adaptive landscape, which represent different levels of potential fitness for different physical and behavioral properties of the species: a narrow diet combined with lower running speed and better defense against predators, for instance. In terms of evolution, it would require the antelope species to accumulate a series of genetic mutations to move from one peak to another, and this may be difficult to achieve. Just as pertinent, if the antelope's predator itself evolves a faster running speed, then the antelope's fitness is reduced, because it is more likely to be killed. In other words, the antelope's adaptive landscape has been changed, with the high fitness peak it occupied now being lower. The antelope species has several "options." If, by genetic change, it evolves faster speed, its fitness peak will be higher once again. Alternatively, a different package of genetic change might bring it to a high fitness peak, such as one in which it can defend itself against predators, perhaps through possessing sharper horns and a collective defensive strategy. An important point about this abstract imagery is that a species' adaptive landscape is constantly changing as the behavior of species with which it interacts also changes.

The wheelwright we spoke of can also be thought of as living on an adaptive landscape, one that describes his potential economic well-being, depending on whether he uses his skills to make carriage wheels, barrels, or rustic furniture. In the pre-automobile era, making wheels would represent a high peak on his landscape, whereas making barrels or furniture would be far less attractive. When the demand for wheels falls with the arrival of the car, the height of the wheel-making peak sinks dramatically, and making barrels or rustic furniture is now much more attractive. And if the demand for rustic furniture becomes strong, through a change in fashion, that peak might eventually become higher than the previously occupied wheel-making peak; that is, the wheelwright can now make more money making furniture than he ever could making wheels.

It is possible in principle to think of any business ecosystem in terms of a network of companies, each occupying a place in its own landscape of possibilities; and each landscape being coupled to many others: those of competitors, collaborators, and complementors. As the landscape of one company changes—perhaps through increased fitness as a result of a powerful innovation—the landscapes of those connected to it will also change: some fitness peaks will increase in size, while others get smaller, or even disappear. A company whose product line is small and unchanging, and whose business environment is relatively stable, will have a simple adaptive landscape, with few peaks and little change. By contrast, a company in which innovation is driving many new product lines, and where the business environment is anything but stable and predictable, will have a rugged adaptive landscape, with many peaks that are constantly changing. Most companies in the new economy occupy rugged, constantly changing landscapes. The utility of this concept is in enabling companies to reach an understanding of the landscape of possibilities that they occupy, and seeing how the change in others' landscapes might affect their own. Because, as companies are members of economic webs, change is certain.

The Death of Competition

The newly emerging web thinking is the way of the future. For instance, John Hagel, a consultant with McKinsey & Company, recently wrote an article in the company's quarterly journal, which he titled "Spider Versus Spider." Web thinking, he opined, "may even represent the opening salvo in the transition from industrial-age to information-age thinking."[8] The reality of complex economic webs, or business ecosystems, changes the way companies operate strategically, if they are to survive in a turbulent, fast-changing environment. In the new economy, strategy based on conventional competition and cooperation will give way to strategy based on coevolution, as companies adapt in concert. "Web strategies turn traditional strategic thinking on its head," says Hagel. "The conventional approach dictates that firms first define their own strategy and negotiate alliances that are consistent with this strategy and advance its aims. Web strategy asserts that the two basic choices confronting senior management are which webs [or ecosystems] to participate in (or to form), and what role . . . to play in them. In other words, firm strategy follows web strategy."[9] As we noted earlier, Intel and Hewlett-Packard have embraced web strategy, but they are pioneers, not yet mainstream.

In traditional business thinking based on head-to-head competition, the bottom line is win-lose: "I win, my competitor loses." But in the more complex, coevolutionary business environment, the bottom line is win-win, because most businesses succeed if others also succeed. It's mutual success rather than mutual destruction. Competition is part of the picture, of course, but only a part. Cooperation and building mutually beneficial networks is important, too. In an influential book published in 1996, Adam Brandenburger and Barry Nalebuff use the term "co-opetition" to describe this joint strategy, a word coined by Ray Noorda, founder of the networking software company Novell.[10] For many traditionalists in business and economics, this death of old-style, head-to-head competition as the number one route to success will prove hard to swallow. That's scarcely surprising, because the idea goes all the way back to the eighteenth century and the ideas of Scottish economist Adam Smith. He argued that if individuals are left free to pursue their own selfish interests, patterns of economic activity would emerge that would serve the greater good, guided, he said, "as if by an invisible hand."

Almost a century later, Darwin incorporated Smith's thinking into biology, in his theory of natural selection. The core of the theory is that individuals act in their own interests, from which the evolutionary patterns we see in the world arise. Competition in this context includes whether one species or another of, for instance, a seed-eating bird will dominate in a particular ecosystem. The invisible hand at work again, this time in the biological realm.

It is therefore ironic that modern economists embraced Darwinian metaphors earlier in the century, raising the notion of the survival of the fittest through bitter competition to the level of a business law, and apparently believing that their business theory was being inspired by laws of nature. In effect modern economists were embracing Adam Smith's economic theory, but in a modern, biological guise. The irony doubled, however, because just as prevailing economic wisdom elevated the power of competition to dizzying new heights in the late 1970s and 1980s in the United States and Europe, ecologists were engaged in a fierce and sometimes acrimonious debate over whether competition really was the all-powerful force traditional Darwinism held it to be. After the feathers settled, there emerged a new view of the world in which competition between species was just one of many factors that shape ecological communities. Rich interplay in the network of interacting species was recognized as at least as important, if not more so.

But the rest of the world has been slow to catch up with this new perspective, because to most people, evolutionary theory is still dominated by the ideas of competition and survival of the fittest. So it is among most business theorists and practitioners.

CEOs therefore have their work cut out. Companies can benefit from species-level improvement in the Darwinian, self-centered sense, but this is of limited value in the longer term. The more important challenge is to create opportunities and adapt to changes in a complex network of other companies that might sometimes be collaborators, sometimes competitors, and sometimes both at once. In other words, the notion of competition as we know it should be allowed to die. A more appropriate, and powerful, approach requires thinking in terms of whole systems.

John Hagel also believes the simple Darwinian metaphor is of limited value in an increasingly high-tech world. "Webs emerge from the turmoil wrought by uncertainty and change," he says. "They spread risk, increase flexibility, enhance an industry's innovation capability, and reduce complexity for individual participants." And, in a phrase that contains interesting biological overtones, Hagel states that "the more companies—and customers—that join, the stronger the web becomes."[11] Similarly, many ecologists believe the more species there are in a community, the more productive and stable the community can be.

The Economics of Increasing Returns

Just as the burgeoning of economic webs is forcing companies to change business strategy, so, too, is it changing the nature of prevailing economics. Mainstream economic theory has its roots in the smokestack economy of the

Industrial Revolution, and is based on the production of commodities, such as coal and iron. Formalized in the late nineteenth century by the economist Alfred Marshall, this said that the more coal you dig, the more you are forced to exploit less favorable resources, and so the return for your effort is reduced; and as you are in competition with other coal mines in the same predicament, prices become squeezed down close toward the average cost of production. This phenomenon, known as diminishing returns, became a central pillar of modern economics, and is quintessentially an equilibrium model of the economic world.

Now, says Brian Arthur, a different economic phenomenon is emerging, which he calls "increasing returns." Although held to be impossible under traditional economic theory, increasing returns makes perfect sense in the ecosystem view of business. "Increasing returns are the tendency for that which is ahead to get further ahead," explains Arthur. "If a product or a company or a technology—one of many competing in a market—gets ahead by chance or clever strategy, increasing returns can magnify this advantage, and the product or company or technology can go on to lock in the market."[12] As a result, a company can make a financial killing, even if its product is competitively inferior. This is a system-level effect, where the inferior product survives and thrives because it is linked to many other products in the community, thus excluding competitors. Increasing returns would not happen—could not happen—in Marshall's world of perfect competition.

One of the best examples here is the dominance of Microsoft's disk operating system, or DOS. Widely recognized as inferior to other operating systems—it was often derided as Dreadful Operating System by aficionados—it nevertheless prevailed and came to dominate the market. In the early 1980s, DOS was one of three competing operating systems, the other two being CP/M and Apple's Macintosh system. CP/M was first onto the market, and was well established when its competitors arrived. DOS was born from some clever tactics by Bill Gates, which included striking a deal with IBM for supplying an operating system for the IBM PC.

For a while, it was unclear which system would become dominant. However, both IBM and Apple encouraged the development of their separate ecosystems, establishing networks of committed users and, more importantly, software suppliers that wrote to DOS or Macintosh standards. Two technological ecosystems emerged, with very different cultures, with DOS becoming the eight-hundred-pound gorilla in the marketplace, through being protected within its ecosystem that Microsoft helped develop. Apple thrived in its own, smaller ecosystem (for a while at least). And CP/M became extinct. The bottom line here is that although the theory of increasing returns predicts that one system was likely to lock in eventually, it cannot predict which one it would be based on the technical merits of each.

Deep Commonalities Between Business and Nature

These parallels between business communities and ecosystems are intriguing. But how useful are they in trying to understand the dynamics of the new network economy, through drawing on what is known in ecosystems? If the similarities between the two worlds are superficial—mere analogy—then they are probably not very useful. But if business communities and ecosystems are common in fundamental ways, as we suggest, then the parallels are valid and provide potentially powerful insights. Do such fundamental commonalities exist? Yes, but that's not to say the two systems are precisely the same. People make decisions in business communities, consciously trying to take advantage of their position in the ecosystem. That doesn't happen in biological ecosystems, so differences are inevitable. But because business communities and ecologies are two examples of the same thing—complex adaptive systems—the parallels are far from superficial, and the ecosystem perspective of business is more than mere analogy.

This being the case, there is some disconcerting and humbling news for business executives. The first rule of complex adaptive systems is that it is almost impossible to predict who is a friend and who is an enemy. Field experiments, in which a predator is removed from a community, illustrate the point. You might expect the predator's prey, species A, to thrive, because it is no longer being preyed upon. But about half the time species A suffers when the predator has gone, because the predator has another prey species, B, which is A's competitor. With its population no longer kept in check by the predator, species B may then push species A to local extinction through being competitively superior. These effects are only one or two steps into the network, and yet we are already in the midst of uncertainty. Venture a few more steps, and it becomes almost impossible to work out combinations of harm and good: complete uncertainty.

In the business ecosystem, CEOs face the same problem of working out who is a friend and who is an enemy, and how this might change as the environment changes. It's not just the competitive interactions that are important in the business ecosystem. It's the entire complex of interactions that matter. Also, being part of an interconnected network of companies—the business ecosystem—has dangers as well as benefits. The benefits include the opportunity to reap great rewards through the economics of increasing returns and through forming alliances. But the same interconnectedness that protects ecosystem members also poses the threat of disaster. When everything is connected directly or indirectly to everything else, changes in one part of the system may be propagated throughout the system, and sometimes organizations may go extinct through no fault of their own. This is an example of small changes provoking large effects, with innocent victims suffering as a result.

These aspects of complex systems—unpredictability and the possibility of extinction because of changes in other parts of the system—are distinctly unnerving to traditional CEOs, who cherish predictability and control. There is a phrase popular among high-technology companies, coined by a leading scientist at Xerox's Palo Alto Research Center, that captures this spirit: "The best way to predict the future is to invent it." This gung ho attitude, says James Moore, is doomed to failure. "We know from studying complex systems that prediction in any conventional sense is not possible," he warns. "Not in biological ecology—and not in business and social ecology."[13]

The most effective leaders in this kind of environment are those who are prepared—often against much of their training—to give up control, or rather the illusion of control. Managers have a choice in the matter, of course. They can choose to take the bold path, give up the traditional mode of control, and thereby secure an opportunity to survive and even thrive, recognizing that they must tolerate uncertainty and anxiety on the way, and recognizing that they must continually experiment with new possibilities. Or they can hew to the safe path, and cling to control in the way they know best, doing what they know best, and thereby secure a brief period of survival, but almost certainly ensure uncomfortably rapid extinction.

PART TWO

The World of Complexity Experience

Preamble

Complexity and Narratives

A man is always a teller of stories, he lives surrounded by his own stories and those of other people, he sees everything that happens to him in terms of these stories and he tries to live his life as if he were recounting it.

Jean-Paul Sartre, *The Words*

We chose the narrative form rather than traditional case studies to present our qualitative data for several reasons. Narratives, unlike linear case studies, allow for the inherent and complex experience of these organizations that you will read about—namely, their contradictions and their paradoxes, their emotional life as well as their economic realities, their purpose as well as their profitability. In other words, instead of writing about what *organizations* do, we write about what *people* do in their organizations, and their *experience* of being part of the organization. Through narratives, we are able to bring to you a slice of life as it presented itself to us as we entered the complex, real-life world of these organizations.

Narratives, we feel, can capture the intangible, nonmeasurable, temporal reality that is often overlooked in analytic writings about organizations. As the psychologist Jerome Bruner speculated, "We seem to have no other way of describing 'lived time' save in the form of narrative."[1] We believe that this mix of scientific principles embedded in personally lived experience moves our understanding of complexity and business toward a greater unity, wholeness, and reality.

We write these narratives in the spirit of seeking truth and understanding through a nonlinear process; that is, through resonance, verisimilitude, life-likeness, rather than the linear, analytic process that seeks truth by means of proof. "In science," says Bruner, "we ask for verification. In the domain of the narrative . . . we ask instead that, upon reflection, the account corresponds to some perspective we can imagine or 'feel' as right."[2]

All these organizations felt that they were unique and revolutionary in how they worked, and they also felt isolated and alone in their struggle to find a better way of working. Although they all come from different lines of business and are of different sizes, nevertheless, from their narratives emerges a collective voice for a different way of being and working, for a different vision of the workplace. We feel each of these stories is in very good company with one another.

When you read these stories keep in mind the principles of complexity we outlined in the previous section. At the heart of how complex systems can adapt is pattern recognition within their environments. Pay attention to patterns that might emerge among these stories—how they get to the edge, how they behave, what they value.

The power of the narrative for constructing meaning is through reflection. In reading these stories, see what stands out for you, where you stand, where your own organization stands in relationship to these narratives. These organizations show that a different way of working is possible. We hope their stories will open the possibility for thinking about a different way of working in your organization. Most of all, we hope these stories will start a conversation about your work and your workplace.

Chapter 5

Muhlenberg Medical Center: Healing Connections

It was the best of times, it was the worst of times.

Charles Dickens, *A Tale of Two Cities*

Twenty-four miles southwest of New York City, in north-central New Jersey, is a place called Plainfield. Plainfield—once farmland, then a village, and later a "town in the country" where city dwellers retreated for holidays—is now the core city of what is known as Greater Plainfield. Here there are tree-lined streets with Victorian mansions in various states of repair and disrepair, alluding to grander times gone by. Surrounding the historic areas are many humble neighborhoods with bungalows built close to one another. In the center of Plainfield is a large empty park, where buildings once stood but were burnt down, casualties of the race riots during the 1960s. The surrounding area borders on devastation—houses abandoned or direly neglected. Like its architecture, Plainfield's community is also diverse—economically and racially. Minorities are the majority, and there's a strong gay population. Plainfield gives the impression of a city struggling to come to terms with itself, caught in disparate vestiges of time.

A leader among the institutions committed to serving this city of 47,000 people is Muhlenberg Medical Center. The hospital, which was established in 1877, is named after the humanitarian William Augustus Muhlenberg, and has a long tradition of putting people first. As John Howard Jr., director from 1935 to 1946, put it: "A hospital is a human institution. Its success is not built of bricks or beds or scientific equipment, but of human beings—doctors, nurses, employees, volunteers, patients, and the public." This human-centered, relationship-based approach to the organization continues today under the leadership of John Kopicki, CEO and president.

For example, the first thing you notice when you approach the entrance to Muhlenberg is Jimmy, who has worked at the hospital for forty-two years. His current position is official greeter for the medical center, which he does with irrepressible cheeriness. But he also assists those leaving the hospital—maneuvering wheelchairs and making sure people have a ride home—all of which has made for more speedy and facile discharges. The hospital could operate without Jimmy; some might think him to be a luxury; but he so impresses, with his embracing spirit, everybody that comes through the door—making people welcome, setting a friendly tone—that it overrides the fact that he is a nonmeasurable benefit. This says a lot about Muhlenberg—a medical center that values good relationships with its customers, right from the start.

Placing value on developing good relationships is particularly striking given the health care crisis in the United States, with economic pressure on hospitals to cut costs, on doctors to see more patients, on nurses to get patients out early—all pressures that transform patients into cost units. As a result, many people feel that the quality of care—that is, care of patients as individuals, not just the medical treatment they receive—has eroded. In a 1998 survey, which compared consumer satisfaction among thirty-one industries, hospitals ranked twenty-seventh on a scale of trust felt by people. Distrust in doctor recommendations has further undermined the physician-patient relationship, a vital dimension to successful healing. In this climate of misery and frustration, Muhlenberg and its care toward relationships seemed an oasis.

Muhlenberg, now a 396-bed facility, is a fairly humble medical center, much like Plainfield itself. The entrance to the center is a kind of solarium, with ficus trees, a fountain with its inevitable coins, scattered pots of poinsettias. Inside the foyer, on the left, is a waiting area that resembles a living room. On the mantel of a false fireplace are photos that you might find at a grandma's house. Nearby stands an information table with hospital services on display. To the right of the waiting area is the extremely successful Express Admissions facility; and further on is the circular information desk—quiet, open, friendly. Nearby is a hallway of offices, one of which belongs to CEO John Kopicki.

In late 1997, Muhlenberg began the process of merging with the nearby Kennedy Hospital, to form the Solaris Health System—one of many such mergers provoked by the turmoil in the health care industry. When you step into the reception area to John's office, you'll be greeted by his assistant, Lou Ciganenko. These days, if you ask to see John, it's unlikely he'll be there. During this time of transition, he's spending more and more time at Kennedy doing what he does best—developing relationships. John doesn't just network; he takes seriously the task of developing trust through support, dialogue, and consensus building. Even though the Muhlenberg staff understands that now they have to take charge as he forges new links with their new and more powerful partner, they miss him. The merger has everyone on edge—anxious about their jobs, excited about the possibilities, curious about the outcomes—and John's presence is a comfort for many. Transitions are never easy, and this one is no exception. Muhlenberg is fortunate to have John navigating the turbulent waters of change—because he's been there before.

Command and Control Culture

The time in question was not a merger, but not unlike a merger either. It, too, was a time of transition, one that John had not expected to be part of, because, in fact, he was planning to leave the hospital. In 1990, after a brief spell as Muhlenberg's chief operating officer, John had an opportunity to join a management culture that was closer to his own style, and so he handed in his resignation. It just so happened that, at the same time, Muhlenberg's board of governors felt it needed a change of direction, a change of leadership. So, too, did the medical staff. As a result, two days before John was to leave, the board asked him to stay and become the president and CEO. He accepted, knowing that what lay ahead would be one of the biggest challenges he had ever faced.

At that time, Muhlenberg had drifted away from its tradition of a people-centered culture. Fran Hulse, vice president of medical affairs, who has worked at Muhlenberg since 1971, and longtime confidante of John, remembers the time prior to John's appointment as CEO in this way:

"It was a very uptight culture. People were extremely reserved and cautious about what they were going to say openly. The CEO's view of management was very controlling—things had to work the way he said they would. Period. What tended to happen was that even senior people felt they couldn't challenge him and expect to survive. This created a climate that was anything but open as far as inviting feedback and comment, positive or negative. And negative had a lot of risk attached to it—if you spoke negatively about the wrong thing, you might just shorten your career at this institution. There was a pervasive sense of oppression, and as a result employees felt constrained and very reluctant to express their ideas and opinions openly."

The Muhlenberg culture of that time—in common with all command and control cultures—had become a culture of disconnection. People disconnected from themselves—what they really thought and felt—as a way of keeping their jobs and surviving the culture. Disconnected from each other through silence, by not giving or receiving genuine feedback—fertile ground for festering complaints. Disconnected from their purpose—forgetting why they were there, becoming complacent and "just doing my job." And, as people in the care profession, disconnected from their care—preoccupied with and living in an atmosphere of fear and suspicion. Command and control leadership generates disconnection; and disconnection empowers command and control leadership. A vicious circle. What emerges is a culture of pained and strained relationships. And over time, disassociation sets in—people forget that they are disconnected.

A Different Way,
a Different Culture

Management that shuns command and control and instead engages people in a genuine way, creates a different culture, which is what happened at Muhlenberg. What follows are stories that illustrate how this came about, stories of cascading connections within Muhlenberg, starting with John's personal conversion as a leader, which created conditions for the culture to transform from one of command and control to one that was more accepting of change and uncertainty. His example of doing and his way of being enhanced that way of being in others and cascaded through the organization and ultimately created a sense of community.

There are evident three simple practices of behavior at all levels at Muhlenberg: listen, respond, let go. *Listen* to the people in the problem. *Respond* by acting on suggestions, providing resources, encouraging, acknowledging, and supporting experimentation. *Let go* and get out of their way and let them do what they need to do. Throughout the Muhlenberg story, these three behaviors, as you will see, continue to reemerge as core behaviors that led to the success of many projects; simple principles that were the source of creativity and adaptability in a complex adaptive system. These behaviors began a healing process in the relationships at Muhlenberg, affecting souls that had stagnated under a command and control culture.

John's story shows us the difficulties and rewards of changing existing modes of bureaucratic behavior and hierarchical thinking in an organization into a culture of change, openness, and connectedness that made the organization more adaptable, efficient, and creative. And a more congenial place to work.

John–Culture Connection: Transforming Cultures

In the midst of a health care crisis, faced with the reality that change couldn't be stopped, John found himself having to change how he thought about change. Leaders, he realized, could no longer command outcomes—it was too complex. They couldn't control their business environment—things were changing too fast. As John said, "If you're an autocratic manager, you're going to have a very difficult time operating in this chaotic environment. You just can't tell people what to do, and think they're going to do it. It just doesn't work that way anymore."

During this time of uncertainty, where a top-down approach to management came up short, John faced different questions. How to tap into people's creativity in the midst of chaos, rather than control their behavior? How to maintain a steadfast confidence that order, although unpredictable, would emerge rather than feigning a certainty? How to foster adaptability and flexibility in his organization? How to shift a culture of command and control, where predictability reigned king, to a culture where there was an acceptance of uncertainty and change? How to open up a closed system whose lines of communication had shut down? And how to bring people along in this transition, knowing that this was the organization's only recourse for survival?

A Personal Conversion

The first step in John's journey was the quandary where he had to give up the notion that he had control and he had to dispel other people's expectation that he had control. He had to learn to let go. A controlling style isn't in John's nature, nor in his avuncular appearance. True, he was trained in a traditional MBA program at George Washington University, but he wasn't interested in being a traditional manager. Rather, his leadership style is more intuitive, his reasons to lead more idealistic rather than egoistic. As the son of a funeral director, John learned early on to have a tremendous respect for people. Perhaps that's why he's attracted to managing organizations that take care of people—like his father, he also services people in a time of need.

Although command and control is contrary to John's nature, giving up control is not easy—even for him. He talked about it this way. "I think, unconsciously, you always want to maintain your control. You really have to fight against that. It's the toughest thing for senior management to do, to give it up. Even when you recognize that you *have* to just give it up, it's hard to have that flexibility, to have that patience. You have to create a new discipline in yourself. For instance, I have to have the courage to let my VP, Mary Anne, go ahead and spend money for which she couldn't immediately demonstrate the feedback. That doesn't mean I'm frivolous; that means that I have to make hard choices when it's impossible to know the outcome. At other times, when I've let go, I'll think, 'What the hell has this proven?' Sometimes I have to grit my teeth to keep from saying, 'Who authorized that!' But I never say it."

John's struggle to let go of control can be explained by his MBA training at George Washington University, which inculcated the conventional management model that leaders are controllers. But for men generally it is difficult, because traditional roles, and the definition of masculinity, demand that men *be* in control. Traditional roles put enormous pressure on men to perform, to produce, to be the answer man—a very mechanistic orientation. Leadership would then naturally be associated with fixing problems, providing solutions, enabling what's disabled, leveraging—also a mechanistic view. And because masculinity is heavily associated with autonomy, it is also about being the Lone Ranger, as John points out: "At a meeting once, there were a couple of CEOs saying, you know, 'I'm so tired of making decisions. Being the CEO, it's *so* hard.' And what I've been able to do is say, 'Yes, it is chaotic, we're out of control. The best we can do is rely on our instincts.' They seemed to respond to that."

On the other hand, letting go gave John a sense of relief. "By God, I've accepted all this responsibility, but it's okay," he says. "I don't know how it's going to turn out. I can't control it. All I can do is try to intuitively work with my people and direct it. I felt, 'Thank God. You don't have to have that total burden of leadership.' "

The practice of letting go initiated a different personal journey for John, where he faced an enormous uncertainty—how his style of leadership would affect the existing culture. In fact, several managers left Muhlenberg soon after John became CEO—some voluntarily, some otherwise—because they couldn't stomach the prospect of John's very different form of management. John called them "culture casualties." Even to this day, many evolutions later, John continues to see this struggle in his people, their wanting him to just take control.

"There are times when people will come to you and want that control decision," says John. "I mean, that's the incredible thing about it. You're all going along as a team, and then suddenly everybody will be looking at you, and you better not disappoint them. They want you to say, 'By God, it's going to be this way.' Sometimes people say, 'We've done this as far as we can. All we want is your final blessing.' At that point they don't want to hear me saying, 'Well, geez, what do *you* want to do?' They really want to have that final blessing from me, that final approval. It's beyond me."

But those who stayed began a powerful conversion themselves—from secrecy to openness, from illusion of control to honesty. In order to move people along toward accepting change and uncertainty, John cultivated an environment that encouraged them to experiment, learn, and contribute. He wanted people to feel that their efforts and contributions were recognized and appreciated. In return, they were prepared to go the extra mile to meet extraordinary challenges with and for him. "Sadly, we are living in a nonaffirming society," John recognizes. "People hunger for recognition, and when they receive it they are extremely motivated, and fulfilled."

A Cultural Conversion

John's *presence* was pivotal to stimulating a cultural change. When his people recounted to us powerful moments that impacted them and affected the existing culture, it was John's way of being with them that instigated the change, they said. Specifically, there were four behaviors that he demonstrated: being open, straight, human, and in relationship. These behaviors proved to be very effective in convincing a skeptical culture that things could and would be different. As John and others attest, although ultimately these behaviors make life simpler, they are hard to do. The organization worked very hard at it and went through a lot of rough times. And it didn't happen overnight. But it did succeed in moving the culture to a different place—a place where there was time to build trust, and time to heal, a place where a stagnant atmosphere of command and control lifted and the air cleared.

From Controlling to Being Open

Vice President Fran Hulse recounts an early event which illustrates the power of being open:

"Early on we started to bring management groups together informally, away from the hospital, to try to get to know each other on a more personal level. The first time we did it, there was a roomful of people, around forty-five, and we asked the questions: 'What are we doing wrong?' 'What do you think?' 'How can we make it work?' Nobody said a word. Here we were putting out all these direct questions, and all you could feel was the silence and the tension in the room. It happened again the second time. It was tough. But by the third time we got together, some of the barriers were coming down. It was incredible to see people relax a little bit. People had to build trust. They had to feel this wasn't just more lip service. I think it was less about trusting us and more about how shell-shocked they were. It wasn't until you saw the reactions of those people that you really appreciated how bad it must have been to work here."

From Secretive to Being Straight

John made it clear in the beginning that it was going to be different. And that people had to decide if they could change—become team players, be experimental, be straight. Fran had her own experience with John being straight with her and encouraging her to be straight herself. In her characteristically passionate, rapid-fire way she recounts *recognizing* her own lack of freedom to be herself in her discussion with him.

"It made me think about the fact that we were conditioned by the previous leadership to do business in a way that was kind of calculating. I mean, not that we were necessarily by our natures calculating and devious. But I think without even realizing it, we were conditioned to a certain way of doing business, where you had to strategize things in the back room so that a certain thing would play out a certain way, even though there were players who never had the whole picture of what was really going on.

"When you do business in a calculating way, you usually don't realize you're doing it, because it is what you do to keep things going, and how you survive. And I think literally John cut through that right in the beginning. He used to do that with me and say, 'You know, you don't have to do that, Fran. Just talk to them. Don't worry about telling them. We're not holding anything back here.' He had to keep reminding us that we're not going to keep secrets here. That we can't do that anymore; it doesn't get you anywhere."

Fran also remembers a powerful moment when John was straight with the organization:

"John came right out in the open on some real big issues with the staff. At employee meetings, held periodically through the year, John would get up and tell people what was going on. 'Here's the story, guys,' he'd say. 'And you've got to know this because we can't deal with this without you. I'm not keeping anything from you.' People listened and they questioned. Several years ago we were in a financially bad position. We had cuts, and it was looking bad. John had to tell them that he was going to have to freeze wages; no raises for that year. He had a full house, standing room only, people sitting in the aisles. He pulled out all the charts, presented all the finances, took them through it step by step. He explained why; he told them what we were going to do. He told them how great they've been. They applauded at the end of the meeting! We sat there and said, 'Can you top that?' Usually you get, 'Nobody appreciates me,' or 'Why am I only getting 2 percent?' They applauded!"

It was an extraordinary experience for the staff to see their leader be forthright with them, to show himself as vulnerable and not in absolute control. It was equally extraordinary for John to see the resilience in his people, that his people could accept very difficult situations if they felt they were part of the process.

From Omniscient to Being Human

COO Phil Brown recounts a time with John:

"John and I talk about personal issues from time to time. For instance, John stopped in last night. He came in to talk about how he was feeling about a family matter, and things that were going on. And that gave me an opportunity to say back to him about how I see him, about who he is. I mean, I could understand, given the difficulties and challenges he was facing at the time, if it had been played out as anger and bitterness at work. But in fact he did just the opposite: coming to me, telling me about his concerns, strengthened our relationship. I said, I understand now more about why you are so caring, and giving, and patient. I haven't often had those types of relationships in a work setting, where those kinds of conversations get going."

By revealing himself as vulnerable, John allowed people to care for him, and gave them permission to be human, too. He himself recognizes that his own frailties actually work to bind him to his staff:

"This management team puts up with me when I go off the deep end. Everybody has to go off the deep end sometimes. Somehow we've developed a tolerance where we don't hold grudges. It's also about the ability to have failure in an organization where people don't jump all over you, blaming and screaming. This gives permission to change. I heard a CEO recently admit he was wrong. He said, 'I pushed my people too hard. We failed. We didn't understand this field, and we're going to take some hits and lumps.' I guarantee you they're going to figure this out and come out okay. When the leader takes responsibility during a crisis, he gives permission for the team to regroup. What normally happens in a crisis is the leadership is replaced or they blame someone else. How many times has a CEO of a company come out and said 'I'll take that responsibility'? I don't see that a lot."

From Isolated to Being in Relationship

So much of what John accomplishes and inspires stems from his way of being in relationship to others, which engenders a sense of mutuality and respect. It even reframes the meaning of charisma and power.

People associate charisma with being slick, razzle-dazzle, a powerful attractiveness. John's charisma, on the other hand, doesn't light up the place but, instead, arises from his sincerity and honesty as a person, and the way he deals with people. Charisma with him is an emergent property—it comes through in his relationship to others. As Fran states, "If anything, you would say he's not that comfortable a public speaker. But when you find that out, it becomes his strength because he's real; he's not a phony. It works in a completely different way. It is John's way of *being* in relationship to people that defines him as a leader, not his position."

A Culture of Change and Care

A culture of change, adaptability, and action did emerge at Muhlenberg, as John hoped it would. And care. Care for the patients, as exemplified by Jimmy's warm and reassuring greeting at the front door, which is so important to people who are sick and often disoriented. It's apparent in the patient-satisfaction scores. When John became CEO, Muhlenberg was rated in the mid- to lower range in patient satisfaction according to a Pressgane survey. The management committee recognized the importance of improving these ratings, and had tried to deal with it in a command and control approach—that is, top-down decision making. But nothing happened. Finally John and the management committee decided to give the problem to the people who knew what needed to be done to improve the ratings. A diverse group of doctors, nurses, and other staff took on the task, and management, in essence, let go and got out of the way. Within a year, the group yielded results that previously were impossible to achieve. For the last two quarters of 1997, their ratings were well above the 90 percentile.

In this atmosphere of change and care, people once again became connected to their work. Mary Anne Keyes, VP of nursing, says she has the best team she has ever had. "It's an incredible experience to come in every day, to believe in what you're doing with people, to enjoy the relationships—that's worth a lot." That's just what John wants to hear. "If we can't come here every day being happy, there's no reason to come here at all," he says.

But no one should imagine this transition from one culture to another is quick and easy. "You have to keep trying," says John, "and you have to be prepared to get things wrong, because you will. You have to be prepared to fail at things." No wonder a common refrain heard at Muhlenberg is "Just try it"—words that heal a connection to work and lead to accepting change.

Listen . . . respond . . . let go . . .

Mary Anne–Janet Connection:
Unleashing Potential

At first, Mary Anne Keyes had mixed feelings about working at Muhlenberg as vice president of patient care. Previously, she had worked exclusively at tertiary hospitals involved with large teaching institutions, and she had grown accustomed to being part of academic circles, where new concepts were discussed and applied. New ideas were important to her, and so she didn't know how interesting a small community hospital would be in the long haul. She knew she could run a nursing department: that wasn't what interested her. The challenge was figuring out how she could do it better and different each year.

"The ability to continuously learn is very important to me," says Mary Anne. "I wasn't sure I could find that here. But I did. In spades." Muhlenberg, she found, was aswirl with innovative ideas about management, principally the idea of using complexity science to generate creative adaptability and implement change, which John had introduced to Muhlenberg a year before Mary Anne arrived. Mary Anne hadn't heard of complexity science before, and at first it seemed foreign and a little abstract to her, couched in a new and strange language. But very soon, in the midst of a collective learning experience, she could see that it wasn't abstract at all. It gave her and her colleagues a new perspective on the day-to-day demands on their jobs, provided a language that named things that Mary Anne knew intuitively to be right but that had no external validation. It created a support system for change.

"What I think the language and the concepts have given us, as we learned these things together, is more courage to *do* things. Sometimes scary things," says Mary Anne. The science says that you have only limited control over where your organization is going, but that continuous experimentation allows you to explore possibilities of change, sometimes leading to dramatic, emergent, unexpected results. "It gives you that willingness to take a leap into the dark, not knowing where you are going to land, but trusting you're going to land safely, and you're going to be okay. For me, that was always the most fun—the seat-of-your-pants kind of stuff. Doing what seemed like the right thing to do."

Validated in her beliefs in trusting that some order will emerge, Mary Anne became what John called "a fearless context changer." But Mary Anne will be the first to tell you that her initiatives for change don't come out of the blue—she listens. She pays a lot of attention to what matters to patients, and what matters to her people.

The Admissions Problem

Soon after coming on staff in 1993, Mary Anne made it her business to spend time getting to know her people and they her, which included janitors and visiting clergy. Through patient surveys and written responses, and asking around the units, one of the things she heard was that admissions was taking too long. It could take up to twenty hours between the time a patient enters the hospital and receives their first dose of antibiotics—that's serious, especially with someone fighting infection. And the endless waits were distressing for the patients. Mary Anne discovered that this wasn't just a Muhlenberg problem: a survey, published by VHA, Inc., a health-care cooperative formerly known as the Voluntary Hospitals Association, showed Muhlenberg to be pretty typical. Mary Anne put herself in the patient's position and asked herself the question, "What must it feel like to experience my organization as a patient?" Lacking patience in the line of waiting herself, Mary Anne's reaction was outrage. "How could we let that happen?" she demanded of herself, and then of others.

Several existing committees at Muhlenberg were looking at the problem, but none was making any headway. So she went to John and asked if she could have a shot at trying something different. "Sure, go ahead," John said. "Do what you want. You have until the end of the year." Mary Anne started up a new task force, pulling people from all the departments, leaving the project open to anyone who wanted to participate, knowing from complexity science the power of diversity and self-organization. Among the twenty who joined was Janet Biedron, who had worked at Muhlenberg off and on since 1975, and had her share of dealings with different styles of management.

From Troublemakers to Stars

Janet, a straightforward, cut-to-the-chase kind of person, with wild auburn hair to match, often found herself stepping on people's toes in the command and control culture. A freethinker, she couldn't accept a decision just because she was told to: she needed to understand the decision, and it had to make sense to her. Consequently, although respected for her technical skills, she was perceived to be a troublemaker. And a troublemaker—as someone who challenges the status quo, who recognizes what's not working rather than pretends it does, who has courage to stand up for what's right rather than conform to what's expected—doesn't do well in a command and control culture that demands compliance. Janet was stagnating in that environment. She stopped opening up; she stopped looking for better ways to do things. She did her job of pre-hospital service, supervising eight people, and did it well. But something was missing in her work—her passion.

When Janet went to the admissions task force, she knew something was different. It was the first time in her twenty-plus years of experience that she attended a meeting chaired by a senior management person. Usually it had been middle management that headed this type of task force. What Mary Anne's presence said to Janet, and to the rest of the members, was that "this woman means business." Although Janet's mostly negative experience with management made her guarded at first, she sensed in Mary Anne something different—a gentle toughness, genuine caring, someone who *wanted* change. The status quo was shifting and Janet began to feel hopeful that there might be a chance to improve something, an opportunity to change and grow.

Mary Anne began the meeting by simply and directly stating that the current admission time was unacceptable. As Mary Anne began to sketch out her ideas and interact with people on the task force, Janet experienced a chemistry of connection with her that held the promise of transformation. "I thought of it as a new beginning for me," she recalls, still moved by the power of the moment. "It was like coming up from the trenches." The connection was mutual. From the first meeting it was clear to Mary Anne that Janet could not only conceptualize what she, Mary Anne, was trying to do, but Janet was the one who could implement it. Their meeting was synergistic, connecting each of them to their passion, their knowledge, and their wealth of experience.

Even though Mary Anne had been told Janet was trouble, that was no trouble for her. "I was looking for someone who could do what needed to be done," explains Mary Anne, leaning back in her chair, arms crossed on her red suit jacket. "I didn't worry about the fact that someone was ticked off because Janet disturbed the equilibrium. In fact, that's what I *wanted*—someone who could shake things up." Mary Anne perceived a troublemaker differently, and appreciated rather than devalued Janet's characteristics, because she is a troublemaker herself. "She drives me nuts," John says, laughing. "Mary Anne has no satisfaction. She'll ask a million and one questions as to why. She has this constant quest for trying to understand, and asking what we can do about it. Unfortunately, that's not always understood by everyone."

Troublemakers are often misunderstood. Their resistance to buckling under cultural pressure is not always seen as a healthy integrity; their challenges are not seen as potentially innovative. In a command and control culture that is invested in predictability and constancy, troublemakers ruffle feathers and need to be put in their place. But in cultures that value adaptability and change, troublemakers are the movers who push organizations to their creative edges, where new opportunities emerge. So it's not surprising that Mary Anne and Janet would have a powerful and healing connection, where they would mutually unleash their capabilities. All the characteristics of a troublemaker that were regarded as bad in a command and control culture now became assets.

As with most task forces, the work quickly devolved to a few people, with Mary Anne and Janet at the helm. Their skills were complementary—Mary Anne had the clout to get things done, and Janet knew what needed to be done, and how to do it. They were on a mission, determined to make the project a success. In less than two months they were ready to set up a two-week pilot project, with Janet overseeing it, and Mary Anne "cheering her on" and getting out of the way. What emerged was something neither of them could have anticipated or predicted: they found themselves with an unexpected, nonlinear result.

Janet knew she had to have the right people for the job; people who could respond to the challenge of being pioneers, people who could come up with ideas of their own and make them work. Here, Janet's long tenure at Muhlenberg was an important asset: she knew everyone, and she was able to choose carefully. "Had we had the wrong people in the pilot, it may have had a different turn," Janet admits. There were lots of possibilities for things to go wrong, or for other departments to get in their way—but instead they got cooperation.

The project was a huge success. In less than three months, admission time was down from twenty hours to eighty minutes. And much of it was due to Janet, who deftly navigated her way around any obstacle, who never doubted the success of the project.

Express Admissions

Other departments quickly saw the benefits of up-front admissions, and support for the project grew. The management committee quickly approved full implementation of express admissions. Again, Janet recruited carefully for the expanded unit. Her approach was to have each person be an expert in one of the skills needed in the unit, from secretary to lab person. Then she cross-trained them. Given that no cross-training courses existed, she developed her own. It took a year for the staff to go from being expert in one thing to being expert in everything. The staff were happy, because their jobs had expanded, they had learned new skills, and their work was more diversified. The staff set up the unit themselves, right down to the Band-Aids, because according to Janet, "The way I looked at it was, 'I'm not going to set up my kitchen, and then ask you to come cook in it.' They had to set it up; they had to make it theirs." She let go and got out of the way.

The project didn't end there; it continued to evolve in unexpected ways, growing and including other departments. The ward nurses loved it because all the admission work was done prior to the patient coming to the floor, and they could focus on getting the patient comfortable. The doctors loved it, because Janet's team was a "can do" unit—any additional services the doctors requested were always possible. Most of all, the patients loved it. And Janet, director of admissions, now headed a department of eighty-seven people who handled registration for both admitted inpatients and outpatients, all the emergency room registrations, two clinical areas at the express admissions, pre-admission testing and financial groups. And many hospitals have replicated the express admission. As Mary Anne says, "Janet is a real star of the organization."

Leadership As Engaging Others

What made the difference for Janet was Mary Anne's way of leading and dealing with people. As Janet says, "For me, what made her management style successful was that I was given freedom, but also guidance. You have to have both—you can't just have space, independence, and freedom without guidance. If she had approached me differently, I doubt that I would have supported her the way I did. But Mary Anne also saw in me what only my mother saw in me," she says with a peal of laughter. "She sees that I'm an honest player; I call it like I see it. If I believe in it, you get one hundred, two hundred percent. If I don't, you get zip. I feel very loyal to Mary Anne. I wouldn't want to let her down."

Mary Anne feels similarly toward John. "I don't want to disappoint John. He deeply cares about the patients and this institution and the people he's working with. I think that most people here would walk over hot coals for him." When people feel they are part of a web of connection and part of a community, then they go the distance for each other, not because they *have* to but because they *want* to.

Mary Anne describes her style of leadership, which is similar to John's—that is, direction without directives—in this way. "I *could* be the kind of leader who says, 'By God, this is what we're going to do, and this is how it's going to be done,'" Mary Anne says, slamming her hand on the table to make her point. "I *could* make everybody do whatever I decided, but it's not the most effective way of managing people." Instead, she argues, it's better to take the time needed so as to involve people in the process of figuring out what change needs to happen, and how to achieve that change. "I think you need people to be engaged in the process," says Mary Anne in her characteristically soft-spoken, reflective way, "and they have to trust that there's a chance they have some sway over what's going to happen. If they feel like there's no opportunity to influence, then you're wasting everybody's time around the table.

"One of the things that makes this approach to management successful is that you're listening to the front-line people, which gives you the ability to pick out a focus people can grab on to. Then give them a little bit of support along the way—it doesn't take much—so they can do what they need to do. And then just get out of their way." In Mary Anne's style of leadership, acceptance is the end point of a project, not its implementation.

"Overall, this approach might take longer in the up-front phase than the more traditional approach," concludes Mary Anne. "But I think it's worth it. Because the other way, you spend a lot more time fighting with everybody telling you why it's not working, and trying to fix it. This way, you don't have to keep explaining it every six months."

Three simple rules, a healing connection, helped transform troublemakers into stars:

Listen . . . respond . . . let go . . .

Janet–Rhonda Connection: Front-Line Wisdom

Charity care, state money given to hospitals to pay for the care of indigent patients, conjures up images of another time, of a Dickensian ethic of social responsibility—caring for the less fortunate. As often happens with many government programs, magnanimous intentions become entangled in the snarl of bureaucratic requirements, and nuisance upstages altruism. The difficulty with the multistep process of charity care is not just that the procedure is complicated, but that it requires information from a population who are often homeless. These people are not likely to be carrying their tax statements for the last five years in their transient bag of meager possessions. Charity care is not a minor issue for Muhlenberg, because it represents 12 to 15 percent of patients, and therefore has a big impact on the hospital. An indigent population creates tension for the hospital between fulfilling its social responsibility and the necessity to achieve its financial margins.

The process of qualifying patients for charity care is so arduous and time-consuming that many hospitals don't even bother. Swallowing the costs seems the lesser of two evils. But with the pressure of mounting economic constraints, ignoring this potential source of revenue is no longer feasible. A popular option is hiring outside consultants to sort through the mess. Although the cost of consultants can be high, the increased revenue still leaves hospitals ahead. That was exactly what Muhlenberg's management committee was considering.

When Janet heard of this plan, it bothered her. "I couldn't understand why they would want to bring somebody from the outside who had no loyalty to the hospital, and reward them. When you have resources here, why not use incentives for your own employees?" Janet had a particular resource in mind—three clerks, paid $8 per hour, who had approached her and insisted that the hospital didn't need outside people. They could do the job, they claimed, because they had a relationship with the people. Because it was their community. In particular, it was Rhonda Owens who would eventually become the heart and soul of the project.

Rhonda remembers how the new approach emerged. "When Janet became responsible for this financial area, she started talking to me, listening to me. That's the key—listen to your people," says Rhonda emphatically. "I had no title or anything. I was just a regular worker like everybody else. Janet just sat down and listened to what I had to say. She was like an angel who came to me . . . she just listened. A lot of employees like to be heard, but nobody listens. I've been here ten years, and everybody knows me now, but they didn't before. Janet makes you want to do better in your job. You don't want to let her down."

While talking to Janet, Rhonda suggested a novel approach for dealing with charity care: go to the patients' homes to get the information needed to qualify them. Janet recognized the force of the idea—the hospital going to the community rather than waiting for the community to come to the hospital. She remembered a time noticing Rhonda talk to a male patient who couldn't fill out a form. He couldn't fill it out because he didn't have his glasses with him—they were at home. Although the many reasons for not filling out the forms may seem small, for the patient, unfamiliar with the ways of bureaucracy, small obstacles can become overwhelming. And the hospital, up to that point, had been unable to overcome them. Hospital administrators thought of all kinds of incentives to draw the charity care population into the hospital, like offering free turkeys or a $100 gift certificate. But none of them were implemented. And the reasons were very simple—eligible people didn't come in because they didn't feel well, because they were disorganized, because they didn't know about the availability of funding for them.

Doing home visits had made sense to Rhonda for quite a while, because she was already doing them on her own time, usually on the way home from work. She had the solution—she just needed someone to ask her. As Rhonda says, "It was not just the fact that Janet listened; it was also that she acted—immediately. When I told Janet an idea I had, she said, 'Great idea,' and she moved right on it. It's not like when you tell somebody something, and then you never hear about it again. With Janet, the next day it's done."

Janet describes the intent of her actions—namely, to mobilize others. "These women were working in places where they weren't recognized as having value. Now they are recognized as having value and are given the space to do what they need to do," she says passionately between gulps of Coke from a jar. "I've always believed that the people who do the work should have the greatest say in how it should be done. When I hire people I tell them right up front—if you're going to work in this area and for me, this is the way we do things. If you have an idea, if you want to make a decision or you want to take action, do it. Don't come to me for every little thing, because there's no way I could manage this department, virtually unassisted as I do, unless I could trust the people who are going to take things into their own hands. They have to feel comfortable that they can make decisions. Not everyone can work in this kind of environment."

Egged on by her staff, Janet argued that the management committee should allow her people to engage in head-to-head competition with the outside consultants. The consultants put on a professional presentation, and demonstrated that, for a half million dollars, they could have charity care benefit the hospital. Janet showed how for less than $50,000, which included a small incentive plan of $18,000 that would kick in only after revenues exceeded the $7 million collected the previous year, her team of five people could offer everything the consultancy offered. And, even better, the hospital would be utilizing its own people and letting its own people benefit from the incentive. She won, and the challenge was theirs.

Rhonda and her colleagues got to work. "I've never experienced such a committed group that worked so hard, so professionally, so diligently," Janet recounts with a continued sense of awe. "This staff was fearless. And the reason they were fearless is because this is *their* community. These are *their* patients. They have a *relationship* with these people. And because the patients aren't threatened, they're willing to work with us."

Within ten months, qualified charity care income had increased by $2 million over previous revenues. From a business perspective, five people generating an income of $2 million would be regarded as highly successful entrepreneurs! So, charity care was a huge economic success. But it was more than that. The cascade of healing connections spilled out of the hospital and continued into the community.

Listen . . . respond . . . let go . . .

Rhonda–Community Connection: Touching the Indigent Community

There are good reasons why Rhonda is known as the Mother Teresa of Plainfield, not least of which is that she herself embodies the spirit of charity care. She sincerely cares and wants to help, and she goes the distance for people. Patients recognize this in her, and consequently trust her. They know her commitment firsthand—she sticks with the patients from the beginning of their care to the end. And in that process of helping, she educates them about a system they don't understand, and she herself learns many procedures, from Medicaid to disability to Social Security. And she does it, not because she wants to be great, but because "it makes me feel good."

Rhonda, who has lived in the Plainfield area all her life, gently touches a fantastic pile of cornrows elegantly draped on her head, smooths her tuxedo-white blouse, and slowly recounts a story:

"There was a patient in the hospital . . . she refused to talk to anybody . . . we have a lot of those. If the nursing staff can't get through to them, they call me. I went up, and tried to get her to open up. She started to cry, and then started to talk. So I just listened. It turned out her family didn't know that she was HIV positive. She didn't know how she could tell them. I told her I would go with her when it was time for her to tell her family. I told her about Plainfield Health Center; that it is very involved with HIV people; that they have counselors there. I told her she can get help there. I told her to trust me. And she did."

But the story doesn't end there. Two days later, the woman, now back at her home, called Rhonda in a terrible state of distress and despair, barely coherent: she and her parents were threatened with eviction, was the fragmented message. Rhonda tried to calm her, and gave her what advice she could. Later, Rhonda went to the woman's house—it was dirty, no food, no heat. They were using the gas stove to warm the place, barely. Rhonda persuaded the woman's parents, who were elderly, to listen to the police who were at the house, and were urging them to be admitted into a nursing home. The parents listened to Rhonda, and a place was found for them. The young woman moved in with friends. Rhonda continues to be, as with many others, a vital resource for this family, as someone they turn to for information, for guidance, for hope.

But it's not easy, given the number of people needing help. Their faith and expectation that Rhonda *will* rescue them, *will* take care of them can be overwhelming. "I just do what I can," she sighs, "but sometimes it's so bad I just don't pick up the phone." In the meantime, Janet is encouraging Rhonda to go to social work school because "she's a natural."

HIV Community

An unanticipated outgrowth of the charity care project was the impact that Rhonda's home visits had on the community. Her high visibility makes her a well-known person in the Plainfield community. They know her by sight. They recognize her car. She seeks her constituency, patiently, persistently, wherever they are: at their bars, at the strip joints, at shelters. And the community helps her, cooperates in tracking patients down. "Many of these patients don't have phones, but I just find them," says Rhonda, and then adds with a confident chuckle, "I *always* find them."

Rhonda's presence in the community and her involvement with HIV patients has become a conduit for creating more healing connections in the community. As a symbol of efficacy and a source of information, Rhonda has become a reference point for many people in the community—someone they all know. Patients in the HIV counseling group at the health center started talking about her. Patients were referring other people to her. And consequently, a population that characteristically tends to be isolated were talking to each other. They were sharing information about resources. They were learning from their friends; they were educating their friends about the system. They didn't do that before. Rhonda had inadvertently forged a connection for the community to itself, an example of a small change having a big effect in a web that includes hospital, health center, and community.

"We talk about the financial incentive," reflects Janet, "but that's not what drives this. What drives these five women is the commitment to the community, to each other, and to the patients." And that commitment has left an indelible mark in the community. The rich web of connections, within the hospital and outside into the community, has kindled a stellar opportunity—a time for all to heal. Not just the body, but also the soul.

Listen . . . respond . . . let go . . .

The Next Challenge

Now Muhlenberg embarks on another journey, the merger with Kennedy Hospital. A survival tactic taken by many hospitals, merging has become an economic lifesaver. But merging is about more than just the financial bottom line: it is also about an ability to nurture a constructive working relationship between institutions that are typically unequal and different, not only in size and economic clout, but often also in their cultures. This is the case with Muhlenberg and Kennedy, with Muhlenberg being the smaller of the two hospitals and having a much more open, human-oriented management practice compared with Kennedy's more traditional management. Two different cultures face each other, with unease on both sides. "I think everyone's anxiety level here is high," says John. "But my people have consistently said, 'Let's just get on with it. Let's find out how it turns out.' It's a kind of an acceptance of life on their part and what is going on in the world, in all its unpredictability and uncertainty. It's incredible."

Chapter 6

St. Luke's: The Ox That Took Flight

One must not always think so much about what one should do, but rather what one should be. Our works do not ennoble us; but we must ennoble our works.
Meister Eckehart, *Work and Being*

In January 1998, *Campaign,* the trade magazine for the advertising industry in the U.K., voted St. Luke's as the Agency of the Year, an award coveted by all the high-powered ad shops in this high-powered business. A tiny agency by most industry standards, having just a hundred people on board, and barely into its third year of existence, St. Luke's should have earned acclaim and praise from its fellow travelers, for its achievement was remarkable by any standards. But mostly it didn't, because St. Luke's is a maverick organization that turned its back on the industry and openly criticized its morals and aggressive work practices, which St. Luke's chairman, Andy Law, describes as being "driven by ego and greed." David Abraham, co-founder and chief operating officer of St. Luke's, is no less disparaging. He says that the industry is run by "money-grubbing, mealymouthed liars."

When they created the agency, Andy and David wanted a company that not only works in a very different way from traditional agencies—indeed from most companies in any industry—but also produces a new genre of advertising based on honesty and ethical values. For an industry that a 1995 Gallup poll in the United States placed second only to members of Congress and used-car salesmen in lack of honesty and ethical values, St. Luke's credo was quite a challenge. "St. Luke's sets itself up as an easy target for critics," commented an editorial in the same issue of *Campaign* that announced the agency's award. "Its policy of replacing offices with 'brand rooms,' its refusal to enter work for creative awards, and its insistence on pulling out of pitches with which it feels uncomfortable can smack of pretension and insufferable preciousness."[1] Noting that the St. Luke's way of doing things is widely regarded as distinctly flaky and weird, the magazine nevertheless acknowledges that the agency "has managed to achieve something different in business."[2] An article in a February 1998 issue of the *New York Times* business section recognized St. Luke's special brand of creativity, by saying that the agency was "coming up with some of the most rule-breaking campaigns on either side of the Atlantic."[3]

The Genesis of St. Luke's

The people who became St. Luke's were formerly the London Office of the New York–based ad giant Chiat/Day, one of the most famous names in the business, with a reputation for being as creative as it was arrogant. During the early 1990s, Jay Chiat became concerned that the industry had become ossified and that creativity was suffering. He formed a team from the agency, including Andy and David from the London office, and charged them to seek a new path, a new set of values, to create the Agency of the Future. In May 1992, the team, which had called itself the Chrysalis Committee, met in Los Angeles, which at the time was in the midst of conflagration and riot following a court decision in a highly racially charged trial. Tucked away safely in a swanky hotel, the committee came to see that the industry, not to put too fine a point on it, stank.

One afternoon during the meeting, Andy and David entered the conference room, placed a picture of Aristotle on the flip chart, and Andy slowly wrote a single word in Greek. (Andy has a degree in Greek and Latin literature.) He pointed to the word and said, "It means 'ethics.' And we think this is what we've been looking for." The rest of the committee agreed, and they quickly developed the notion of nothing less than a moral crusade to introduce an ethical vein in the companies they worked with. So entranced was Chiat with the idea that Chiat/Day could be a force in changing the world that he installed himself on the committee. His tenure didn't last long: three hours. The committee told Chiat that, like charity, the crusade would have to begin at home, because the agency itself was sick, with its employees ground down, its profit sharing geared to enriching top management, and its creativity lackluster. Chiat exploded, stormed out of the meeting, the Agency of the Future history, and the Chrysalis Committee moribund.

A few years later, in January 1995, the huge communications conglomerate Omnicom Group announced that it was acquiring Chiat/Day, which, it said, would be merged with a TBWA, a much larger, rival agency known for solid, if unexciting, work. Andy was told that his job would be to bring to the merged agency the maximum amount of business with the minimum number of people, and that stock options would soon make him rich. "I was appalled by the idea," Andy recalls. "I was going to have none of it." He returned to the London office from a meeting with Omnicom executives, drew a line across the office floor, announced that he was leaving the agency, and urged others to decide what to do based on their own best interests. One by one the thirty-five people in the room crossed the line to Andy's side. "It was an incredibly emotional experience, incredibly tense," Andy says. "Because we had no idea what we would do."

Despite their different perspectives, Andy and the people at Omnicom had developed a decent working relationship, and this allowed Andy to negotiate a deal whereby he and David would acquire the London branch of Chiat/Day from the parent company for $1 and a slice of future profits. Within weeks Andy and David had given away their newly acquired company.

"As soon as we could get ourselves organized, we all gathered in a hotel near here and I said, 'All right, we're on this desert island, what is the perfect company? What is the best company for ourselves? What makes sense for us?' " Andy recalls. "A lot of words came out, emotional concepts, like 'friendship,' 'cooperation,' 'trust,' 'being proud of the company.' I realized that we were being asked to invent something as a human being rather than an outside body that we were all going to have to fit into." The result was the notion of an organization with virtually no hierarchy, no bureaucracy, where everyone could say what they wanted, wear what they wanted, and come in when they wanted. Where no one would have personal offices. And where the usual linear process of creating ads would be abandoned, in favor of a chaotic, nonlinear method that focused on brand rooms (that is, offices devoted to current clients). "We wanted to unlock the human potential trapped in conventional business environments in order to enhance creativity and competitiveness," recalls David. Some of these innovative elements of work practice had been present in the group's previous incarnation at Chiat/Day, but it would be taken to extremes in St. Luke's. But what was very different from Chiat/Day, and is unique in the business, is that everyone would have an equal share in the equity of the new company, from Andy the chairman to Rose Hamilton the housekeeper. "That way you get rid of the ego and greed problem," says Andy.

As a cooperative, the group felt the agency shouldn't be named after themselves, and so St. Luke's was chosen, because St. Luke is the patron saint of artists and doctors, which was thought to resonate with the agency's goal of creativity and healing. "The nature of the name and the fact that we are all equal shareholders means that the company can live on beyond us," explains Andy. "We didn't want the usual ego-driven few years of intense activity, followed by lucrative sale of the company, making a few top people rich." The agency would be governed by a five-member council, called QUEST, which stands for a legal structure for running a cooperative entity, a qualifying employee shareholder trust. Employees would vote people onto QUEST, whose function, among things such as nurturing the agency's culture, includes setting the chairman's salary. And so St. Luke's was born, this utopia of equality, mutual respect, and purveyor of ethics in an otherwise unethical industry. A beautiful butterfly had emerged from the long-moribund chrysalis. The first year was hell.

Ethics in Business

St. Luke's is housed in a renovated toffee factory of Victorian vintage that most writers describe as being "on the fringes of Bloomsbury," which has a nice intellectual aura to it, Virginia Woolf and all that. In fact, it is much closer to London's biggest red-light district, King's Cross, reflecting the agency's desire to be physically as well as philosophically distant from London's adland in swanky Soho, and on the fringe of things. At the doorway is a plaque that reads as a dictionary, "entrance, *vb.*—entrancing, entranced, to fill with delight, Entrancement, entrancing, *adj.*" Inside, it's chaos, or at least looks that way. The foyer vaults two stories high, the walls painted a riot of sea foam green, raspberry frappé, black-light rose, lit by huge Victorian windows. Next month it will be different colors, because through a lottery someone gets to choose a set of colors that takes their fancy of the moment, and over a weekend the place is chromatically transformed. And the same every month after that.

Simple furniture is scattered casually here and there, including a long, curved blue couch. Hanging over a long, curved reception counter, all metal, is a papier-mâché ox with wings, image of St. Luke as he took this form in flight in Dante's *Inferno*. A few people are working on computers at desks by one wall; more are to be seen in a room just off the foyer. An open metal staircase in the middle of the foyer reaches up to a mezzanine. As people walk in they pick up a mobile phone from a bank of them on the wall, a morning ritual.

People wander back and forth, dressed casually, in army fatigues, T-shirts; black is big. Short-cropped hair is big, too, for the young men—and they are all young, in their twenties and thirties.

We wait for Andy for a while, until someone suggests we should go to the chill-out space in the basement. Just outside the room is a line of personal lockers, decorated idiosyncratically to each person's whim by an artist in residence. In the chill-out space, Rose is busying herself behind a buffet counter, papers are spilled over half a dozen refectory-type tables, someone is working on a large sketch of what looks like a man in a space suit, and two men are playing table soccer in the corner. All whitewashed, rough brick walls, the chill-out space spills onto a patio via French doors, where a couple of people chat over coffee. We install ourselves in a tiny "library," whose contents range from Mary Daly's radical feminist book *Gyn/Ecology,* a book titled *Ethics in Practice,* and Peter Senge's *Fifth Discipline.* It's a cramped, disheveled space, with unpacked boxes of books and papers, and a computer. The whole building, or what we'd seen of it up to that point, looks like nothing we'd encountered anywhere.

Andy eventually walked into the chill-out space, a phone at his ear, chatting. He went over to Rose, exchanged casual greetings, picked up a cup of coffee, and then shoehorned himself into what little space remained in the library. "Sorry I'm late," he said with a smile. You got the feeling that this was the norm, not the exception, a consequence of the free-flowing pace of St. Luke's. The son of a vicar, Andy is a man of medium build, dressed in a black shirt and black pants, with thick dark hair and pensive brown eyes. You would think him more a poet than one of London's more famous business figures. Before long he was telling us that he draws on Greek philosophy in his business world. "It sounds pretty ridiculous, I know," he began, "but you realize that some of the things that went on in the Greek city-states and their understanding of democracy and how people work together and what happens when they don't are pretty instructive for what we do now." The fact that all who work at St. Luke's are equal shareholders is a good example of Aristotelian distributive justice, after all.

We asked Andy about ethics in the advertising world. First, he said that St. Luke's doesn't call itself an advertising agent, more a creative communications business. "We want to communicate gracefully," he explained, "and we want to sell products genuinely, because the truth about a company is more powerful than any slogan you can fabricate." He told us about a large, international company that wanted an advertising campaign that dwelt only on the good things it did. "We said, we'll do it only if we can talk about the negative side of the business, too. They couldn't bring themselves to do that." Another agency took up the task, produced the kind of campaign the company wanted, and finished up being the target of environmental protesters. "One day business leaders will realize that being honest with the public is not just the best way to work, but the only way to work in the future," Andy said. "But it could take a while."

As for internal ethics, the duty of companies to their people, Andy argues that the single most important responsibility for a company is the fulfillment of its people, a notion of personal transformation, a notion of personal growth. At St. Luke's, this translates to everyone feeling that they can contribute, be involved not only in the day-to-day work in a genuine—not lip-service empowerment—way, but also in financial decisions, the direction of the company, and so on. "You have to believe that everyone is brilliant," he explained. "Because if you don't, you've automatically limited them. So we leveled the organizational structure, and said everyone is brilliant. That's why we shared out the company equally among us." To most companies, this is not the typical bottom line, which is profits. "To me, profits are like breathing," Andy said. "You need it to live, but it's not what you live *for.*"

An Upside-Down Swan

Despite having a common vision and being a tight-knit community, St. Luke's first year was hell, because the group was in the chaotic throes of breaking an old way of working and seeking a new one, a novel way whose chances of succeeding no one had any clue about. In the vortex of uncertainty, people were grumpy, bewildered; there was a lot of backbiting. "We had no mold to follow," remembers Robbie Sparks, a typographer who's been in the business for almost thirty years. "This is traditionally a high-pressure business, with people ground down for the financial benefit of others or for themselves. I've seen so many marriages fail because of the pressure. I've seen friends have heart attacks. We knew there had to be another way, but we didn't know what it was. We knew we wanted to try this different way, but it was hard, very hard." David remembers it this way: "Our desire for ideological purity conflicted with our need to survive as a business. We argued about how to balance financial realities with creative and philosophical ideals. It got sticky, but it was worth the struggle."

On a day-to-day scale of work, one of the hardest things for many people was not having a personal desk. People were supposed to come in in the morning, pick up their mobile phone, and then find somewhere to sit. If there was a client team meeting going on in which you were involved, then you'd go to the brand room. Even if there wasn't, you might go there anyway. Or to a quiet room to work on a computer. Or to the chill-out space, where a lot of St. Luke's work goes on in a distinctly nontraditional environment. "It's really difficult at the beginning," Sue McGraw told us. An account manager who had been with St. Luke's just six weeks when we visited, Sue was still in the midst of adjusting. She had come from one of the largest, most famous agencies in the world, which was very hierarchical, very aggressive. "I'd say, 'Okay, I'll go to the client room today,' and maybe do that for a few days, and that began to feel comfortable. But then I'd say, 'Oh, I'd better go somewhere else today, because I'm not supposed to be in the same place all the time.' It can make you feel quite uncomfortable and disoriented."

Sue told us that she was getting used to it, and was also getting used to the idea that she could contribute when and how she wanted. "That was very difficult, too, to begin with, because in my previous organization, in most organizations really, you're usually told what to do," she said. "It can be very disorienting being asked, 'What do you *want* to do?' " Some newcomers don't fare as well as Sue, she told us, and they hide themselves away, physically and in terms of coming forward with ideas.

These days, newcomers are entering an organization where most people are already at ease with this apparently chaotic work environment. In that first year, however, *everyone* was a newcomer to a new way of working. "I remember that time as being full of extreme agony, frustration, and despair, for everyone," recalled Andy. "People were pleading, 'Where are we *going?*' 'What are we *doing?*' '*Why* can't we have our own desks?' I said, 'I just know that having offices is wrong. This is an experiment, and I don't know if it will succeed.' " Andy told us that he deliberately stepped out of the organization, in the sense of not trying to make it go in one way or another, just seeing what might unfold.

Andy didn't know about complexity science at the time, but he was doing what the science would advocate under the circumstances of seeking dramatic change. He was taking an organization that was, if not exactly mechanistic, running in a fairly stable, comfortable mode of operating, and then deliberately pushing it into chaos. The pain of the process was obvious, from what he and others told us, and the swirl of confusion was described as hard to tolerate.

What happens in this state is that the organization is slowly exploring new paths of interaction, new dynamic avenues, incorporating elements that work and rejecting those that don't. The system is moving gradually toward the emergence of something that works as a whole, even though it doesn't feel like it at the time. Not until a critical mass of working elements is reached does the new pattern emerge, and when it happens it happens quickly, as through a phase transition.

"We struggled with how to make decisions that were accountable but still effective," is how David describes the challenge of the first year. "We failed to run the company properly the first year, failed massively," is how Andy remembers the process. "Instead of creating a place where everyone was happy, we created bitterness and uncertainty. Then toward the end of the year optimism began to flow, and we were on our way." The phase transition was complete, and the agency was now in the zone of creative adaptability.

There were a few casualties, of course, because the free-flowing, apparently chaotic mode of working is not for everyone. "There was one guy who just couldn't function without an office with a door, and a secretary," Robbie told us. "He went back to a bigger agency, and that was probably best for him. The way we do things at St. Luke's might not be the best way of working, and we will keep changing it, building toward something better. But now we've come this far, there's no going back."

We keep using the phrase "apparently chaotic," because that's how St. Luke's looks to visitors, and it can feel that way, too, for people working there. "Most companies want to look like a graceful swan," Andy suggested to us, by way of analogy. "They see themselves as an image of beauty and order, attractive and in control. Meanwhile the feet are going berserk under the water, making the thing move. We see ourselves as an upside-down swan. Deep down we know where we're going and we think of ourselves as attractive. But all you see are the feet waving around crazily. I think it's more playful that way."

From Linear Progression to Nonlinear Teams

Andy and David's intuition about the benefits of disposing of personal desks was that it would encourage more casual interactions among people, breaking a static office into a free-flowing environment in which serendipitous encounters would be centers of unexpected creativity. "I sat opposite someone for two years in my previous agency," Sue told us. "I got to know him very well, and we became good friends. But I now know that it was at the expense of interacting with a lot of other people in the agency." Mark Lewis, an account director, told us that the benefits were huge. "It's fundamental to the process of creativity here," he said. "It may be hard and irritating in some ways, but it keeps us in contact with one another."

Just as they felt that having no desks would be creative in a nonlinear way, Andy and David believed that similar creativity could emerge from breaking the usual linear progression of producing work for clients and instead forming nonlinear teams. Mark described the traditional process to us. "You have an account-handling department, which gets the brief from the client," he began. "The account-handling department then talks to the planning department, which is probably located somewhere else. A creative brief gets written, which gets passed to the creative department, which in most agencies is on a different floor, you know, the floor with the pool table, casual dress, and all of that. Then you wouldn't see anything for a month. Finally the creative work gets back to the account-handling department, which then tries to sell it to the client. Usually, the client will say, 'That's pretty good, but it's not quite what we had in mind.' And the whole linear progression begins again. It's a slow, iterative process, full of air locks, people aggressively defending their territories."

At St. Luke's the whole linear process is folded into one space, the brand room, where it becomes nonlinear. "Everyone who's involved in the account gathers in the brand room," Mark explained, "including the client. The client is involved throughout the whole process, so there are never any surprises, never any 'it's not quite what we had in mind,' because the client is *part* of the process of creativity." One consequence of the client's constant involvement, said Mark, is that the client is usually much more willing to go with what he describes as "more dangerous work, more cutting-edge work," because the client has seen the ideas unfold, been part of the process of unfolding, and is not simply confronted with a wild idea out of the blue after months of silence.

As important as the client's involvement, however, is that the brand room provides a mutual space for all the people involved. Each brings their own expertise, but not a territory to be defensive over. "Everyone sits around—the account handlers, planners, creative people—and those meetings go crazy," Mark told us. "They're real brainstorming sessions, and we get to solutions really quick, because we're not pushing against each other; everyone comes together and it explodes. The planning is happening, the creative work is happening, and then, instead of saying, 'Okay, we've got the brief, let's think about strategy,' we start writing ads immediately and we start working out whether the strategy is right or not. Everything just goes crazy really, really early on."

Sue compares the experience with that in her former agency. "You spend less time talking to a thousand different people about the same thing," she explained. "The team process is important because, rather than everyone having their own little jobs that they do and then write a piece of paper about it and pass it on to the next person, everyone sits together in the same room and talks. Differences get resolved on the spot, rather than passing a piece of paper to someone and waiting three days to get a response. Here, that takes half an hour." The whole nonlinear process is much more dynamic and less controlled than the traditional mode of working, because a greater diversity of people is interacting at any one time. It's a perfect example of a complex adaptive system operating in the creative zone, from which unexpected ideas emerge.

Chaotic? Certainly. Creative? Apparently so, if one is to believe what the industry press writes about St. Luke's products, such as the *New York Times* comment we cited earlier. The linear progression mode of working encourages ego, because each person feels a need to defend their contribution, which is done in isolation from everyone else's. In the nonlinear team process, where each person can contribute ideas in any sector of the process, not just in their area of expertise, ego is much less of a problem, because it is a collective, emergent process. This is not to say that there are no big egos at St. Luke's. There are, of course. But the nonlinear process serves to minimize the "I" and enhance the "we." For this reason, St. Luke's refuses to enter the agency's work for industry competitions, because, Andy explained, "Prizes usually go to individuals, not to teams, and ours is quintessentially a team effort."

The Problem of Growth

Growth is always a big issue with small, successful companies, particularly when the creativity of the organization depends on a culture that is very human-oriented, and depends on rich interactions among people who know and trust each other. Beyond a certain size, a group is simply too big for everyone to know everyone in this way. At St. Luke's, this issue is addressed by what Andy calls the "magic number rule," which simply means that when a group exceeds thirty-five people, it splits. "With larger groups, it's not possible for people to care enough, for people to know what's going on," Andy explained. Coincidentally, anthropologists talk about magic numbers in hunter-gatherer societies, with the foraging band being about thirty-five people. So, again, Andy and David appear to have hit on something fundamental through intuition.

St. Luke's began life with thirty-five people on board, and three years later there were more than a hundred, divided among five groups. The pressure to grow has been great, particularly as the agency's notoriety burgeoned. "We want to grow, but we want to grow slowly," Andy said. "We avoid taking on business that would stretch what our people can work with in the way we want to be able to work. Sure, you can push people and make a lot of profit, but that's not our style. We are making a lot of money anyway." Recently the agency turned down a potential client—a $90 million account—because Andy felt his people were working at maximum capacity. Not that pressure doesn't build up sometimes. During 1997, for instance, when the staff doubled from fifty to a hundred and new accounts were coming easily, pressure started to mount, and, said Andy, "it started to get tense, with people fighting with one another, everyone working too hard, we were getting overheated." The creative work was still good, he told us, but socially the agency was suffering, people were suffering. "So in the early summer, we said, Enough. We stopped taking pitches. We wanted time to cool down. We called it the summer of love." It was out of this that the decision to split from two groups into five was made.

Such decisions are usually made during annual October 18 retreats, St. Luke's Day. "We go away every year to reinvent the company," Andy said. "As you grow, you have to change, to assimilate the people who came on board during the last year, so that the company reflects them, too, not just what it was like before they came." But the overheating of 1997 was too severe to wait for the away day, and so October 18, 1997, became a celebration of that change, not its initiator. The St. Luke's way of working is a continuous experiment, Andy insisted, and it will change through continuous evolution, continuous reinvention. "We don't know where we're going," Andy conceded, "but we know we would never go back to the old way of working."

But even though the magic number rule may preserve the social and creative milieu within groups, it cannot escape the reality of size. "When you split into groups, to retain the spirit within each group, you still have people from other groups you might not talk to as much anymore," said George Porteous, an account manager who's been at the agency since its birth. "Wandering around the building these days, there's a sense of anonymity, an absence of the spirit where everyone knew everyone else when there were just thirty-five of us. But don't get me wrong. We do need to grow, as an example of how business can change." Mark Lewis points to an issue beyond simply knowing people's names, an issue that all small, crusading companies face. "In the beginning, we all shared a vision of a cooperative group, committed to certain values," he explained. "At first, new people wanted to join because they shared those values. But now that we're a hot agency there's the danger that people will want to be here because, well, we're a hot agency. If you are in London and want to be in advertising, that's the kind of agency you want to be with. We have to be very careful about hiring these days."

St. Luke's may be a hot agency, it may work in the most extraordinary human-centered way, and it may, as someone told us, be a workplace where you can be yourself and not hang up your persona at the office door, as so often happens in business. But it is not utopia. Paradoxically, St. Luke's can feel cold to outsiders. And newcomers often have a miserable time for the first six months. People have disagreements, as people do. Bad decisions are sometimes made. The phone system is far from perfect. People often find their phone missing, or the battery run down when someone else used it. The lack of personal space makes people less concerned with maintaining the physical appearance of the place than they might otherwise be. There are pockets of resentment about the equal sharing of equity. And even though the ratio of men to women is roughly equal, the great majority of the senior positions are occupied by men. The continuing process of growth will make these problems more difficult, not easier, to deal with.

But, as Robbie Sparks told us, growth can be good, too: "We sometimes get set in little micro cultures, and hooked to a way of doing things. Growth gives you an opportunity to transform yourself, to create a wider landscape." David agreed. "Growth here is driven by a thirst for experience more than for cash," he told us. "Without growth, individuals have to repeat projects too often and they go stale. Without the goal of climbing the hierarchy, because there isn't one here, people need experiential goals."

The Community Connection

It took St. Luke's about fourteen months to emerge from chaos into a working cooperative. Andy and David are now wondering how long it will take for the company to connect with the community, which, guided by Aristotelian prin-

ciples, they believe it must. The agency's continued growth is forcing the issue, because the toffee factory can stretch no more to accommodate the business. A bigger space is needed. Andy explained an idea the agency is toying
with: "Suppose we went to the local education authority and said, 'You've got
all these wonderful Victorian school buildings, and they have huge lofts. How
about if we renovated the space we need, and pay you rent?' " This way the
agency would not just be located *in* the community, but would be a contributing part *of* the community, a part of the social and economic web. "I don't like
checkbook charity," he told us. "It's too easy, and it's not being genuinely involved."

"Integrating the company into the local community would feed our appreciation of the lives of real people we are talking to through our ads," David told
us. "It would also provide us with a more fulfilling use for our profits than
spending them on expensive corporate space in the West End [of London].
Clients would see we are in the laboratory of real life. But how can we make it
work? Well, we are just starting to find out."

The agency has already spotted a suitable school nearby, which, by coinci-
dence, is also called St. Luke's. "I mean, it's simple and elegant," Andy en-
thused. "Something great will come out of the association. I don't know what
it will be yet, but I know it will be great. As a company, we will be breathing
something into the community, helping to transform it." Andy describes his relationship with David Abraham as complementary: "I have the vision, and
David makes it happen." The community connection is certainly an extraordinary vision, and it will take David's talents to make it happen. "Now, we are
only a small company," Andy noted. "But what if IBM did something like
that? What if Coca-Cola did something like that? They have all these big office
buildings in Atlanta, standing empty at night. When we've done it, we'll start
asking others, 'Why don't you do something like this?' " Why not, because
even an ox can take flight.

• • •

During the first day we spent at the agency, a journalist from the *Los Angeles
Times* was also visiting, an elegant-looking woman, dressed in chic business
black. As she was leaving she whispered conspiratorially to Andy, "It's okay,
you can tell us the truth now. Where *is* your office?" Andy laughed when he
told us the story. "They just don't get it, do they!"

Chapter 7

VeriFone: High Tech–High Touch

On the edge of a new millennium, on the brink of a new stage of human development, we are racing blindly into the future. But where do we want *to go?*
Alvin Toffler, *Future Shock*

In the spring of 1997 Hewlett-Packard Co., seeking to secure a firm foothold in the nascent market of electronic commerce, agreed to buy VeriFone in a one-for-one stock transaction, for $1.18 billion. Under the leadership of Hatim Tyabji, VeriFone had grown from annual revenues of $31.2 million in 1986 to $600 million in 1997. Hatim, in his negotiations, ensured that VeriFone would remain autonomous. VeriFone would continue to run independently, under its own name, its own options.

The VeriFone success story can be attributed to a clear toughness in execution of ideas, to astute business strategies, to an unswerving commitment to a vision, to an innovative product line. Their "culture of urgency," the collective immediacy of this virtual company, has been written up in several magazines and in one of Tom Peters's books. But this is only half of it, and according to Hatim, not the most important half. And it is the half that business minds often don't want to know about. Alongside a tough business sense exists a deep regard for humanity—a level of human compassion and caring within the VeriFone culture that, if not unique, is at least exceptional in the high-tech industry or any industry for that matter. As Hatim puts it:

"Revenues and profits for a long, long time have been a by-product to me. An important by-product, yes, and as a rational businessman I have an obligation to my shareholders. But the record speaks for itself. We have delivered. And I think that's what people sometimes find hard to relate to, because they are often looking for absolutes in life, and they say, 'oh, yeah, touchy-feely, so you can't deliver the numbers.' There doesn't have to be a sharp division, a dichotomy; it's not something that has to be black or white. They very much can and do coexist; they are both visible all the time. And it's that degree of caring, being sensitive to the people in the organization—that's what really makes the organization tick."

We had known that VeriFone was organizationally flat, promoted rich, open communication, and favored a global distributed influence over central control, which follows the principles of complexity science in business, and was why we wanted to include them in our study. But, until we visited the company, we had not seen or heard any mention of care as an organization principle. Because care has the capacity to enhance connections and relationships among people, their organization, as a complex adaptive system, is likely to be more creative and adaptive. And there was no doubt that this is what VeriFone had become, in a very tough business environment.

In the Beginning

Until the early 1980s most credit card transactions were processed manually, which meant a lot of paper, which in turn meant time and money. But Bill Melton had an idea—to provide a simple electronic check verification system, and in 1981 he incorporated VeriFone to do just that. Remember the days when you would write a check and the retailer would call a mysterious number that would tell the clerk if you were a bad check writer? Not so long ago, really. VeriFone initially provided this service for local retailers in Hawaii, which is where Melton lived at the time, and within a few years the company was dealing with credit cards and moving to the mainland.

Today the evolution of that idea can be seen as the little gray box we all slide our credit and ATM cards through, which serves retail merchants, gasoline service stations, convenience stores, supermarkets, health care providers, government agencies, and consumers. To date, VeriFone has shipped more than six million systems supporting more than two thousand applications to customers in more than one hundred cultures. The little gray box that initially opened the gateway to the credit card payment system would later in 1993 lead the way into the complex world of electronic commerce. It was VeriFone that coined the term "transaction automation," which has since been adopted by competitors as well.

Bill Melton, being a renegade entrepreneur, also had a vision about a company that would totally outsource everything—selling, manufacturing, R&D—because he wanted a company with maximum flexibility. That meant it couldn't be weighed down with bureaucracy, something that instinctively collided with his entrepreneurial spirit.

Bill's first product, VeriFone Mark I, was developed by Hong Kong engineers. When it came back from Hong Kong in 1982, it was a complete disaster—a 50 percent dead on arrival every time it was plugged in. In its debut presentation, the little gray box did more than not cooperate—it burst into flames. During its second presentation, it started playing the radio. Bill knew he was in trouble; he knew he couldn't be going back to Hong Kong to try to explain all the problems. Although he was a great believer in the outsourcing concept, he realized that certain core competencies had to be developed in-house. He therefore used the informal contacts he had developed in Hawaii, a group of guys who got together to talk about microcomputers, and made them an offer they couldn't refuse. As Will Pape, chief information officer of Veri-Fone and now "ambassador," recounts:

"He lured a bunch of people on board. He lured me," Will says in his wry understated Santa Fe way, "with a promise of getting no money and getting stock in a company that was basically bankrupt." Why would he accept such a deal, especially since he had recently sold Spellguard and was thinking about an early retirement? (Spellguard, by the way, created algorithms for microcomputers that became the first commercial spell-checker system for personal computers.) "Intellectually Bill's offer was an interesting challenge. It looked like it could be something."

Bill enlisted Carl Chang, a very enlightened and creative engineer who worked for Spellguard, to deal with the hardware problem. He got the 50 percent hardware failure down to 10 percent. Will undertook the software challenge. The code, written in Hong Kong, was virtually impossible to fix—lots of bugs and no documentation, so he started from scratch. Together Carl and Will created an operating system and put a language on top of it, which allowed them to develop new applications. Will's concept, which continues as the platform for VeriFone, was that they were "providing a software delivery system for financial institutions to competitively differentiate themselves through software."

At this time, there were five employees in four locations. From the beginning VeriFone was a virtual, decentralized company. And that reality continues today—there are around 3,500 employees in fifty-one locations around the world, with greater than half of VeriFone people now outside the U.S. Widely dispersed employees who have lots of interaction and share information may sound impossibly unruly to most. But Bill saw a solution: electronic mail and online databases would become the company's lifeblood. From this emerged a paperless culture that made secretaries obsolete and neatly placed responsibility for communication into the lap of each employee, who now average sixty messages a day.

By 1986, the first year they broke even, VeriFone had around $30 million in revenue. Neither Will nor Bill had run a company with that amount of revenue, and they recognized that they weren't the people to be the symphony conductor for the growing VeriFone. Bill formed a team of people who put together a short list of potential candidates that would then go to subordinates, who would do the final interviewing.

The practice of subordinates hiring their boss, and the enormous amount of time spent reinterviewing people (sometimes as many as eight times), and involving many people in the organization, not just the senior executives, reflects VeriFone's commitment to getting the right people on board from the start. It may take longer but it pays off in the end. In an industry with an average turnover of 18 percent, VeriFone's current turnover is less than 12 percent.

Among the final candidates for CEO back in 1986 was Hatim Tyabji, whom they recruited from Sperry Corporation, a huge, centralized bureaucratic organization producing expensive mainframe computers. Hatim couldn't have come from an organization more diametrically opposed to the entrepreneurial, decentralized, informally managed VeriFone. Hatim had joined Sperry in 1973 as a young program manager, with three years of experience. For the next thirteen years, he rose through the ranks, and at the time of his interview with VeriFone, he was the number three person of a company of 77,000 people, with 25,000 people reporting to him.

Will Pape recalls Hatim's first interview in this way:

"My first question to him was, 'How fast do you type?' My question infuriated Hatim. He literally bounced out of his chair. At that point even his secretary had a secretary. If he ever got e-mail it was a piece of paper on his desk. I said, 'With all due respect, sir . . .' and I proceeded to explain what kind of company we were, an e-mail, paperless company. He is so bright. He understood instantly and sat back down and said, 'Well, if this goes further, how fast do I need to be able to type? I don't type at all.' We told him, 'Thirty-five to forty words a minute, and you can survive.' His response was, 'I'm a betting, sporting man. If this goes further, I tell you within six months I'll be able to type at that rate. But if I do, you owe me a box of fine cigars. And if I don't, you put up what you want on your side.' At that point, I knew we were going to get along real good."

Hatim won himself a box of cigars.

The idea of being responsible for your own communication came from a basic concept from the Green Berets, who train individuals so they can operate on their own without logistical support. When teams get large, the amount of communication required to keep them all in sync is so great that the overall productivity drops. It's the notion that small numbers of individuals empowered by computers without having to have an intervening logistical army can move faster than anyone else. This is a very complexity-oriented notion. A guerrilla warfare approach suited VeriFone, whose competitors, such as IBM, AT&T, and Panasonic, were huge, organized regimental armies, operating in a bureaucratic manner. VeriFone may have been outnumbered, but they had an advantage—they, like gazelles, were agile and nimble.

For newcomers at VeriFone this adds up to culture shock. Vice president of corporate development Roger Bertman remembers his initiation into a paper-less culture this way:

"I had a master's in computer science, but I had not touched a PC. It was like backlash. I always had people to answer the phone, do the charts, do my calendar. I came here and the first thing that hit me was e-mail. It doesn't matter if you're a VP or general manager or clerk, you're going to be on e-mail. Everything in the company is online—travel requests, purchase requests. I was pretty worried initially. Executives think they don't have time to do all this stuff, but at the end of the day it takes more time to have someone else manage your calendar, write your documents. By eliminating the middle person, I end up saving myself a lot of time, and I do a better job."

For us, the realization that we were dealing with an unusual company came with the initial call to set up interviews. "Roger Bertman, here," was the response after the first ring. It's a bit disarming to have a VP answer the phone, and disorienting to find no need to navigate through bureaucratic layers. Something like expecting to push against a locked door only to discover it is wide open. Not only was he accessible, he was helpful. He offered to arrange several days for us to talk to various people. Not much self-important ego here. We found this to be true with everyone we spoke to—very busy but very cordial, open people. What we were experiencing was the living practice of the VeriFone philosophy.

The Little Blue Book

Most companies have a mission statement. But how many companies have a pocket-size blue book with the company philosophy written in seven languages? Pocket-size, so it can be conveniently carried around by employees as a reference to guide their decisions. Multilingual, to reflect that no one culture dominates, that headquarters is everywhere.

Establishing a moral philosophy, a family mission statement that would guide this global company, was Hatim's first task as CEO of VeriFone. The seeds of the philosophy preceded him, but it was Hatim who moved it from an oral tradition to a written one, who formalized the VeriFone philosophy into "a system of motivating concepts or principles; the system of values by which one lives," as it says on the first page. Guided by these ethical principles, VeriFone would emerge as "a company that cares," "a human company." Their *way* to do business, a human-centered approach, would blaze the trail, they believed, for how people can do business in the twenty-first century.

We came to see that the VeriFone philosophy is not an abstract vision but a daily practice. Their focus on care—care for their customers and co-workers, caring about meeting commitments—is what gives VeriFone an edge over competitors. As Will told us, "Lots of companies are embracing technology but they're ignoring the people side of it, which is the organizational structure, the mind-set, the environment." With the exponential increase in the growth and use of technology, the product is no longer the edge for companies. Now it's the service, the quality of relationships that they are able to form that differentiates them from their competitors. Alvin Toffler's prediction in 1970 that with high tech comes a need for high touch has come to fruition.

To grow a company in the way that VeriFone managed to grow can be attributed to their commitment to a "we"—a "we" that recognizes the inextricable web of interdependence, that shares values, that strives toward ethical behavior. From this moral foundation, which guides interactions and thus the quality of relationships, has emerged a collective identity—the VeriFoner.

VeriFoners told us that they are truly committed to the eight principles in the blue book that constitute their philosophy. Following are those principles, the source from which a culture of care and efficient urgency has emerged. The way we want to illustrate these principles is by having VeriFoners speak of their own experiences, in their own words, telling us what it means to live, not just espouse, this philosophy—the clarity it engenders, the difficulties that surface. As people talked to us of their experience working at VeriFone, pleasures as well as tensions emerged. Paradox and contradictions are also present—an inevitable reality for people living and working on the edge where possibilities shift with the change in circumstances.

1. We are committed to excellence.

As a way of life, excellence is reflected in how we design and build our products, provide service to our customers and behave toward each other.

We take pride in the products and services we provide. . . . VeriFone's growth and success will be a natural by-product of the respect and loyalty we earn from our customers.

Gerry Wentworth, Human Resources Manager:

"It's a feeling of accomplishment, the pride that I have working here. My ego and self-esteem is not attached to what title is on my business card. I'm proud to say, 'Yeah, I work for that company that makes those little gray boxes.' When I was interviewed for my job, I had never heard of VeriFone. Someone showed me the gray box, and I said, 'I know who you are.' After the interview I saw these boxes every place I went. There's something prideful now in taking our talent to the Internet. There's a healthy sense of self-esteem here which makes me want to make a better contribution. If we miss our numbers, it's personal. We are here to see how many good things we can produce and sell. But the soul of VeriFone is bonds. So there is loyalty because you don't want to let down your fellow employee.

"The backdrop of this culture is a sense of urgency, immediacy, or 'we need it now.' Everything is a priority, by definition, but you need to prioritize otherwise it becomes panic. I'll prioritize by not only who has the squeakiest wheel but what will be the most fun to accomplish. I'm not saying that's correct but that's the way I work. Sometimes we forget about having fun with work. We have to remember, it's not rocket science. We're making important decisions and they shouldn't be neglected, but we have to look at them in context. I think people often forget that this is a place to have fun every day. There has never been a day when I was taking my morning shower and thought, I don't want to go to work.

"This sense of urgency also crosses boundaries into my personal life. I don't mean the personal life being infringed upon by the work life. When someone wants or needs something, I don't wait. I do it now. It's just this normalcy in speed to get things done that comes from working here. It's our way of being there for each other and our customers."

2. We are dedicated to meeting our customers' needs.

Our products are tools for helping customers solve business problems.... We go the extra mile to bring solutions to our customers.... Excellence begins at home.

Will Pape, Chief Information Officer:

"One reason we decentralized, and you have to have a good reason to decentralize, was that we could rapidly put a whole team together that is close to our customers. The team would be responsible for customer maintenance but also engineering what is necessary for the customer. This meant that our people could take care of what the customer needed, the changes that needed to be made, right there on the spot. Our competition would take everything back to Tokyo where everything was coded. Whenever you have those long-distance linkages, it's likely to lose a lot of meaning. It's the old rumor game: the phrase goes around the circle and comes out totally garbled in the end. I don't think that works. But when you put a team literally down the street from the customer, who meet frequently with them, who know what needs to be done, and they go back and do it, and then the customer drives by and sees the lights burning late, knowing their work is getting done, that you are committed to their needs, they deeply appreciate what you do for them.

"VeriFone is a very focused company. We make sure we deliver what our customers want, but we're also leading our customers. You can't predict where you'll go, because the soul of our organization—these organic relationships and the business environment we're in—changes every six months; it's like asking the bronco rider how the bull is; but you have to be in the lead position. We're responding to market forces, not just sales calls. What we're doing now is way ahead of where the consumers are today. If not, we lose it all tomorrow."

3. Each individual in our organization is important.

... help identify opportunities for growth ... encourage continuing education ... reward, retain, promote those individuals who contribute to the achievement of corporate goals ...

Katherine Fines, Director, Operations, NextGen Systems:

"VeriFone is remarkably free of politics, remarkably free of sexual and cultural bias. But it still exists; we're not perfect. But it's less of an issue here than anywhere else I've worked. We're striving to achieve respect for each individual for what they can bring to the table, what they can contribute. We look at each individual on their own merits and people really do try to live that."

Michael Gilman, Sales:

"There was a point in my career that I was ready to leave the company. I was tired of what I was doing—the same customers for five years. The day I was leaving, processed all my papers, collected my checks, Hatim finally realized I was leaving. Hatim and I go way back; we worked on some big opportunities together. He gave me the biggest hug, stood there and hugged me for thirty seconds. It was very emotional. I think he was upset that I might go without saying goodbye. Then he said, 'You're family, goddamn it. You can't leave.' For a CEO to do that is uncommon. Usually you think of CEOs as being remote. It was moving to have him care, to be my mentor. It's good to be valued. In Silicon Valley, it's unusual. I told him I needed time off. He accepted that and then he added, 'There is something very dynamic going on in this division. You might like to be part of it.' Now I'm part of a very small, entrepreneurial team, just six of us. It was a good decision to stay."

Katherine Beall, Vice President, Human Resources:

"Our VeriLife program shows our commitment to people. We have VeriPal, which is a pen pal program for children of VeriFoners. We even do that in our factory in Taiwan where not everyone has a lot of e-mail access. We set up kiosks so that the children can come in and use the computers there. We have VeriKid, which is an exchange program where VeriFone children can go to different places around the world and stay with a host VeriFone family. We have eight scholarships for students of VeriFoners to go around the world. We have VeriShare, where employers volunteer their time for community efforts. We did it in a China plant and it was something that was completely foreign to them. They had a great blood drive. We encourage further education and training and have an online campus called the VeriFone Virtual University.

"The biggest contradiction we struggle with is on the work and family issue. We really care about the individual employees and their families, but at the same time we're just driving relentlessly. No one is going to tell you that you look really tired, go home. If you can't moderate yourself in this fast-paced environment, you lose the balance. Here the problem is not getting people to work more, but getting them to work less."

Mary Sue Bizzarri:

"After that hurricane in Miami, some people in the company lost everything. People went down to help them get back on their feet. Those people who initiated the action were given an award for their humanitarian efforts. Another instance is the VeriGift program, which was created when a young man in sales had a terminally ill wife and a group of people got together and said we ought to do something. He's losing his wife, the center of his life, and now he's getting this financial punishment because he doesn't have enough days off. Now there's a program in place where you can donate vacation days into a pool and those who need extra time, get it. Those people who initiated the VeriGift program got quite a bit of recognition."

4. We work as a team in a spirit of trust and cooperation.

. . . together we do more than we could as individuals working alone . . . we respect each other's abilities and contributions . . . we depend on each other . . . we assist and support each other . . . we share the rewards together . . .

Katherine Fines:

"The more diverse a team we have, the more successful we'll be. Everyone gets involved—from all departments. You put them on the team and tell them go make it happen.

"We've had the lone cowboys in our past, and still have them from time to time. They've done some wonderful things for the company, but we find that we need them less and less and want them less and less. As the company grows, it's more and more focused on a team effort. The individual contributor just doesn't work very well anymore. Things are too complex. No one person can do it all.

"When we hire people, we're looking for interesting people—no shrinking violets need apply here. VeriFone doesn't hire them. We self-select. We have questions we ask them in the interview process which are designed to find out if they'd fit. We ask, for example, 'What was the most fun project you ever worked on?' You get them talking about something they really like doing and that's where you find out what kind of person they are. We ask, 'How did you handle a difficult co-worker or difficult situation?' You can figure people out from a technical perspective by reading their résumés, but that doesn't tell you how well they work with others. It's hands on, it's 'create your own job here,' it's 'can you handle this? Do you like working in a place where the ground shifts under you all the time? Do you need more stability? Perhaps you should apply elsewhere. If you're a flexible person, you'll do well here.' The people who do really well here, who stay, who progress, are those who have the ability to connect with others.

"Sometimes people walk in and don't understand that you actually don't have a secretary, and that you, too, are supposed to stand in line at the photocopier. If they can't handle that, if it's beneath them, if they're better than the person down the hall who earns less money and has less education, then they're not going to work out here. Because, here, no one is really better. Everyone has a contribution to make to the team effort."

5. We focus accountability for every assignment. .

. . . the people who know best how the job should be done are the ones doing it. We involve employees directly in the management of their own areas of responsibility . . .

Katherine Fines:

"There isn't any training at all for the jobs here. It's sink or swim. It's, 'Hi, we want you to create a tax department. We don't know what that means, but we assure you, you'll figure it out.' Well, of course, that's what I wanted. At VeriFone, you're empowered to do the job, to do what has to be done to deliver to customers. It's up to you to take charge of your career. That also makes you responsible and accountable."

Curt Lindemer, Corporate Treasurer and Director of Facilities:

"The guiding principle is accountability—accountable to serve the customer, accountable for results, accountable for asking for help when you need it. If people feel unsupported and don't let it be known, they will probably stay unsupported. If they vocalize it, it's a high probability they will get support. Managers provide support in the form of open communication—how can we structure this to allow you to succeed? And it's okay to make mistakes here, as long as you learn from them."

6. We believe in open communication.

. . . we promote informal and open dialogue throughout the company. . . . through e-mail, any employee may reach the entire company instantaneously . . . we respect the right to be heard . . . we invite our customers to communicate with us through e-mail . . .

Gerry Wentworth:

"VeriFone is a leading example of a virtual company. But you can't work in this environment without a tremendous amount of trust in the person who's reading your e-mail. It's so different from being in a room talking with someone. So much communication comes from body language, eye contact. When you're reading an e-mail from the other side of the world with no cue or clue, you have to trust the intent of the person making the communication. For instance, last night I was ranting and raving about a compatriot of mine. How could she do this! My fiancée said, 'You've got to be misreading it.' When I met her in the morning, after I cooled down, before I even said anything, she said, 'In this situation it was, I've got to do this and then apologize rather than asking for your permission and having a no.' I said, 'I hear you. It's done and over. Let's move on.' "

Mary Sue Bizzarri:

"I think what's very interesting about VeriFone is the fact that most of the people you work with, you never see. The drawback is you can't just walk into someone's office and say 'I just had a great idea.' It's difficult to have these free-flow discussions especially when that somebody is in a different time zone. On the flip side, you get to travel a lot because you need to meet the people you're going to be working with on a project for many months. Also in an office, you see who goes to lunch with whom, who's working on what with whom. With e-mail, there are all these invisible relationships.

"The constraint of e-mail is that it makes communication more formal. You also have to be much more careful about what you say in e-mail because it can be sent anywhere. So you have to develop a relationship over time to figure out where the boundaries are with that certain individual. When you communicate with people whose native language isn't English, you can't use slang, jargon, abbreviations. You have to reread everything you wrote to make sure the sentences are structured in a way that doesn't confuse the message. But the benefit is there is more openness in getting information, which, for conducting business, is paramount. I can write to anyone in the world for help in solving a problem. And you get responses within twenty-four hours."

Will Pape:

"Face-to-face interaction is the most effective communication bar none. We maximize our customer interaction. Being in front of the customer is one of the most important things we do.

"Internally, we realized being decentralized as we are, that having ad hoc meetings didn't work. Then how do we compensate for not having face-to-face interactions? We developed a process of setting the annual calendar. Every six to eight weeks [senior managers] get together for a week in different cities, face-to-face, to work out our problems. We are intensely involved—all day, five or six hours sleep, and we start again. We end up having more face-to-face time with our colleagues than they have in companies who have management on the same floor but don't see each other.

"One of the things we have in our communication culture is a log-on secret—where there is no way a message can be traced back to that person. That person can send to anyone they want, say anything they want. We did it as a relief valve. You need an informal communication channel. If you don't have it, authorities will not know what's going on. We wanted to give them a mechanism whereby if they whistle-blow they can do it anonymously, and we take those messages seriously. The way I feel about e-mail is that when you encourage people to speak frankly you had better be prepared to not like everything you hear."

Katherine Beall:

"The benefit of an e-mail culture is that I can communicate effectively and quickly and I know everyone is getting the same message. The downside is that it can provoke what I call a 'forward edit syndrome,' which is, 'I get the e-mail, I'm going to forward it, and therefore I'm done.' What it means is that I'm passing a lot of the work on to others and saying I did my part. So we have to work on that but also teach people to pick up the phone. E-mail is never going to take the place of building relationships by the phone or face-to-face."

7. We are an international company.

. . . not just another multinational company . . . we decentralize our development, manufacturing, sales, and service centers . . . we endeavor to understand and adapt to cultural norms wherever we operate . . .

Will Pape:

"We don't focus on VeriFone France, VeriFone Spain. There's one and only one VeriFone. We don't file financial statements and don't file stock on every location. Only one company. We're a global company, a very different perspective; it's a whole. Therefore we need to allow certain cultural practices to happen in different countries. Our objective in going into other countries has always been to look at all levels of the staff—have local management at each operation, develop a professional as well as a blue-collar infrastructure, and to allow certain practices to happen in different countries. The fact that country A isn't the same as country B doesn't make a difference.

"Being an international company you become more patient and you can't slide in this environment; you have to make an effort. Problem definition invariably comes up in a global environment, because people from different cultures see problems differently. The interesting thing for me is 'How can I see it that way?' And by talking about it and learning to see it their way changes me. Usually a group coalesces on a problem definition that's totally different than when they walked in."

Mary Sue Bizzarri:

"I have developed friendships in amazing places. My best friend in the company lives in Singapore and we probably see each other only three times a year. I have friends on virtually every continent. The difference working here makes is that I don't go on vacation and see the Taj Mahal. Instead I go to India and see people there who actually work for me, who have become a part of my life, who complain because I'm not there for enough days so that they can make me dinner. Working here has certainly deepened my experience as a human on this planet."

Katherine Beall:

"When you're working remotely and as dispersed as we are, you have to have a lot of confidence in what you're doing and be self-directed because you can feel very insecure about what other people are doing in other locations. But in developing global relationships that don't depend on face-to-face interaction, what brings people closer together is the feeling that they're a VeriFoner. It doesn't matter where you are in the world. There isn't a lot of distinction in our minds that's based on geography. I think we've pioneered the global company. Instead of this U.S.-centered mentality, we are global citizens, recognizing people for just being people. I've learned over the years that everyone is a contributor, and that it's important to be a better listener and more open to different ways of doing things. The American way is not necessarily the best way. We have a real edge in really valuing people all over the world and I guess a lot of companies will come to that, too, and we've already been there."

8. We live and work ethically.

. . . we fulfill our commitments . . . treat others with dignity and respect . . . are honest and fair in all transactions . . . it is our duty to make a positive contribution to the communities in which we operate . . .

Katherine Beall:

"I joined VeriFone for one major reason—it professed to be an ethical company. Ethics are not paramount in most management philosophies that I know. Three months after I joined VeriFone, we had our first disappointment from Wall Street. For a new employee, that's pretty frightening. Hatim sent an e-mail to every employee that said that we hadn't met our quarterly numbers and that the stock was going to drop. But, he added, we aren't going to lay off anyone. We would not travel and we would cut other expenses instead. I can't tell you what that meant to me to see that, as opposed to some of the tactics other companies take when these things happen.

"During that time, Hatim had done an all-hands meeting in Dallas where I work and he was down in my office, and he said, 'How do you think everyone's doing?' And I looked at the man, and he cared so much—I knew he was suffering. And I said, 'Well, Hatim, I think the meeting went well, and the fact that you look awful makes the employees feel better.' So as for ethics, I've never been disappointed.

"At one point, we found ourselves with some money accrued for management bonuses and we were talking around the table on how best to disperse it. But then Hatim said that if there were bonuses for managers and not the rest of his people, then he wasn't going to take it either. So in our typical, outside-the-box thinking we said, 'Wouldn't it be more meaningful if we give everyone two days off with no one on e-mail?' We called them celebration days. We sent letters to our customers telling them we were taking these days off to celebrate our success. The best thing was that we knew no one was going to call us and we wouldn't have three hundred e-mails waiting for us. Everyone absolutely loved it. What could have been management's gains and greed turned into something for everyone.

"We don't always live up to our philosophy, but the fact that we know what we're driving toward and we know what the guiding principles are is a cohesive thread. For instance, I heard employees outside my door say, 'Boy, I think the VeriFone philosophy is a bunch of bull. We aren't doing this right.' What I say to myself is, one, thank goodness they know there's a philosophy, whether we're living up to it or not, and two, thank goodness they can say whatever they want and not feel there's repression."

Will Pape:

"I constantly refer to the book, three to five times a week. It's automatic. It's not the exception. It's the rule. A couple of years ago we were looking at the economics of a particular office that was pretty expensive. So the decision was, What to do? Do we shut it down, do we merge it with another office? We went and took a look at it. In our discussions, the principles of accountability and dedication to meeting the customers' needs and the importance of the individual were very clear at this office. We ended up cutting some costs but we left the office in place. We wanted to make sure we continued to meet a particular customer's needs. There's always accountants telling you if you were centralized you'd have all these economies of scale, but you lose the human touch with your customer. This is the strategy we use for going forward—people not technology."

• • •

The VeriFone philosophy consists of simple practices that create conditions and a safe environment for emergence—of teams, of innovations, of productivity. Their strong ethical base of care and appreciation of diversity makes for rich interactions from which, within the organization, a sense of a global community and a collective identity emerges, and outside the organization, a robust interdependent economic web with other companies. Their e-mail culture, which allows for abundant and open communication, generates a well-connected, even though dispersed, system. Also, e-mail breaks down hierarchies, which fosters mutuality in interactions—an important element for moving toward the zone of creative adaptability. These testimonies also show that not everyone is or has to be on board with the VeriFone philosophy. Diversity of opinions and fluctuations are healthy in complex systems. After all, isn't complete consensus, which often means suppressed differences, a cult?

Hatim—Leader As a Moral Compass:
"Do as I do, not do as I say."

It was five to seven in the morning. We were waiting for Hatim in the lobby of Hotel Sofitel in Redwood City, California. We had two precious hours to talk to him over breakfast. Two hours, for strangers to develop a relationship of trust; two hours to engage and try to capture the essence of the man.

He strode briskly across the lobby, dressed informally in racing jacket and sneakers, his eyes alert and attentive, with just a subtle weariness in his shoulders. We knew he traveled 500,000 miles that year to see customers face-to-face and to visit sites. That could explain it. But he told us later jet lag was just a matter of mind over body. We also learned that he slept an average of four hours a night and started the day at five o'clock. We soon learned weariness is the last word one would use to describe Hatim.

If there are two words that describe Hatim they are intensity and passion. Intense, in his focus, his direction, his commitment, unequivocal in his perspective. He sets high expectations and expects results. Passionate, in the depth of his care for his company, his people, his customers, his commitments. This sense of discipline and values was clearly shaped by his Jesuit education in Bombay, India, where he developed his hard-driving nature and what he would describe as "a fanatical sense of ethics and integrity." Being a Muslim growing up in a Catholic school also prepared him to be a global leader—he encompasses and flourishes in diversity. "I took enormous pleasure from going to Mass in school," he recounts. "I felt peace. Even today. What does that have to do with being raised Muslim? It doesn't matter what religion you have. If difference didn't matter so much, we wouldn't have had Bosnia for starters."

Paradoxically, Hatim, trained in a hierarchical system, is himself antihierarchical. He has no office per se. Through e-mail he is accessible to anyone who wants to reach him. And he responds—immediately. His privileges, such as flying, are the same as anyone else in the company. He mostly flies coach.

A Philosophy of Care

The first year was a difficult time for Hatim. There were nights when he would turn off the lights, not knowing whether there would be money in the bank to turn them on again in the morning. But business issues are business issues—

"you work through them," Hatim said. What was more traumatic were situations dealing with people and their way of working. There were those who wanted to run VeriFone the way most high-tech companies are run—ride roughshod over people, discard them. But Hatim doesn't function that way. Instead he held tightly to his hope that they would be able to change their thinking. Finally he had to say enough was enough—some changed, some were fired. "It would have been a lot less traumatic if I didn't care." Like trees, organizations also need pruning to grow strong.

We found a complete consensus at VeriFone that Hatim's influence on the company—everyone calls him Hatim—is enormous. As Roger Bertman says, "The *soul* element of the business, that's what Hatim is about. He engenders it. People are incredibly loyal to the guy. And it's mutual. He's on the road constantly; he knows the VeriFone people around the world; he looks out for VeriFone. He's tough, he expects a lot, but he also cares on both a professional and personal level."

And this caring manifests in a multitude of ways. He goes the distance for his customers. One time in Paris, during a downpour, Hatim couldn't get a taxi to drive eighteen miles out of the city for a meeting. He couldn't leave the customer waiting and instead of canceling or disappointing the customer, he ended up going on a sales manager's 600cc Honda motorcycle. He arrived at the bank soaked, but on time, which, needless to say, impressed the customer.

His care for his people manifests in his consistent acknowledgment of their contributions. "You don't forget what other people have done, and you give them their due. And it's not something that happens on Monday the 15th. It's something that happens every day, in some way, shape, or form."

Hatim draws strength and gratification from his unwavering sense of ethical commitment. He doesn't give a damn what people think, he told us. Instead he does what he believes is right. He doesn't waste his time on "self-serving networking." Instead he develops relationships, constantly attends to them, which ensures that VeriFone, as a complex adaptive system, maintains itself in a state of high creativity, high adaptability.

With Hatim there is little room for doubt, but he does accept uncertainty. "Doubt has to do with whether you're going to go forward or whether you're not. There is no clarity of direction. I have no doubt, but I do have uncertainty. Uncertainty is accepting the fact that you may or may not succeed."

He has no tolerance for pat answers, for silver bullets, for panaceas, for the sound-bite culture. Instead he pays attention to the "being" not the "doing," and is endlessly patient and constantly working at maintaining a culture of care. "The culture is very difficult to put in place; it can unravel very quickly. People have asked how I maintain the culture. You must work at the being. The being is the cause; everything else is a manifestation of that being. That being is caring. Human beings being human beings, that message has to be repeated multiple times. Then it may be understood. And it starts with you. As a leader, *you've* got to care. It's got to come from within you."

Hatim has no tolerance for superficiality, what he calls the "veneer of denial." Instead he looks beneath the surface. "You're dealing with human beings that by definition are extremely complex. We all have our strengths, our weaknesses, our insecurities, our egos. The real key is to take a deep interest in people. And try to do your best to understand what their insecurities may be and then work with them. When you reach out to them, they will reach right back. I think that's tremendous. Some say, 'Hatim, big deal. That's common sense.' That's true. The issue is practicing it. The most profound truths in the world are the simplest. Except they don't get practiced."

But is this caring really necessary for business? Plenty of companies succeed very well without it. "I feel sorry for them," says Hatim in his characteristically definitive way. "If you measure success only by financial parameters, then I don't want anything to do with them. I say shame on people for thinking like that. They're not aiming low—they're not even aiming. For me, that's not enough. Because at the end of the day, you've got to live with yourself." It's no wonder that when he shaves in the morning, he says he loves what he sees. Care nurtures individuals for who they are, and it cultivates rich interactions, or relationships, among people, which, as complexity science shows, leads to a more effective organization.

Hatim admits he makes a lot of conventional businesspeople uneasy. Whether you like Hatim or not, he is a "do as I do person." "I would never ask somebody to do something that I wouldn't do myself." And what Hatim does is nothing less than extraordinary. He leads by example; he is a moral compass. Hatim embodies the kind of leadership necessary for the complexities of a global organization. To have the freedom that VeriFoners have paradoxically requires an even stronger leader—with unflinching vision, a sense of direction, and strength of conviction—like Hatim, who is everywhere and nowhere. VeriFone demonstrates that, when combined, freedom and strong leadership is a new way of doing business in the twenty-first century.

The Merger—The End of the Beginning

The merger with Hewlett-Packard was done in record time. Hatim attributes the efficiency to a common chemistry among the players. "We liked each other, we trusted each other, and we got the job done. They are very good people. They don't operate on the Attila the Hun principle of rape, pillage, burn, like some companies. And our people are good people, so the chemistry has worked." Hatim's care for VeriFone guided him in his negotiations. Fiercely protective over the VeriFone family, he made sure they were taken care of, made sure he didn't leave his people in the lurch. "When I'm negotiating, I'm negotiating for my people. The core of my value system is trust and caring. I will not let anything compromise that or subvert it."

And it is this focus on care and integrity that supersedes everything else, including money. "Chief executives often get a very lucrative retention package when mergers happen; and I'm talking millions in this case, because we've been a very successful company. So we're sitting with Hewlett-Packard and they ask me to sign on for a minimum of two years. And then they ask what I have in mind for a retention. I said, 'This is what I have in mind. One, I will give you my word that this acquisition will be the most successful acquisition you have ever done. Two, I want nothing in return. Three, I will sign nothing. I'm not asking for anything in return.' I guarantee you they didn't know what to make of it."

Shortly after the merger, VeriFone held a gala dinner for their worldwide sales meeting. Hatim spoke to the group in his usual fashion about the metamorphosis of the company. Never speaking from a prepared text, instead he has another reference point—he speaks from the heart. "The employees know when Hatim speaks he's speaking the absolute truth," Katherine Beall observes. "He means it from the heart, and it's often emotional because you know that he's speaking directly to you about what he really feels."

In his closing remarks, Hatim talked about change, knowing that with the acquisition people were feeling a degree of insecurity. But people were also feeling a little insecure about whether Hatim was going to continue to be with them or not. As Katherine noted, "I can guarantee you whatever speech he would give, people would interpret that as, 'that sounded like his last speech.' " He gave personal anecdotes and among them he talked about sky diving with his sons to illustrate how he dealt with change and fear.

"The story is very funny when he tells it," remembers Roger Bertman. "You could see he was scared out of his mind, standing up there with one leg hanging out of the airplane. But you just do it. He conveyed a sense of humanness and vulnerability by saying, 'Hey, you know, I go through this insecurity, too.' Then he said, 'Are we going to change? We are going to change. Have we changed a lot? You bet. And we're going to keep changing.' People wonder how Hatim is dealing with being part of HP. I can't imagine that it's that easy. There is some sense of loss, naturally. But he's dealing with it very well, running the company like he always runs the company."

What happened after the speech is not what one would anticipate to see at a typical corporate meeting. Hatim's assistant, Sharon Schwartz, described it as follows: "As he got to the end of his talk, he came down from the podium and onto the dance floor, so he was level with everybody. Being out on that huge floor, he looked small and vulnerable. He closed with saying that the two most important aspects of his life were in that room: his family, his wife of twenty-eight years, and his sons; and his people. It was very emotional for him and for everyone else. He got a standing ovation, and then a flood of people went onto the floor to be with him."

Hatim himself was amazed at the amount of raw emotion that flooded toward him that day. "They were crying and hugging me. They were touched at a very deep emotional level. We are an extremely emotive group. It was unbelievable for me. And the most wonderful part of that is nobody can take it away from me. Wall Street can't take it away from me. HP can't take it away from me. They can't take this bond we have. That bond is what drives me. I have always maintained that in business, people are looking for pat answers, for panaceas. The answer is here," he said with a simple gesture. "It's here in the heart."

E-mail from Hatim to VeriFone
Subject: My retirement
Date: 98-05-12; 10:51:31 EDT
From: Hatim
Over the years I have written many e-mails to you. This one I write with extraordinary emotion. I am announcing today that I intend to retire from VeriFone.

I am intensely proud of the company we have built over the last twelve years. We created a transaction automation industry, and remain the industry leader. We have extended the boundaries of our industry from the merchant countertop to payment processing, Internet commerce, and consumer solutions. We have dramatically grown our business, both in revenues and geographic scope. Our products, operations, and facilities are truly world-class, meeting quality standards to which many companies can only aspire.

My heart swells with pride even more as I reflect on our organization—that is, each and every one of you. It is only through your incredible dedication and hard work that we have manufactured and shipped millions of electronic payment systems. It is your talent and creativity that has led us to breakthroughs in new products and new markets. It is your focus and determination that has allowed us to achieve the seemingly impossible for our customers. And it is your strong ethics and character that have guided us to "do the right thing" in everything we do.

For the near term, I will remain as active in the company as ever, and do all that is humanly possible to provide a seamless "passing of the baton." . . .

As for my plans, my wife, Durriya, has strongly advised that I take time to "smell the roses." I concur with this advice; however I believe you will agree that this cannot be a full-time activity, as there are only so many roses that one can smell! . . .

I have one character trait that runs to excess—it is my sense of caring. I care deeply for VeriFone and its mission. I care deeply for our customers and partners. And above all, I care deeply for each of you. It has been a privilege and joy—indeed, the pinnacle of my career—to work with you and build our company together.

Durriya and I will forever be grateful for being part of the VeriFone family. We wish you good health, much happiness, and continued success. We will miss you.

With warmest regards,
Hatim

● ● ●

The last we heard, Hatim was, as he told us, "having a blast" in his retirement. Apparently there are plenty of roses out there.

Chapter 8

Cornelia Street and River Café: Food for the Soul

> *We aim at something more sublime and more equitable—the common good, or the community of goods. . . . We demand, we would have, the communal enjoyment of the fruits of the earth, fruits which are for everyone.*
>
> François Babeuf, *Manifesto of the Equals*

The restaurant business is notorious for the elusiveness of bottom-line success, with the majority of start-ups failing to survive more than five years. Traditionally, restaurants struggle for survival in a highly competitive environment, but in reality the dynamics are much more complex than that. There are two stories about restaurants here, the first of which was inspired by something we read in the *New York Times* about a group of restaurants in New York City that seemed to embody certain complexity principles, particularly in terms of business ecosystems. We visited the restaurants several times, spending time with the owners, talking about their very special experience as part of that ecosystem. The result is "Cornelia Street." We arrived at the second story serendipitously, when we visited a restaurant in London simply to eat there. We quickly realized there was something different in the way the restaurant worked, and so we arranged for an extensive visit of observation and interviews with everyone, from owners to dishwashers. The result is "The River Café." Buon appetito!

Cornelia Street

To New York food writers, Cornelia Street in Greenwich Village is the new "in" location to eat, where tiny restaurants are booked up a month in advance.

Although the restaurateurs are enjoying the fame and the business it brings, Cornelia Street is more than just an epicurean Mecca to them. "There's something magical about the neighborhood," says David Page, co-owner of Home, which he opened with his wife, Barbara Shinn, in 1993, thus initiating the evolution of what he describes as "a true community."

When Home opened, there was just one restaurant on the street, Cornelia Street Café. Since 1977, it has been a kind of salon for poets, writers, and musicians to whom food and wine was merely an accompaniment to more serious intellectual endeavors. By the end of 1998, diners had half a dozen venues to choose from on this one-block-long, tree-lined street, offering American, French, Italian, Moroccan, and Cuban cuisine, and a raw bar. "The diversity of food available here is one of the strengths of the street," David told us. "But the real strength of the community is that we see each other as friends, not competitors. We're constantly borrowing from each other when we run out of things. You don't see that much in the restaurant business."

The restaurants form a supportive social web that is also good for business, since the critical mass of eating opportunities is a magnet to customers who speculatively cruise the street to see what takes their fancy. And when one restaurant is full, cruisers can spill over into others that have seats available. The street's fortunes have fluctuated through the years, and the recent renaissance is just the latest blossoming. A constant, however, has been the fact that the street is embedded in an old Italian neighborhood blessed with the kind of specialty stores for which European cities are renowned but are fast disappearing in most urban environments in America.

Within a one-block radius of Cornelia Street there's Florence meat market, now in its seventh decade; Faicco's pork store, established in 1900; Zito's bread store, which still has ancient coal ovens that were installed seventy years ago; and Murray's Cheese Shop, a relative newcomer, which opened its doors in 1940. This network of food purveyors was vital to the most recent emergence of the web of eateries, as David explained to us: "I encouraged the restaurants that came after us to use these neighborhood stores. It was an important philosophy for me, to build these connections, this community." As had happened to some extent in earlier times, the restaurants and food stores have come to form a loose economic web, or business ecosystem, in which, as David noted, "everybody benefits."

Before the Renaissance

Cornelia Street, in the heart of Greenwich Village, was laid out in 1794, on the farm of Robert Herring, who named it after his granddaughter. It has had an interesting history, Robin Hirsch told us over coffee at the Cornelia Street Café, which he founded with two equally inexperienced and impecunious partners more than two decades ago. "In the nineteenth century it housed the stables of the rich," he learned while researching an article to celebrate the café's twentieth birthday. "During Prohibition, it sheltered one of New York's most famous speakeasies. In the early 1940s W.H. Auden moved in at number 7, in the late 1940s Anatole Broyard opened a bookstore at number 20; for eleven years into the early 1950s James Agee had a writing studio at number 33; and in the late 1950s Joe Cino opened his café at number 31, where he established Off-Off-Broadway theater." In 1977, when Robin and his friends opened their café in just one room modestly equipped with a little toaster oven, much of that history had been erased and there were just two restaurants on the street. One was Sabor, a Cuban establishment, and the other Restaurant Leslie, with innovative French cuisine that catapulted the owner, Leslie Revsin, to culinary fame and a subsequent move to a swanky establishment uptown. "That represented a brief flicker of food fame for the street, a harbinger of what has recently happened with Home and the other restaurants," said Robin.

That flicker was insufficient to brighten a street that was otherwise pretty run-down and wracked with warring factions, which included a Mafia presence, a coterie of building superintendents who wallowed in bitterness and alcohol, and an Italian family and friends who lived over what was to become the café, and were distinctly unhappy about the prospect. "The supers used to sit on the opposite side of the street cursing us roundly while we were getting the café together," Robin said. "The store we renovated had been a junk shop and it was a horrible mess. For two months we built, scraped, sanded, plastered, plumbed, and painted, and did the intricate dance one has to do with authorities who live beyond Cornelia Street." Then, miracle of miracles, on July 2, 1977, the café opened. Also miracle of miracles, when the supers saw the grinding hard work come to completion, the disgruntled onlookers applauded, apparently recognizing the determination of Robin and his partners. "It was a moving moment," Robin told us.

No such miracle transpired with the Italian family, who continued to harass the café for years, taking the owners to court on numerous occasions and pretexts. "They once tried to set fire to the café," Robin recalled. "They poured boiling water on our heads. And every morning when we arrived, we'd find the locks sealed with glue." These and other tensions on the street have long since gone. Not everyone was as unwelcoming to Robin and his partners as the upstairs neighbors, however. There was a French potter around the corner, who made a vase as a housewarming gift, which still stands on the café's bar. In return, the café's first art exhibit was of the potter's wall ceramics. Very soon, and without deliberate intent, the café became a venue for poetry readings, stage performances, and music. "The whole scene just emerged unexpectedly," Robin told us, "probably because the three of us were into the arts in various ways. The café was not just about food. It was about food for the soul." Shortly after the café opened, Calvin Trillin wrote an article in *The New Yorker,* saying that the café was a benchmark for what Greenwich Village was all about.

Robin, the son of refugees from Hitler's Germany, grew up in England, and yet felt rootless. "I looked on myself as a wandering Jew," he told us. "But as soon as the café's doors opened, I felt at home at last. I realized that if I stood still long enough, my life would pass through these doors." There were hard times, but the café survived and even prospered at times, and became the social focus of the street. "I remember riding my bike back to Cornelia Street on the night of the great New York blackout of 1977," Robin told us. "It was pitch black. And then I saw the café, ablaze with candlelight. All the street was there in a huge spontaneous party, singing, dancing. We were giving away all the food in the fridge. It went on through the night, and we all went swimming in the Carmine Street pool at six the next morning."

As a constant on the street, the café became a haven of calm for the new restaurateurs, while their contractors wrested order from the chaos of renovations. We asked how Robin felt when he saw David Page in the throes of transforming the now defunct Sabor into Home, a tiny, simple restaurant serving simple, homey food. "I said a prayer for him," said Robin, remembering his own, earlier travails. "It's very tough to pull off something like that, especially in New York."

Home Coming

We met David and Barbara at Home, on a sunny, mild March morning. The restaurant has just twenty-four seats in the main dining room, and an equal number in a small, secluded garden, whose existence is a complete surprise, given the restaurant's ultra-urban location. Wind chimes were jingling a lively tune in the breeze. Even in winter, this little verdant oasis is small enough to enclose, heat, and use on all but the coldest days. Wine bottles stand in orderly lines on a few shelves, and rows of the restaurant's homemade preserves and pickles like you'd find at a farm stand form about the only decoration in this diminutive establishment. The floors are wide wooden boards, and the wooden chairs are the kind you expect to find in a favorite aunt's modest cottage. The coed bathroom is indicated by a picture of Julia Child and James Beard. The hostess answers the phone to a potential customer, saying, "Yes, this is Home," and, "No, wear what you like; we're very laid-back here."

David and Barbara are both from the Midwest, David from a small town twenty miles west of Oshkosh, Wisconsin, and Barbara from Toledo, Ohio, "two towns that most Americans think of as just names, not real places," said David. David and Barbara root their mode of doing business in what they call the Midwestern ethic. "You get to know your neighbors," Barbara said. "You knock on their doors. You give them support when they need help. And you know they will help you when you need something." The simple "borrowing a cup of sugar" mentality was what nurtured the emergence of the new Cornelia Street community. In complex adaptive systems, simple rules of behavior are the bedrock of what emerges.

The two met in San Francisco ten years ago, where David worked in several restaurants, including Masa's, Café Americain, and Postrio, while Barbara was doing fine art photography. They enjoyed the pace of life in the Bay Area, but took the 1989 earthquake as signal that it was time to move on. "We decided to move to New York City," Barbara recalled. "We got in our truck and drove for six weeks across country, on the back roads, not the highways, and not knowing where we were going. David kept saying, 'Don't worry, as long as we keep going east we'll be okay.' We camped out every night, except one time when we stayed at the Flying B Ranch in the Black Hills of Wyoming, because we wanted a steak real bad."

Once they were in New York, David and Barbara worked in various restaurants in Manhattan, David as a chef and Barbara as a waitress, but with no immediate plan to have a place of their own. But an idea seeded by the example of a friend eventually became their plan. "We formed the firm conviction that it should be a small restaurant, a family restaurant, because then you can be involved with everybody, the people you work with, and your customers," David explained. "And we wanted to be part of a community, really involved. That's why we came here, with all these food stores in the neighborhood, these little streets, the ethnic diversity. And we wanted it to reflect the values of what we grew up with in the Midwest, in the food and in the way you form relationships with your neighbors. I know it might sound stupid, but this thing is relationship-driven."

When they heard that the restaurant Sabor had closed, David and Barbara moved quickly to secure a good deal, and proceeded to create a little piece of the slow-moving Midwest in high-powered Manhattan. Home opened its doors on April 1, 1993, and before long was attracting favorable reviews in the food press, something all restaurateurs view as both a blessing and a curse. A blessing, because it brings recognition and the possibility of survival. A curse, because the flood of customers with high expectations can sometimes strain the resources. In Home's case, the first resource to crack was the napkin supply. "We were using cloth napkins, and we needed to try to borrow some when we ran out one night," Barbara recalled. "The café didn't use cloth napkins, so we tried to find some in SoHo, but people said effectively, 'Oh, you're that funny little restaurant three blocks away . . . we don't have any . . . and anyway, we can't be sure we'll get them back.' There was no trust."

At this point in our visit, Rebecca Charles joined us, a twenty-four-year veteran of the restaurant business, as a chef in various establishments in New York and Maine. In 1997 she became an owner for the first time, when she joined forces with Mary Redding and opened Pearl, an oyster bar, where Restaurant Leslie used to be. "Don't you just love Cornelia Street," she asked us, more expressing her own feelings than seeking an answer. "It has a very special atmosphere. It reminds me of streets in Paris, with little restaurants and stores." We talked about the travails of running a restaurant, where you can break your back with hard work, only to see your creation fail. It is also notorious for a high turnover of staff, particularly with chefs, who, when they make their mark, usually want to open a place of their own. "The most difficult part is trying to find people interested in the same journey," David told us. "The journey is a sense of something greater than a team. It is a team, of course, but it is more about community and family. There's not a lot of young people who can see that."

With Home's success established, David and Barbara opened a second restaurant, Drover's Tap Room, on Jones Street, one block over from Cornelia Street, and a take-out place, Home Away from Home, on Bleecker Street. With a total staff of seventy-five, management requires more than just being the head of a family. "There is a hierarchy, of course," David said, "but that doesn't mean I don't have a relationship with the dishwasher, a high-five kind of relationship. But the guiding principle is giving people room to make their own decisions. It's a matter of trust." Barbara agreed. "No one can make the perfect snap decision all the time," she said. "So you have to help people do their best, even though it isn't perfect. You have to hope they make a good decision on their own. It's about stepping back and resisting the urge to control everything, and that's not always easy. But that's the only way people can grow." Rebecca strongly supports this complexity science principle of allowing distributed influence: "You have to trust people to make good decisions, even if they are not the ones you would have made yourself."

Growing with people, supporting them in their dreams and ambitions, is essential to David and Barbara. "What is important in people's lives is the knowledge that they can succeed," David explained. "Barbara and I opened a restaurant five years ago with nothing, no money, and now we have something we can call our own. Not long ago Melissa, our pastry chef, went off to open her own pastry business in Brooklyn, and Robert, the sous chef, left to open his own restaurant in South Carolina. I love it when people have dreams like that, and make them happen." Not everybody grows and leaves, they told us. For instance, Augustine started as a dishwasher and is now the sous chef. "That's quite a jump," David said with pride in his part in the young man's development. Rebecca explained that the restaurant's owner provides the continuity and memory of the place, with people constantly coming and going. Her description evokes the image of a standing wave in a river, with the shape persisting while water molecules are constantly passing through it.

For David, Barbara, and Rebecca, the key to nurturing a creative, responsive work environment for their people, and for generating a relaxed, welcoming atmosphere for their customers, is to be genuine, to be authentic. "When you have waiters saying to customers, 'Hello, I'm James. I'll be your waiter this evening,' all delivered over a big, plastic grin; that's just awful," David grimaced. "It's just not genuine, and customers know it. We try to teach our staff to be real, and the best way to do that is to be real yourself. It has to come from you. These principles can be very effective, but it is difficult, and we are still figuring out how to do things. And we sometimes get it wrong, wrong, wrong." Although they had not heard of complexity science before we talked to them, David and Barbara had obviously come to many of its principles intuitively, in this case the principle of establishing effective relationships through their own authenticity.

Making Connections, Nurturing Evolution

Rob Kaufelt cut his business teeth in the food business, first by running a family-owned chain of supermarkets, and then in the gourmet store business. When he got divorced in 1988, he moved from New Jersey to Greenwich Village, installing himself in an apartment on Cornelia Street. Financially secure, he was wondering what his next move might be in terms of work. One day while in Murray's Cheese Shop Rob overheard the owner lamenting the loss of his lease and the impending end to a half-century-old business. "I asked him if he wanted to sell," Rob told us. "He said, 'I've nothing to sell, because the lease is ending.' I knew that a store at the corner of Bleecker and Cornelia Streets was vacant, and I was determined to reopen Murray's there." He did, in the spring of 1991.

"I loved the idea of perpetuating an old established business, and of working with cheese," Rob told us. "In supermarkets, it's all about commodities and numbers. But I'm interested in real products. Cheese is wonderful in many ways. It's peasant food. It's indigenous. You have to nurture it. Working with the quality and range of cheeses we do at Murray's makes you part of an elite network of cheese stores, like Formaggio in Cambridge, Massachusetts, and Neal's Yard in London. It's part of the soul thing." Of course, the need to visit his suppliers in France and Italy, which he does every year, is no hardship for Rob, a bonus really.

Rob quickly established himself as part of the network of food stores in the area, and, in addition to lecturing about cheese at various culinary schools in the city, he conducts walking tours of these stores for their students. "Zito's bread store is my favorite," he said. "It's run by three Italian brothers, one of whom is in his eighties and the other two in their seventies." Rob told us a story about the spirit of the store that he said had a big impact on him. "I was in the store one day and a woman came in, not a local, and asked, 'Is the bread fresh?' Charlie Zito exploded, and yelled, 'Get out.' The woman was bewildered, and said, 'What do you mean?' Charlie said, 'Nobody comes into my store and asks if my bread is fresh!' He is fiercely proud of what he makes every day, and has been making every day for more years than he cares to remember. 'I'm sorry, I didn't mean to offend,' the woman stammered. There was no appeasing Charlie. 'Get out,' he said again. I come from a background where the customer is always right, where you just swallow whatever customers say. The idea that I could tell a customer to get out of my store if I want to, and not go out of business, was very liberating for me."

Not long after Rob opened the reincarnated Murray's Cheese Shop, he met Susi Cahn, daughter of the co-owner of Coach Dairy Goat Farm, one of the store's suppliers. Susi was dating Mario Batali, an up-and-coming chef at Café Tabac in the East Village, which was very trendy at the time, and much favored by celebrities. Consequently it was very hard for mere mortals to get a table upstairs, where stars such as Madonna ate in rarefied seclusion. "On my wife's birthday, we joined with friends, two couples, and went over to Tabac, but they refused us a table," Rob told us. "We talked to Mario, who pitched a fit to the owner. Mario can be quite volcanic, you know. He threatened to walk out on the spot. Well, we got our table upstairs. Mick Jagger was there. The women in our group were very glamorous, and by the end of the evening people were trying to find out who we were, thinking we must be very important or something. It was very funny. The owner was all obsequious, and kept coming over to make sure everything was fine, and saying that we must come back soon. We never did."

Not long afterward, a store closed on Cornelia Street, and the landlord wondered whether Rob would like to open a restaurant there. Rob wasn't interested, but he knew that Mario was ready to strike out on his own. "I contacted Mario, and he jumped at it," Rob recalled. "I helped him work things out, and the rest is history. Restaurant Pō was born, and after a few months it became very successful." A devotion to food showing in his frame, the red-haired Mario is as enthusiastic about his work as he is energetic, as viewers of TV's Food Channel know from his antics on his daily programs, *Molto Mario* and *Mediterranean Mario.*

"We had no idea about Mario's plans, until one day not long after we'd opened he knocked on the door and told us he'd just signed a lease down the street," David told us. "It was during brunch, so we invited him in and drank Bloody Marys all afternoon in the garden as a celebration." Mario's arrival was precisely what David and Barbara hoped would happen. "We were overjoyed, because we knew that more restaurant traffic would come on the street," Barbara said. "We'd have more people around in the same business, forming the nucleus of the community we hoped would emerge."

"When Pō opened we had a difficult time for the first three months," Mario told us, "partly because we didn't have a liquor license." An Italian restaurant with no wine! Mama mia! "David was already successful, and at the end of each evening he'd come around with ice-cold beers for me and my partner, Steve," said Mario. "He'd say, 'We did a hundred covers tonight,' while we'd only done maybe thirty. So the beer was a booby prize! David and Barbara were very supportive of us; they are special people, and they should take a lot of the credit for making Cornelia Street into what it became." Before long, Pō was reviewed favorably in *New York* magazine, and customers began to flood in to taste the magic of Mario's kitchen. "I said to Steve, 'You're going to run out of napkins!' " recalled Barbara. "He said, 'Yeah, yeah,' not believing me. The very next night he was knocking on the door saying, 'Can I borrow some napkins, please.' It was very funny. We hunted around and found some pale blue ones, not our usual ones. They loved the color."

Barbara told us of the time she worked in a restaurant in SoHo, where, she said, people viewed newcomers as competitors, and certainly didn't help them out in a crisis. Not so on Cornelia Street. "Giving is just giving when it's done right, with no expectations," David explained. "If you can do that, then you get it back." There's a biblical proverb to the same effect. Pō was just the first in the evolution of the new restaurant community on Cornelia Street, a gradual weaving of a social and economic web. Andalousia, a Moroccan restaurant, soon followed in Pō's path. Then Le Gigot, a French bistro. And most recently Rebecca's Pearl and a Cuban restaurant, Havana. "The street welcomed me with open arms," Pamela Decaire, co-owner of Le Gigot, told us. "It's a wonderful community. We are all separate and distinct, but we help each other out when someone needs something." As Rebecca told us: "With the atmosphere that exists on the street, it's just the natural thing to do. We're neighbors, not competitors."

The emergence of the Cornelia Street restaurant community resembles what ecologists call succession. This happens when ecological communities become established in a previously barren environment, with one new species at a time becoming part of an increasingly complex, interacting network. As time passes, a community whose dynamic is more than the sum of its parts emerges, behaving in ways like a single organism, a superorganism. So it is with the social and economic web of Cornelia Street, with the critical mass of restaurants drawing potential customers to the location, not just to any particular restaurant, and so all of the restaurants benefit; and with the restaurants supporting and being supported by the network of food stores. Cornelia Street may not be unique in the nature of the interdependences that have emerged there, but it is undoubtedly special in the *degree* to which the social and economic web has developed. It is unique, however, in the players' awareness of the complexity-oriented dynamics of the system they've created and in the deliberate way it was nurtured, particularly by the owners of Home, where it all started.

The River Café

March 1997

An extraordinary accolade in an issue of *The New Yorker* seduced us to make the journey from Central London to Hammersmith, in West London, there to seek out the River Café, a restaurant on the banks of the River Thames. The River Café, suggested the article, "is the best Italian restaurant in Europe."[1] The comment had chefs from Palermo to Turin snorting in indignation. And it was enough for us to find time in our schedule to see if this could possibly be true. Set amid modest row houses and humble English gardens, the River Café's location is unprepossessing, especially for a restaurant that is widely credited with transforming and elevating standards of cuisine in London since its debut a decade ago. But it was to be something other than the food that would cause us to revisit the Café six months later, in September.

While savoring the restaurant's cucina rustica, peasant food, on that first occasion, we began to sense that the working atmosphere was somehow special, an almost palpable spirit of community, of family, a fluctuating dedication to, on one hand, delivering simple but extraordinarily good food to its customers, and on the other to mutual care and support among its people. The atmosphere was distinctly familiar to us—it had a *feeling* about it, a sense of community and connection, the same feeling we experienced in the other organizations we were working with. "Yes, you're right," our waiter told us when lunch was over and the press of serving a full restaurant had ebbed, and we felt it was appropriate to engage him in conversation. "This place *is* different. There's respect here, for everybody—the chefs, the wait staff, the dishwashers, everybody. If there's one rule here it's, 'If you see a job that needs doing, do it,' and it doesn't matter what the job is or who you are, you do it. We have the usual workplace problems, of course. People are people, after all. But this is like no restaurant I've worked in before, and I've worked in a few."

Our waiter told us about the culture of the restaurant, and how the spirit of the place emerges from the dedication of the two owners, Rose Gray and Ruth Rogers. What he was saying struck a chord with what we had seen and heard in other businesses that were guided by complexity science, except that at the River Café it was all by intuition—no one had heard about the science, Rose told us when lunch was over. She explained that she and Ruth had started the restaurant with little experience as chefs, and none at running a restaurant. Both had trained as graphic designers and had worked with the same publishing company. "All we had was a shared passion for Italian food, simple but exquisite ingredients, simply cooked," she said. Rose had lived for four years in Lucca, Tuscany, and Ruth spent part of each summer nearby. "If you have the best ingredients, you don't have to mess about with them much; in fact you *shouldn't* mess around with them much. If you respect the food for what it is, something wonderful will emerge from simple cooking."

Rose, with her lean face, penny specs, and short gray hair, has the appearance of a school principal, but the warmth of a beloved aunt. "Ruth and I both come from large families, and we wanted to create a restaurant that captured the community feel of domesticity, a feeling of family. We wanted to create a place where you can enjoy the best food and cooking, not one of those temples of haute cuisine where you are made to feel privileged that you have been allowed to enter its portals and eat its prized offerings."

The River Café might not be a temple of haute cuisine, but it soon became a kind of busy, artsy salon for celebrities: Woody Allen eats there, as do playwrights John Mortimer and Harold Pinter; Tina Turner has a penchant for hugging the waiters; and cooking greats such as Julia Child, Marcella Hazan, and the late Elizabeth David have eagerly made the pilgrimage to the Hammersmith eatery that one writer described as the apogee of "gastro-erotic Nineties London chic."[2] But we were interested not so much in the restaurant's stardom and acclaim; rather, we wanted to know how the restaurant works, what engenders its culture, what its values are. We arranged with Rose to spend a full day at the restaurant when we would return to London in September. We agreed on a date, and Rose told us to arrive at nine in the morning. Alex, the restaurant's greeter, would meet us and arrange our visit, Rose promised.

September 26, 1997

9:00 A.M.: The wood-burning oven is lit, visual and sensual focus of this high-tech yet casually chic restaurant. The architecture is studied simplicity: the dining area is an unfussy rectangular room with white walls, a deep blue carpet, and a burnished steel bar running along one of the long walls, and pearl-glass windows casting diffused light behind it; the opposite wall is all glass windows and doors, giving a view onto a grass courtyard and Harrods warehouse (now abandoned) brooding in Victorian decay on the far bank of the River Thames. White linen drapes tables ringed by simple stainless steel and cane chairs. The only extraneous decoration in the room is the shadow of a clock face projected on the end wall, and a huge vase of blue flowers atop the bar. Charlie, the manager, sits nursing a cappuccino at a table near the door, reading a newspaper. Low voices drift from a few people in the kitchen, unseen behind a wall at the far end of the room. It's a brief oasis of quiet and calm as the day begins at the River Café.

Alex wasn't there when we arrived at the appointed time. "Have some coffee," Charlie said, when he saw us hovering by the open door. "Alex will be here soon." He went on to explain that, although technically he is the restaurant's manager, "we aren't into titles here, no hierarchy; it's all very informal, even though the food is expensive and a lot of famous people eat here." Charlie described himself as a newcomer, having been at the restaurant for two years. "There's not much turnover here, and that's unusual in the restaurant business," he said. "That tells you a lot about how people feel valued. And, best of all, it's *fun* working here. Listen to that." About a dozen people had arrived as we'd been talking with Charlie, and, as they were donning their starched whites, there was a lot of laughter, and someone singing. "In most restaurants there's a lot of tension and sometimes animosity between the wait staff and the people in the kitchen," he went on. "Here, we all work together, and so we feel a common purpose. You'll see that in a while, when veggie prep gets under way."

Alex finally arrived, wreathed in smiles and apologies for being late. Young and chic, in keeping with the restaurant's decor, she sat at our table, managing to pull the tablecloth onto her seat, spilling coffee everywhere in the process. "Oh bloody hell, Charlie, it's going to be one of those days." Charlie cleaned up the coffee lake, amid much bantering, while we found another table. Alex told us of the support people feel in general at the Café and her own experience in particular. She said that Ruth and Rose are very sensitive to people's personal lives, and not just because this can influence the way people are at work. "They are very understanding when people have trouble at home," Alex told us, "and they will do all they can to help. But they don't tolerate someone's bad mood being expressed in bad service to our customers. And, don't get me wrong. This isn't some ideal paradise, all smiles all the time. Sometimes people get to hate each other, and you might have feuds for a while. If they persist, someone has to go, for the health of the community, and it *is* a community here." Complex adaptive systems are very sensitive to positive relationships, which can promote creativity and adaptability. Equally, the effects of negative relationships also pervade the system.

9:30 A.M.: Laundry arrives, bright orange sacks stacked by the door. One of the chefs is sweeping up outside around the pile of wood that fires the oven. Someone is setting tables. Four chefs, dressed in classic kitchen garb of blue and white checked pants, blue and white striped aprons, white chef's jackets, and chef's clogs, huddle around a table in the corner by the window. A ritual that occurs twice a day, every day, is beginning: menu planning, working with a list of what's in the fridge and must be used up, and a list of what will come in fresh that day. The process takes about an hour, and at the end, one of the chefs makes a list of jobs to be done and gives it to the prep captain, whose role is to make sure all the jobs are done by the time customers arrive. There's no allocation of jobs; people choose what they want to do. And anyone can be prep captain. The authority fluctuates day by day.

"Our menu emerges from the bottom up," Garry, one of the chefs, told us. "It's a more organic, instinctive process. You have to taste the food first, then decide what to do with it. Most chefs do it the other way round." The chefs told us that Ruth and Rose's philosophy is to use what's in season, and then select the best quality, just like an Italian grandma would. "It keeps you in touch with the seasons, the cycling of nature," explained Pete, another of the chefs. "I love this season, the autumn. The grouse will be coming in soon, and white truffles." You can hear the chefs' love of food in their voices. Not so much a reverence for the food, but a respect, a deep connection, a delight. "Food is alive here," Pete added. The chefs keep a ten-year record of their menus, handwritten twice a day, and they constantly refer to it, to guard against repetition. "We try not to repeat colors and flavors too often," explained Ashley.

We wondered whether the twice-daily menu ritual was stressful. "The strengths of what we do are also our weakness," Garry responded. "So, yes, it can be very anxiety-making, but the chaos of it all makes you very creative. Some restaurants do the same dishes week after week. You get very good at it, of course, but it loses inspiration." There's more freedom, but less control with the River Café way of doing things, which operates in the zone of creative adaptability, and there are often last-minute scares, when dishes don't work out as envisaged, they told us. "Yesterday, for instance, we did tuna with horseradish, but it just wasn't right, so we changed it at the last minute. That's frightening," said Ashley, the third of the four chefs. "But it pushes you; I love the challenge when it's, 'Okay, we've run out of calamari, *now* what do we do?' There are lots of chefs who can't live with this kind of uncertainty. We've had people come to work here and they are shocked by what we do. 'What the hell is going on here?' they ask. I know I wasn't sure that the lack of hierarchy and lack of discipline was a good thing, having been in a very hierarchical, aggressive kitchen previously. But then I began to see the creativity of it, and I now love it. And if you don't, then you leave. That has happened." Creativity out of chaos.

The twice-daily orchestration of the symphony of dishes brings the staff to a point of deep mutual respect. "In the traditional restaurant kitchen the head chef shouts orders and everybody cringes," said Pete. "I was in a restaurant once where the chefs actually threw knives at each other. I'm not saying we don't have our difficult moments, when the pressure's on or something goes wrong. We're not perfect, I'm not suggesting that. But there's a mutuality here that I haven't experienced anywhere else, an equality, and support—tremendous mutual support." At this point a man delivering meat came in, sporting a bright red shirt, dark complexion, and a three-day stubble—very Mediterranean-looking. "Is anyone in charge here?" he asked. Good question.

10:30 A.M.: Tables are being set outside. Someone is gathering herbs from tubs in the courtyard. A line of wait staff is behind the bar, all wearing crisp white kitchen jackets, preparing vegetables, an oddly linear sight in this distinctly nonlinear environment. Someone bitches—more or less playfully—about having to pit the olives *again!* Mostly they chat, laugh, and occasionally break into collective chorus. Playful.

The wait staff told us that they like to be involved in food prep, because it brings them close to the food they will be serving later; that it creates a camaraderie among them and a bond with the kitchen staff; that the freedom to choose jobs, rather than being told what to do, is liberating, even though some jobs are tedious; and, yes, disorienting at first, because it is not what most have experienced at other places of work. And it's fun, they told us. They feel appreciated and, most important of all, trusted. "You can slack off from time to time," said Sam, one of the wait staff, "and people will pick up for you. But you can't do that too much, because that becomes an unfair burden on the others. Because you feel trusted, it makes you want to do your best."

Their enthusiasm and oneness is palpable. They are a medley of young artists, actors, and students—and all River Café handsome. There's a paradox of authority, they said: everyone is equal, but some are more equal than others:

Those who have worked longer have more influence, but everyone can make suggestions, give feedback, and they do. "But you don't feel anyone is looking over your shoulder," said Sam. The air is filled with the aroma of chopped tomatoes, roasted peppers, fresh basil, garlic—we are bathed in a flowing kaleidoscope of sensations.

Ruth arrived at 11:30, looking serious. She huddled with the chefs, and went over the planned menu. She has the final say. Normally, she and Rose exercise this role, but Rose wasn't in the restaurant on this day. And the prices for the dishes were set. She looked into the kitchen, chatted with Charlie, and, satisfied everything was in order, relaxed and smiled. "My first principle is respect, respect for everyone who works here," began Ruth, after we found a quiet corner to talk. "If you involve everyone equally, you get a culture of commitment, a strong work ethic, everyone working together, everyone *wanting* to work together, and having fun doing it. If you treat people well, create good working conditions, encourage their growth through experience, engage in constant dialogue, a powerful commitment emerges. That way, everybody benefits." It all sounds like good, down-home common sense, and it is certainly a way to create a coherent organization with a common purpose. But, unlike Ruth and Rose, many leaders find it hard if not impossible to pull it off.

Ruth, an American from upstate New York, told us that when she hires people she pays as much, if not more, attention to a candidate's social mind-set as she does to professional skills. "You can help people grow professionally," Ruth said, "but changing someone's mind-set is much more difficult, and the right mind-set is very important in a place run the way we run the River Café."

Ruth extends this care, this respect, to the food she gives her people. "Most restaurants give their staff poor food," she said, "but here, they eat what the customers eat. I think that's important; it sends an important message." The first goal of the restaurant is to produce the best food possible, Ruth continued. The second is to make people feel happy about their visit. "You have to be nice to your customers," she explained. "No, you have to *want* to be nice to customers. I know that I'll go back to a restaurant if the food is good, but I won't go back if I'm not treated well, in an open friendly way, no matter how good the food is."

We asked how she and Rose came to their mode of management. "Well, I have friends who run large organizations, so that gave me some insights," she said. "But mainly it's a very hands-on thing, an intuition about people. We both had eaten wonderful food in people's homes in Italy, and we wanted to re-create that kind of eating experience. We wanted it to be like a family, to *feel* like a family. It's not exactly that, of course, but that's where the restaurant's soul comes from. Sometimes I think what I'm doing isn't quite right, but I'm arrogant enough to be confident that what we do is okay."

At this point, Ruth's husband, Richard Rogers, joined us. An architect with the design of the Pompidou Center, in Paris, and the Millennium Dome, in London, as part of his considerable portfolio, Richard played a key role in the genesis of the River Café, as well as in its design. First, it was through his Trieste-born mother, Dada, that Ruth first tasted real Italian food, sparking a passion in her for cucina rustica. Second, the restaurant is part of a warehouse complex that he bought in 1986, with a view to creating a community of businesses. "I wanted the community to be like a family," Richard told us. "My office is over there, there's another architect, a model shop, a print shop, and there used to be a record company and a place that made stained glass." Some three hundred people make up the community, sixty of whom work at the River Café. Regular weekly softball games (Wednesdays) and social gatherings (Fridays) play a key role in fostering connections. And everyone can get a discount lunch at the restaurant, which started life with the modest ambitions of being the community's eatery. It evolved into much more than that.

"In architecture, the environment is critical," Richard continued. "I love space, the fluidity of space, the space between things." In complex systems, fluidity of space and the space between things are the pathways of creative emergence. After he bought the warehouse complex, Richard had one of the buildings taken down, to create what is now the green courtyard in front of the restaurant. "It gives that essential *feeling* of openness, and it's a place where people gather and meet, where unexpected things happen." We had certainly seen that earlier in the day, but now the courtyard was empty as the pace of lunch preparations picked up and everyone was now inside. "This is always a tense time for me," Ruth said. "The preparation's almost done; the customers are going to start arriving soon. It's all very theatrical. At 12:30 the curtain goes up, and you'd better know your lines. It's theater. It's show time."

12:30 P.M.: The wait staff has finished prep. Everyone has tossed off their kitchen whites, and is wearing just exactly what they want. No formal black and white here: casual chic, following Ruth and Rose's philosophy, of everyone being allowed to express themselves as they wish, be themselves. The first customers arrive, and before long every table is filled. Charlie is like a dragonfly, flitting back and forth, making sure all is in order, his territory safe. The wait staff are like water boatmen, sliding to where they need to be. Ruth stands at the end of the bar, by the kitchen, inspecting every plate before the wait staff takes them to the tables. Another unique meal at the River Café. Order out of chaos.

Cooking is in some ways the epitome of emergence: a few ingredients are brought together in simple ways, and what is created is more than the sum of the parts, the definition of emergence. But at the River Café, complexity science is embraced more profoundly than that, even though it is not named as such. The simple rule of saying, "The menu will change twice a day in response to the environment" (that is, what foods are available at any particular season), forces a level of adaptability and creativity that is absent in a restaurant where the menu remains the same for long periods. But, as with any business, there are mechanistic aspects to the River Café in action, too. "You have to work in a mechanical way, as well as being creative," Ruth told us, "it's a blend of both ways of being." The creativity is in conceiving the dishes and in their execution. The mechanical way is in making sure there are plates and silverware and glasses sufficiently available, getting the four dishes at a table to be ready at the same time, and so on. "Of course, the creativity part is more fun!"

4:00 P.M.: Only one table remains occupied, a group of men and women from a local media company. The wait staff for the evening shift have started to arrive, and are donning their kitchen whites in preparation for veggie prep, chatting, laughing. The morning staff, about twenty people in all, have gathered plates of food buffet style from the bar, and are sitting at a long table in the courtyard, enjoying the autumn sun. Ruth sits at the head of the table, and talks about an article in a magazine she holds up. People listen closely. She addresses some general gripes, about smoking, for instance. And then she walks around the table, stops, talks intimately to someone about a concern she has, her hand on the person's shoulder, a delicate balance between reprimand, guidance, and care. The food preparers can be heard singing heartily at the bar. Four chefs sit at a corner table inside, starting to plan the evening menu: the second cycle of the daily ritual at the River Café is under way.

Chapter 9

DuPont: Down on the Plant

Now join your hands, and with your hands your hearts.

William Shakespeare, *Henry VI*

The small town of Belle lies ten miles east of Charleston, the capital of West Virginia, one of the poorest states in the country. Belle lies on the banks of the Kanawha River, which flows from North Carolina and through the Appalachian Mountains, a verdant rural setting. But the footprint of industrialization has impressed itself heavily on this community, which huddles beneath the looming presence of a huge DuPont chemical plant, a mile long and a third of a mile wide, sited on the banks of the Kanawha. Built in 1926, the Belle plant was the first commercial synthetic ammonia facility in the U.S., and the first producer of commercial nylon intermediates. The abundance of cheap coal and salt springs in the region was the reason DuPont located a plant in Belle, and three generations of the town's citizens have lived daily with the less than pleasant sight of the huge storage tanks and manufacturing plant, and the acrid odor that typically used to attend such facilities. There developed an uneasy balance of the town's people being grateful for the work the facility brought to the community, and their resenting its impact on their sensibilities.

By 1987 the community's resentment had deepened to include a deep suspicion and distrust of the plant and its managers, a corrosive fear that a catastrophic accident could pose mortal danger to the town's people, and a belief that the managers simply did not care. The enmity between town and plant was as palpable as the odor-laden air. The plant itself was in a state of decay, physically and psychologically. Outdated equipment needed to be renewed, and most of the manufacturing processes were inefficient and wasteful, leading to quality and cost concerns; the need to revamp was unavoidable. The workforce of about a thousand—down from a high of five thousand during World War II—was frustrated and angry, and there was a deep rift between managers and their people. Accidents were far higher than was the DuPont standard. The plant's managers were myopic about their place in the community, and were unaware of the changing economic and social environment. Executives at DuPont's head office in Wilmington, Delaware, had lost confidence in Belle's management to deliver the needed results, and there was every expectation that the plant would be shut down before very long.

When Dick Knowles arrived as Belle's new plant manager in April of 1987, he knew he faced an uphill battle, both to get the plant working efficiently again and thus avoid the loss of jobs, and to heal the relationship with the surrounding community. A veteran of DuPont whose father was a plant manager before him, too, Dick was by habit a command and control manager, something he'd absorbed from other managers around him throughout his career. You had to be tough and rough to show you were in control, he learned. You often shouted at people, used bad language, and sometimes demeaned those below you. This was not how you behaved in your social life or in the community, but that's the way he'd learned it was supposed to be when you walked through the factory gate; that was the way you showed you're the boss. Given his impressive physical frame, the intensity in his face, and the sternness in his voice, you can see how easily Dick might intimidate lesser beings.

Dick had not gone willingly to West Virginia. A few years earlier he and his wife were divorced, and Dick had fallen in love with Claire, who worked in human relations at the same DuPont plant in Niagara Falls, New York. Upper management frowned on the relationship, deeming it improper for the plant manager to be amorously involved with another of the plant's employees. So it was West Virginia or else for Dick. Reluctantly, he took the lesser of two evils, and set about salvaging Belle, beginning in his well-practiced style of heavy-handed management. But Claire had touched something different in Dick, a softer, more human part of him that had lain unnurtured. And during his eight-year tenure at Belle, Dick underwent a transformation in his personal life and his style of management. He came to see that the way you get the best out of people is not to bully them but to reach out to them as human beings, to let them see *you* as a human being.

Gradually Dick developed a style of management practice that is advocated by complexity science: namely, valuing people for themselves, attending to relationships, stripping down hierarchy, including everyone in a rich web of information flow. It was a slow, painful process—for Dick and for his people alike. Only when he was five years into the transformation did he learn about complexity science, and realized that he had converged onto this new style of management through intuition. That realization was enormously validating for Dick, knowing that he wasn't alone in his difficult journey, and it gave him the courage to go even further, to be even bolder. The results at the end of Dick's tenure speak for themselves:

- Injury rates were down by 95 percent.
- Environmental emissions were reduced by more than 87 percent.
- Uptime of the plant increased from an average of 65 percent to 90 to 95 percent.
- Productivity increased by 45 percent.
- Earnings per employee tripled.

There were improvements in other areas, too, areas that defy ready quantification. People's morale increased dramatically, for instance. And the relationship between plant and community transformed from outright antagonism to mutual respect. Belle went from being a liability for DuPont to being one of the company's strongest plants. And all this was done with most of the same people who had been at the plant when Dick arrived eight years earlier.

In what follows, we show how this metamorphosis came about, in Dick's own words.[1]

Key Management Tool: Shoe Leather

Even before I got to West Virginia I heard how difficult things were down there. People began to call me on the phone, managers complaining about their co-workers. I'd hear stories about some incident or other that I assumed had just happened, and then I'd learn that it was years back. Boy, did they hold grudges. That tells you the psychological state of the place—it was like a sick person in need of healing. So, when I arrived I already knew that hourly workers and the managers distrusted each other, I mean big-time. And some of the managers were at each other's throats. So I decided my first objective would be to meet everyone, every single person in the plant, within six weeks. You do that by walking around, just talking to people, listening to them; that way you tap into the life of the organization. I did that for five hours a day, every day, and I continued doing it throughout my eight years there. Boy, did I go through a lot of shoe leather.

The first issue I felt I had to tackle was the poor record of safety, which was unacceptable at Belle. There were just too many accidents, and yet managers were abdicating their responsibility on this, always blaming someone else. And the hourly people were getting punished a lot, sometimes deservedly, sometimes not. I tried to stop all that and make supervisors accountable. I was very command and control on this, just saying how it had to be. Period. It was brutal. We fought like hell. We'd argue. I demanded that managers know what was going on. In one of my first weekly managers meetings someone said, "We had an injury last night." I asked what had happened. "Well, I don't really know." I asked who had been hurt. "I don't know." I asked how long the man had worked at the plant. "I don't know." To me that was intolerable, that the manager should be so lacking in information, or interest, it seemed to me. I blew my stack. I tore the guy to pieces in front of everyone. He was really humiliated.

We used to have business meetings twice a week, out in the plant, in the laboratory, the control room, shops, all over the place. There'd be the leadership group, including me, and we'd talk to groups of folks in the plant about safety or what they were working on. I used to dread those meetings, because the folks would just light into us, telling us we were doing a lousy job and that they could do things a lot better. They could see the plant was losing products over the years, and that their employment was threatened. They complained that management wasn't doing anything about it or asking for help. They were very frustrated.

After a couple of years things started to get better, and I'd start to make real contact with people. I remember one meeting with about forty mechanics and their managers, a group that prided itself on being ornery. It turned out that before the meeting, unbeknownst to me, one of the supervisors had said, "Don't make waves with Knowles." So I went in there, and we got through the first part of the meeting, and I said, "Any questions?" All forty guys just got up, turned their chairs around, and sat down with their backs to me. And I'm the boss for God's sake, the boss of the entire plant! I panicked. "God, what do I do now?" I said to myself. I knew if I walked, I was dead. If I lost my temper, I was dead. I just stood there, and finally told all the managers to get the hell out. So I'm in there alone with forty backs for company, the place was silent. I got myself a cup of coffee, and sat down, looking at their backs. I don't know how long we all sat like that. It seemed like an hour, but maybe it was only a few minutes. I was sweating. And then I said, "You know, this is a real lonely job. Are you guys going to talk to me?" Within a minute they turned around, and we had a wonderful meeting, people being honest about their concerns, not just complaining. The back-turning stunt was the guys' way of punishing their bosses for having told them not to make waves. It was very funny afterward. We really connected.

Meanwhile, the managers were milling around outside, wondering what the hell we were talking about in there, and afraid I was going to raise hell with them. I did. By telling the mechanics not to make waves, the managers were trying to stop communication, and it was a very clear lesson to me how important communication is. I mean, that's why I spent five hours a day walking around and talking to people. And I'm talking about open communication, authentic communication. It was hard, but I eventually got managers to see that it was as important to admit when they screwed things up, and to tell the guys that they would try to do better next time, as it was to talk about successes. Initially, the managers blanched at the thought, but then they went out and did it. People gave us credit for owning up to our mistakes.

It's so important for managers to be honest and to admit when they don't know something, which is the case a lot of the time. What typically happens in many companies is that managers will do a study of some proposal or other behind closed doors, and then descend from Mount Olympus with The Truth. The people at the front lines usually see right through it, what's wrong with the plan, and so on. Then they self-organize and make the thing work anyway, saving the managers' bacon. We found that it is so much better if you say to the folks, "Look, we don't know how to do this. Help us, please." You win two ways. First, you get better solutions, because the people up against the problems have a better feel for the best solutions. And second, people become more fulfilled because they are involved and they see their ideas valued. People begin to discover meaning in their work. You develop a real community that way. There were people at Belle who when I arrived were just doing their job, and barely that at times. And within a couple of years, they were really pulling their weight, and enjoying it. You could see it in their posture, how they walked, in their faces. I like to see that. And the plant works better, too; you can see that in the bottom-line numbers.

Creating Teams

I often cringe when I think how brutal I was at the beginning. I knew I had to be tough, because the safety issue had to be addressed fast. Command and control doesn't have to be brutal, but that was my habit. At the same time, Claire was encouraging something else in me, a more human approach, but it was slow to develop, because I didn't have a model for how to be. At Niagara Falls, I had developed a way of working with the community that was very human-centered, where I used information to bring people together, where information was free-flowing, like air. In organizations, information is often hoarded by managers as a means of control. I began to feel that what I had done in the Niagara Falls community might transform the organization at Belle, and become more efficient and more competitive. It was a slow process, and it began with creating teams, genuine teams.

The management group had been trying to work as a team for a while, but not very successfully. At our Monday management meetings we agreed we would score ourselves as a team, on a scale of one to ten. Everybody was obliged to speak, and so sometimes they'd tell me I'd done something to screw them up the week before. So I had to behave well and not jump all over them, which was my natural inclination. This stuff hurts, you know, but I think it's how we learn. We went along for four or five months with a score of about seven, which I felt wasn't good enough. We weren't making progress, and I was getting madder and madder at these jerks because I felt they couldn't get their acts together. It didn't dawn on me at first that maybe I was the problem. But one day I was talking to Alan Gilberg, a consultant who had helped us to become civil to each other, when I realized I was the problem. So I went to the team and said, "Maybe what I'm doing is disenabling you folks. Would you be willing to talk to me about that?" All but one of them spent about an hour telling me how great it was when I wasn't there, and what a jerk I was. They said I'd jump on them, wouldn't let them finish sentences, that I'd be really hard on someone if I thought they'd done something wrong. It wasn't fun to have to sit there and listen to all this stuff, I can tell you. There was a lot of pain in me, and I cried a bit after that.

I suggested that from then on at meetings on the plant I wouldn't sit at the head of the table, which was a kind of power seat. Instead we'd have what we called a surrogate manager take that position, who served as a communications coordinator. I said I'd sit at the side of the room and be a coach for what's going on, an observer, and the surrogate manager would lead the meeting. Because these were multilevel meetings, it meant that often the person leading the meeting was less senior than those he or she was leading. The very first week we did that, our management teamwork score went way up, and it stayed there, so it became clear as a bell to me how badly I'd been screwing them up. It's the only time I've ever really seen a step change like that. Our next task was to try to get the same spirit in the rest of Belle.

We talked about the challenges we faced in the management group, we read a lot, and we visited other DuPont plants where teamwork was strongly developed. One of them, in El Paso, Illinois, had been working this way successfully for ten years. We were very struck by what Dick Page, the plant manager, showed us. It was a list of "treatment of people principles," which guided people on how they could work together. We realized that such a body of principles might help us navigate the turbulent times that were buffeting us; they'd be like the poles you hold on to in a crowded, jostling subway car so you don't fall down. We also realized that we had to be absolutely genuine about this; playing games would spoil everything. At this point we faced a dilemma. For instance, we'd heard of other plants that tried to do this from the bottom up, and as the body of principles rose up through the levels of the organization, something got lost at every step. By the time top management got involved, so much had been lost that the end product was a nice but meaningless statement hung on a wall. This way of doing things is counterproductive, because it generates cynicism, and nothing changes. We decided to do it differently at Belle. The management team would draft a set of principles similar to El Paso's that we as the management team wanted to live by, and then ask everyone in the plant to help us do that. We hoped that if we walked the talk of the principles, others might follow us. It was an invitation.

The Treatment of People Principles are as follows:

1. People want interesting work—work that makes good use of their abilities. Boring jobs de-motivate and alienate.
2. They want opportunity for learning and growth and opportunity to apply the skills applied.
3. They can be trained (that is, they are able and willing) to do several different jobs.
4. They want equal opportunity to advance and try different work.
5. They want responsibility in their work, some degree of decision making.
6. They "want in" on decisions that affect them.

7. People expect management to lead, not abdicate. People look to management to make its contribution in those critical areas where employees do not have the requisite orientation, knowledge, or resources.

8. They expect a leadership team to be consistent and predictable.

9. People want to be part of a winning team.

10. People want to know what's going on at Belle, in the department, and in the company.

11. People want to be informed about the business and get early feedback on the performance of their part of the operation.

12. They want fair pay and knowledge about how the pay system works.

13. They have a need to relate to others in the job.

14. They want rational rules and a minimum of regimentation. People want a say in the rules.

15. They want to be treated like people—people have ego needs.

We posted the list of the principles all around the plant—in control rooms, labs, shops, offices, and lunch rooms, and effectively said, "We want to use these principles to lead the plant, and would you help us? These principles are not yours, but would you help *us* live by them?" So, we put ourselves right out there, totally exposed. The initial response was cynicism and disbelief. People said, "You're not going to do this." But after a couple of months of a generally negative response, the people began to see that we were really trying. They then had a grand old time pointing out our deficiencies, where we were falling down on the principles, and so on. It initiated many conversations about what we were as a community and how we could work together, that we shared a common goal.

It was a difficult process, particularly for managers who were used to an us-them relationship with their workers. For us in the management team, we needed a lot of support from each other, and we often had to bite our tongues when we were being criticized. The shift took about nine months, and what had started as a set of principles for the management team was eventually embraced by just about everybody. It was amazing to watch the trust slowly germinate. As a result of this swirl of conversation in the plant, we made two changes in the list. The first was to insert "most people" for "people," because the folks told us that they knew of other people who didn't share the principles, although I never encountered anyone who rejected them. The second change was to add another principle: "People always want the issue of security addressed; they want to know what will happen to them as change occurs."

While nine months might sound a long time, I was surprised by the speed with which the transformation happened, given the magnitude of what we were doing. It was faster than any of us in the management team had experienced for such a process of change, and we felt that the heat we had taken had been worth it. Particularly so, because it dissipated the negative energy that had been crushing us, and hindering what we wanted to achieve in the plant as a whole. The change in culture was amazing to watch, and to be in the middle of: trust replaced suspicion; openness replaced guardedness; cooperation replaced recalcitrance; "them" became "us." If this sounds too good to be true, all I can tell you is that this is one of those rare occasions when it was both good and true. It formed the foundation for all the change efforts we made in the time I was at Belle.

I'll give a couple of examples of how change opened up. One of our first change efforts was replacing the outdated pneumatic instrumentation for controlling one of the chemical processes with an electronic system, which improves operability, gives higher product quality, and lower emissions. Traditionally, this kind of switch-over is done by an outside group of engineers, and involves building a parallel process for use during the early stages of start-up. That's usually necessary to get you through the teething troubles as the operators overcome their resistance and slowly get used to the new system. This takes time, and a lot of angst before the new system is running smoothly. We said we wouldn't do it that way. We'd let our own people be involved and do the whole thing. The operators and mechanics worked with the engineers the whole time, so they knew what was going on, and could have their input. We didn't build a parallel system, because we were confident that we wouldn't need it. We didn't. We did the shift-over in half the time and half the cost that it normally takes, setting a new standard for the company as a whole. And because the operators and mechanics had been so involved in the design process, and had become so committed to making it work, the new electronic control system started up quickly, and was fully operational in a few days. It is a wonderful example of the effectiveness and efficiency you can achieve by involving front-line people in change that affects them.

A second example was in 1993, when we decided to strip out layers of supervision, flattening the organization, and giving more control to the people doing the work of the plant. At the time, each work shift had a shift supervisor, seven or eight first-line supervisors, and a crew of eighty or ninety operators. Our plan was to reassign the first-line supervisors, which meant that the operators had to be able to make a lot of decisions on their own. We did a lot of work helping the teams of operators develop the skills they'd need, and developing their confidence. When we launched the new system, we had a couple of former front-line supervisors on hand to help the teams, but not in their traditional supervisory roles, more as coaches. Most of the people loved it, because they were learning and because they had more authority. From then on, self-organizing teams were at the core of how we did things, with people contributing if they wanted to, and they did. The plant performance improved, and morale blossomed.

Discovering Complexity Science

The new style of leadership we were developing was tremendously liberating for me. As we moved from our static, dull, inflexible hierarchical structures to something that's near the edge of chaos, it was stimulating and fun, but it was also scary. Many times when things weren't going right—and that often happened, believe me—we had to struggle with the temptation to fall back to what seemed like the safety of the old command and control structures. The thing was, we were doing this in a vacuum, winging it, and we weren't sure we were on the right track. We felt very isolated. Then in early 1992 I came across James Gleick's book on chaos theory, which isn't quite the same as complexity theory, but something in it clicked for me, because it sure felt that what we were doing was chaotic, but also creative.[2] It intrigued me, but I didn't know what to do with it.

I was talking on the phone to a colleague one day, and he said, "You know, there's a group of people looking at this chaos stuff; it's called the Chaos Network." He gave me the phone number of the guy who was running it at the time, Mark Michaels. I immediately called him, and he understood what I was struggling with. I about fell over when I heard that, because at that point I had no one to talk to. Mark told me about the second annual Chaos Network Conference, which was due to be held in a couple of weeks' time in California. This was in the fall of 1992. I changed my schedule so I could go, and told my boss only that I was going to a conference on organizational development. I was very excited, but my heart sank when I arrived at the hotel: it was called the Dream Inn. I thought, "If those folks back home ever find out I went to a chaos conference at the Dream Inn, they are going to kill me."

It was a wonderful three days, because I discovered fifty people who understood what I was doing. I thought, "I'm not crazy after all." I got a vocabulary for what I was doing, and courage to continue with it and take it further. I met Meg Wheatley, who was talking about chaos, not complexity, but it was tremendously validating.[3] I read her book going home on the plane, and almost cried. I felt like I'd come home.

I asked Meg to visit Belle, and she saw that we had a laboratory of a thousand people, struggling with new ways of working that most people were just theorizing about. Her visit, with her colleague Myron Kellner-Rogers, gave us a big lift.

One of the biggest struggles was how you keep things under control if you don't do it in the old way. If you leave behind control by directives, dictating results and outcomes, how do you keep things from falling apart and losing focus? I developed this image of a bowl, a safe container that gives people freedom to experiment, to create improvements in serving our stakeholders more competitively. When people feel free to experiment they will try lots of new things on their own, many of which might not go anywhere or will simply fix a specific problem, and that's important. But a few experiments will lead to big, unexpected outcomes. It's the complexity principle that small changes can sometimes lead to large effects.

The bowl gives you order and freedom at the same time. It's a kind of paradox. It's the leader's job to create the bowl through our conversations about our vision, our mission, our principles, our standards, our expectations. The leader creates the conditions that make it okay for the people to grow, and an enormous energy gets released. People discover that they can make a difference, meaning begins to flow, you get discretionary energy flow. That's the difference in energy between doing just what you have to do to keep from being fired, and being fired up and doing the max.

I'll give you an example. I was walking through the plant one day and ran into an operator who was walking fairly fast and had a bundle of papers under his arm, and he was in overalls. I said, "Mike, how are you doing?" He said, "Oh, I'm doing fine." I asked him what he was doing that day, and he said, "I'm project manager for this new tank car unloading spot. I'm working with the operating instructions and mechanical instructions, and I've got a meeting to go to. See ya!" And off he went. I mean, that's the kind of work engineers normally do, not operators. Just a year earlier, we had almost fired Mike because of some environmental upsets where he lacked the required focus in this work. He didn't have any enthusiasm; he was careless. He had completely transformed, and had energy and enthusiasm for his work and the new things he was doing. You can't buy that energy; you can't force it. And if you try to go in for performance systems and bonuses, you can't get it either, because people come to see them as entitlements very quickly.

Another example. In our new way of working we encouraged people to join teams when they thought it was right, to make decisions on their own when they thought it was right. So, I got a call from an operator, Becky, one day, all upset. She had come in for the six o'clock shift, and had heard a couple of folks on a music show on the radio complaining about all the pollution from our plant. They'd seen plumes of white vapor coming from the plant the previous night, and had assumed they were some noxious chemical. It just so happened that that night had been clear, with a bright moon, and the steam plumes were very visible, very beautiful, I thought. Becky knew the plumes were water vapor, not toxic chemicals, and she took it on herself to call the radio folks and invite them to visit the plant. "They're coming next Monday," she told me, "and I want you to meet them and talk to them. Then I'm taking them around the plant." Now in the chemical industry in this country, talking to the public is very prickly. You'd normally get public affairs people and sometimes lawyers involved, be very secretive, and be told what to say. Not at Belle.

Becky, who was an active participant in the environmental teams, knew what the situation was, and she felt free to do something about it without asking me first; she had a good sense of the bowl. Monday came, and it was a great visit. The folks went all over the plant, and had a good time and learned a lot, and they got to know us and saw what we were trying to do. They spent the next two weeks on the radio talking about what a great place the Belle plant was and that we were neat people. Becky's initiative made that possible. Most people know what to do, if they have a good sense of the bowl.

Knowles's Scare Fair, and the Community Connection

When I came to Belle in 1987, the plant was very inward-looking, and managers had created a protective shell around themselves, cutting off the plant from interacting with the community. I knew that was wrong, because it exacerbates the suspicions the town's people have of this big facility right there, full of chemicals that can potentially harm or even kill them. A lot of the suspicion comes from ignorance, as I had learned from working at the Niagara

Falls plant, which is just four miles from Love Canal. Remember the Love Canal story? That was back in the late 1970s, when it was discovered that people in houses built on top of a chemical landfill were getting sick. A lot of environmental legislation governing toxic chemicals in this country was driven by that incident. And a lot of the public's suspicion about the industry was driven by it, too—rightly so. I learned the hard way at the Niagara Falls plant that the only way to break through that suspicion is to be open. I learned that to be viewed as a good neighbor, you must be seen as a responsible citizen, and I was determined to break through the protective shell at Belle, by inviting the community to come and see what we were doing, what we were struggling with.

At one point, we were having five hundred people a month visiting the plant, people from the community, school kids, environmental groups, customers, businesspeople. I wanted to show we had nothing to hide. I remember one night we had a Girl Scout group come and spend the night on an outing to the plant. I don't know what they were up to, but one of the leaders of the group worked at the plant, and arranged the whole thing.

It worked the other way, too, because I spent a lot of time in the community, as much as 40 percent of my time, just talking to people, setting up programs in schools, talking to the local fire chief, environmental groups, and so on. I drank a lot of beer with Norm Steenstra, the head of the environmental movement of West Virginia. The protective shell was gone, and the boundary around the plant was now much more like a permeable membrane, with information flowing across it, going both ways.

This connection with the community became very important in January 1992, when Pam Nixon and the Local Emergency Planning Committee began a campaign to have the chemical companies in the valley talk about worst-case scenarios, what would happen when major spills occurred. Pam was chairperson of the Citizens Concerned about Methyl Isocyanate (MIC)—that's the gas that killed three thousand people in Bhopal, India, in 1984. She had been one of 145 people hospitalized in 1985 by a leak of a different chemical in the nearby town of Institute. So she had reason to be concerned, because the deadly methyl isocyanate is made in the valley, principally by Rhône-Poulenc. We had similar material at Belle, though not in such large quantities. But she had been prompted to act because new legislation, the Clean Air Act, would require chemical companies to publish worst-case scenarios, but not until March of 1999.

There are a dozen chemical plants like Belle and Rhône-Poulenc in the

Kanawha Valley, which is known locally as Chemical Valley. The community of a quarter of a million people in the valley therefore had legitimate concerns, especially because the local geography means that leaked gases would tend to stay in the valley and disperse only slowly. I spent a lot of time talking to Pam, and I knew we had to respond, but it took us two and a half years. For the first six months managers from the different plants spent a lot of time crabbing about the whole thing, trying to figure out how they could avoid getting ensnared, because it seemed like a no-win situation to them. Finally I said, "Look, from my experience at the Niagara plant I know we've got to go out there and be proactive and try to frame this story honestly, but in a way that doesn't kill us." This approach is consistent with Responsible Care, a safety initiative of the Chemical Manufacturers Association, of which we were all members.

We set up two committees, a technical committee and a communications committee, with people from the community and the industry. We invited the president of the Sierra Club of West Virginia and other environmental leaders to join us, which made some industry people nervous. The other managers didn't like the idea, but I insisted that the committees would be chaired by people from the community, not by us, otherwise the committees would have no credibility. We had one huge clash in the valley with one of the managers, who said, "This thing is really entirely out of control. We're going to have to tighten this up." He was really scared and angry. I said, "No, we set this thing up and we're going to do it." Other people agreed with the guy, and said, "Well, we don't think you ought to do it that way." I said, "Fellas, I don't care what you do, I'm going to tell them about the worst-case scenario with the ammonia tank at Belle. You make your own decisions, but you're going to have to explain to the media why you didn't share your stuff." For me to break ranks with the rest of the managers was big stuff, but I felt this was the correct decision for our plant, for DuPont, and the community.

An incident the very next day sealed the argument. There was an explosion at one of the plants in the valley; three folks got hurt, and one of them died. There was no more resistance to going ahead in an open and honest way after that.

There were endless meetings over the next year and a half, some of them acrimonious, but most people stuck with it. There was a lot of media coverage during that time, a lot of it very critical and suspicious. At one point the *Charleston Gazette* wrote a piece that said we were going to be lying, even before we had a chance to say anything. We realized from these kinds of concerns and from all the talks we had with the town's people that it all centered on a single issue, which was clearly stated to me by Mildred Holt, co-chair of the Citizens Concerned about MIC: "We know that you folks can kill us—just tell me what you are doing to prevent that happening." We planned a two-day event, which we called "Safety Street: Managing Our Risks Together," which was to be held at the convention center in Charleston on Friday and Saturday, the 3rd and 4th of June 1994. On each day we would share the background and have booths to give people specific details on worst-case scenarios and the prevention programs. There was to be a formal presentation on the first day, followed by booth displays. The environmental groups were also going to be there, with their booth displays. Effectively we would be saying, "We have twenty-nine different ways of killing you, and here's what we are doing to try to prevent that from happening." It was a tricky but true tension.

About six weeks before the event, Mary Frances Beloidt, the communications committee chair, said, "You know, people are not going to come and hear your dull plant managers at the convention center on a nice Saturday in June. If you want people to hear, you've got to go to the shopping mall." I realized it was a great idea, and my job was to persuade the other plant managers to go along. They resisted strenuously, saying that it was a stupid idea, that you lose control. When some of the Chemical Manufacturers Association members heard of it, they got real uptight and people were calling it Knowles' Scare Fair. When the other plant managers talked to their wives, they saw it was the right thing to do. These women know how things work. During the entire process of developing these communications, the Chemical Manufacturers Association and my own management were very supportive of what we were trying to do. They realized that this is what Responsible Care is all about.

The Friday came around, and it went off really well. The *New York Times* described the citizens' assessment of the event as "enlightening, if chilling."[4] Near the end of the formal presentation I was to show the first scenario, which was about our forty-million-pound ammonia tank, and what a worst-case scenario would look like. I was very nervous, being the first one. There I am sitting in the front of the auditorium of seven hundred people, waiting to tell them these chilling facts, and feeling a little antsy and vulnerable about it. I looked up, and I saw all these school kids coming up to sit with me. They were the kids from the local school we'd been developing programs with. So, I'm sitting there with all these kids around me, feeling the support of innocents in the midst of these grueling facts, feeling their trust, knowing that it said something about the community feeling we had been building the past two years. It was hard not to cry. I still get emotional about it when I think about that.

Five thousand people came to the mall the next day, and it was amazing. Lots of kids running around, people asking questions, we really got through some barriers, built some trust. I'm not saying that it was all plain sailing after that. I'm saying that if you are open and honest, authentic in what you are trying to do, you can build trust. But the trust we built was fragile, and needed constant nurturing. We still had a long way to go, but it was a vital journey to take because the Belle plant—any business for that matter—is not isolated in the world. We are part of an economic web of suppliers, customers, and competitors, of course. But the community is part of the web, too, and you can never forget that.

I left Belle seven months after the two-day event, after a stint of eight years, which is almost three times as long as is typical for a plant manager. Senior executives loved the bottom-line numbers we were producing, but they were puzzled by the, for them, alien way of management I had developed. I said, "Look, the results are really good, aren't they?" They'd say, "Yeah, but you're not on the plant enough. You've got to be on the plant more." I knew that spending almost half my time in the community was important, as the Charleston event showed. I'd say, "The plant's running really good, isn't it?" And they'd say, "Yeah, but you're getting too much press outside. We don't want to be this visible." There were a lot of "yeah, buts." I knew it was time to go.

Complexity: Both/And

After eight years at Belle I was a different person as well as a different manager, and I can only say that I find it much more fulfilling to be in there with the folks, struggling with them, not just telling them what to do. They taught me a lot of good stuff. I had been struggling with trying to make sense of what I heard in church about values and humanity and with what happened at work. I wasn't happy with myself as I'd got more and more disconnected from people as people. I'd always been trying to make the world a better place, and I found that this new way of working is a way you can do that. I had stumbled onto a key principle of complexity science long before I even knew there was such a science, that if you pay attention to relationships in a genuine, authentic way, your organization will be much more able to adapt and change. And people will feel better about themselves and what they are doing. We *can* make our workplaces more humane; people *can* become fulfilled; people *can* become whole people at work. And we *can* get good business results, too. It's not either/or, it's both/and. I think that's pretty important.

So, it was a compelling journey for me. It's spiritual work, it's very lonely work, and it's very hard work. Some nights I would go to bed and just pray, and say, "I don't know if I can get out of bed in the morning and carry on." If I hadn't had Claire's love and the support of the people there, I couldn't have done it. We are all much more alike than we are different. We all have our hopes and fears; we're all quite fragile, and we need each other. People are much more intelligent than you think, and can achieve more than you might think. There are egos as big as mountains that constantly get in the way, and I constantly struggled with mine. We are all carrying an enormous amount of pain, and we need to care for each other, love each other, and be open to each other's pain and caring.

This way of operating has to be so open and the authenticity has to be so deep. You cannot play games, or you'll go right back to the old hierarchy stuff. I'm not content to sit back and say, "All this complexity stuff is really sexy and neat, and feels like living trees, is mystical, but we don't know how it works." That's okay, for a start, but there's much more to it than that, and I think we *do* know how to do it. I don't think you can sell this stuff intellectually. I mean, it's not a spectator sport; you have to step into it. I'll give you an example that might sound simplistic, but I think it's fundamental to honoring the complexity way of management.

A few years before I left we were having problems with the welding crew. I won't go into all the details, but there was one guy on the crew, a crusty old guy, always making trouble and being difficult. So I went to him one day and said, "Will you teach me how to weld, please?" He grunted something that I took to be agreement. I put on coveralls, and went out and sat with him in his welding booth, and learned that welding is a really refined skill. I put on a mask, and couldn't see a damn thing. Anyway he showed me what to do, and I produced something that looked like a porcupine! It was a real mess, but he was gracious enough not to laugh at me. The guy never got to be super-friendly, but we never fought after that. We had reached some kind of understanding; we had welded a connection that was real.

Chapter 10

Babel's Paint and Decorating Stores: The Tower of Babel

> " 'Come, let us build ourselves a city, and a tower with its top in the heavens, and let us make a name for ourselves, lest we be scattered abroad upon the face of the whole earth.' . . . And the Lord said, 'Behold, they are one people, and have all one language; and this is only the beginning of what they will do; and nothing that they propose to do will now be impossible for them. Come, let us go down, and there confuse their language, that they may not understand one another's speech.' So the Lord scattered them abroad from there over the face of all the earth, and they left off building the city."
>
> (Genesis 11:4–9)

"Babel" is composed of two words, "bab" meaning gate and "el" meaning God. Hence the gate of God. A related word in Hebrew, "balal," means confusion.

Babel's Paint and Decorating Stores is a $4.5 million revenue business generated from four stores south of Boston, Massachusetts, and employs thirty-five people. To hear the owners, Vic and Jeanne Babel, talk about their business is to hear, as if genetically encoded by their namesake, the modern version of building the Tower of Babel. Like the people of Babylon who wanted to build a city, the Babels strive to build a sense of community within their town, and in their stores—where employees are more like one big family and where customers can feel at home. And, like the Babylonians, they seek to "make a name" for themselves—to be recognized as the best in their business and leaders in their industry and in their community.

Rather than just selling product, the Babels see a higher purpose to their work as paint retailers. Their "gate of God" is, as Jeanne told us, "to add beauty to people's lives" by offering an extensive range of color for people's homes and by providing an interior decorating service in their stores. As they say, they don't sell paint, they sell color. "Paint is sold $15.99 a gallon. Here you are, ma'am, see you later," said Vic. "Color is a lifestyle feeling. It's working out customers' situations, and offering them good advice. It's being part of their lives." Their sense of aesthetics is easily coupled with their commitment to their community of Norwood, Massachusetts. Donating paint to good causes is one of many ways they contribute toward creating an attractive local environment, and how they and their store play a central role in community life.

Like the Babylonians, the Babels also feel outside forces pushing against them as they try to build their tower of recognition, aesthetics, and community. There are, of course, the normal pressures that small businesses face that are relentlessly demanding and taxing. For instance, the store is closed only four days a year and is open seventy-six hours a week, which means that Vic and Jeanne sometimes work all those seventy-six hours, and then some, when the stores are closed, for attending to noncustomer issues.

The Babels also feel the forces of the rapidly changing world of retail, where "Big Boxes," such as Home Depot and Home Quarters, mega hardware and decorating stores, are changing the business environment, chipping away at the market and pushing small independent paint and hardware stores out of business. Two of these Big Boxes—120,000-square-foot, architecturally identical boxes—are within a three-mile radius of their Norwood store, and finding themselves "scattered" like the Babylonians is a present and lurking threat for the Babels.

The Babels also face an economic climate where the unemployment rate in the state of Massachusetts is at an all-time low, making it even more difficult to find reliable and committed retail people. As a work population, people working in retail tend to drift and go to the highest bidder, and are becoming less willing to work the ten hours a day that is often required.

In their ongoing struggle to build a tower in a labile business environment, the Babels also find themselves dealing with the fallout of the first Tower of Babel, that is, the confusion of language. As Vic put it, "You have to speak a thousand tongues. You have to be able to speak to the local townspeople as well as upscale newcomers; to contractors as well as to 'the woman with the quart' who wants color direction and guidance; to employees, who leave exactly at five when twenty people are waiting to be served; and to those who aspire to be interior decorators; to suppliers (wallpaper, fabrics, paint dealers); to bankers; to the Chamber of Commerce; to accountants; to other paint stores; to the community—fund-raisers, functions, the arts. You have to know all the different languages in order to be successful."

In the midst of this chaotic and confused environment, they have an unusual objective that's uncanny in its appropriateness to the Babel name. Vic and Jeanne venture to do what was undone—to find a common language that can join this entangled polyphonic economic web, and in so doing, perhaps recover a buried possibility. The common language they seek is a shared vision and a shared meaning of business itself, in all its complex and spiraling dimensions. Perhaps with one language, as the Babylonians originally had, the Babels would be able to open the gate where "nothing that they propose to do will now be impossible for them."

The Growth of a Small Business

With fourteen million people self-employed in the United States, at a time when entrepreneurship is driving the economy, and what *Fast Company* magazine in January 1998 called America as the Free Agent Nation, the Babel story illustrates the quintessential American dream—how a small entrepreneurial effort, a mom-and-pop paint store, can successfully grow and evolve with the times.

Victor Sr. and Mickey Babel, Vic's parents, opened their family-run operation, Babel's Paint and Wallpaper Store, in 1950 in Norwood, a small mill town that would eventually develop into a sprawling suburb. Their tiny store of four hundred square feet had three phones, every inch of space was buried in merchandise, and paperwork was piled high everywhere. With only one little aisle available, customers' agility was tested as they bushwhacked their way through the pandemonium. The store's appearance bordered on the comical. Paint cans spilled out onto the sidewalk; the Babels' station wagon, parked in front of the store, held all the wall coverings. Customers would pick out their selections from the back of the car, which was known as "the Babel bus."

Vic's involvement with the store was not what you would call a marriage made in heaven. "I hated the paint store when I was growing up," he told us. "I couldn't hang out downtown with my friends because, not only did my father not want me to, but also you had to walk past the store to get there, which really made it impossible. Everyone knew me because of the store, so anything I did got back to my family real quick. And, starting at six years old, I had to work in the store with my brother, Frank, during the summers."

But business apparently ran in the family blood, and Vic went on to get his business administration degree from Northeastern University in Boston. After graduating in 1970, he interviewed with large companies but, in the end, felt disillusioned. "The people I saw in positions of power were making good money, but they looked to me like they were brain dead," Vic told us. "And I thought, 'I'm going to be like that guy in thirty years.' My father suggested that I work in the store between interviews. I hated it at first, and I really hated it when my father would tell people that I was going to join him. I just wanted to scream, 'Get me out of here!'

"But I started looking at the customers. My parents had a great base of customers, a good core of nice people. That's all you need. There were relationships here. I started to like the towny life—knowing people in the town, being in the Knights of Columbus, local golf tournaments, joining the Chamber of Commerce, that kind of thing."

Unlike his brother, Frank, who went on to successfully climb the corporate ladder at General Motors, Vic decided to give the family business a go. What spurred him on, besides liking his customers, was his competition, Owen's Paint Store (a pseudonym), which at that time, was the biggest paint store in New England. "He was wicked," Vic said, referring to the owner. "If he found out we had a good product, he'd make suppliers stop supplying us with it. You could have that kind of clout in those days. He contributed little to the community. He treated customers badly, too. For example, if we had a Min-wax stain and he didn't, and a customer asked him if anyone had it, he'd say no. Customers would come into our store, just to check with us. When they would find that we had what they needed, they'd leave saying they'd never go back to Owen's. What he was doing was wrong, and I wanted to do it right. I knew what he had at his store and I sent customers to him when we didn't have what they needed, because that's part of customer service—satisfying the customer's needs, and making it easy for them. Even though Owen's had this beautiful showroom, we had a core of customers who were willing to shop in our store, despite the crammed four hundred square feet. Their loyalty hooked me. I wanted to be there for them, too. I wanted to be the best paint store ever."

In the mid-1970s, the store space next door to the Babels opened up, and they expanded to nine hundred square feet. In 1979, the property was sold, which ultimately catalyzed the transformation of the Babel store. "The new owners of the property were rich people," recalled Vic, "just doing business. I loved the people on the block, and I wanted to see what these new owners' attitude was. I arranged a meeting with them, and told my brother, Frank, he had to come with me to this one. We'd been paying very low rent, and the new owners were going to double it, which still wasn't high, but that wasn't the issue. The issue for me was 'who are they as people?' They pulled up in a Mercedes, and we sat down to talk. I said, 'Okay, this is what I want. I want the Christian Science Reading Room out; I want the pizza place out. If you do that, I'll occupy the three corner stores.' They said, 'No problem.' I walked out of that meeting and said to Frank, 'I'm getting out of here. They'll do the same to me for the highest bidder.' That got us off the pot."

Expanding a business in the midst of a recession is not what most retailers would consider a wise strategy. But Vic was willing to take the risk. In part, it was the Babels' strong community presence that made the transition possible. Vic knew an old-time realtor who found him a good deal—an old windowless warehouse in the center of town that had once been a catering business. Although it was overrun with cockroaches, it was ten thousand square feet, which could become four thousand square feet of retail space.

Since the Babels had a vital presence in the community, the bank took a chance with them, even though, if they looked only at the numbers on paper, they probably shouldn't have. Putting up as equity a three-apartment-house building he owned with Jeanne, Vic was on his way to growing the business. He hired an architect, Dennis Carlone, to design the interior of the building and to paint a false facade on the exterior. The false facade completely transformed the stark cinder-block structure. With false painted windows, window boxes, and even a cat sitting on a window ledge, what had once been an eyesore in the community became a visual attraction. Inside, the store was colorful, cheerful and playful, with visual novelties like a large plane suspended from the ceiling. Playful and novel interior design reflected the spirit of the Babels' business, and would become a trademark for all their stores. At the same time that he expanded the store, Vic upgraded the quality of his products. He changed paint suppliers and took on the high-quality paint of Benjamin Moore; he expanded their wallpaper selection, bringing in high-end coverings, such as Schumacher.

The new store opened in 1980 and was an instant, huge success. Not only was it a very attractive and resourceful place to shop, finally there was space and organization. Changing paint lines proved to be a wise strategy, too. The Benjamin Moore paint brought in a wave of business, and long lines began to form at the store. Vic had tapped into an unmet customer need for quality products at reasonable prices. "The first week we opened the new store I said, 'I've created a monster!' " said Vic, recalling the crowds of people that filled the store. But Vic didn't become complacent with his success. "I kept thinking of ways to improve what we were doing. You try to put yourself in the customers' heads, and try to imagine what they want. I used to go to paint stores in every town we visited to get ideas, which drove Jeanne crazy."

At the time of the store's opening, Vic's father had several debilitating strokes, which left him wheelchair-bound and unable to speak. The store had become completely Vic's venture, although his mother and sister, Kathy, were part of the team, and still are, helping out when necessary. Shortly before his father died, Vic wheeled him into the new store. "He was grinning from ear to ear. Then he began to cry," Vic told us with quiet emotion, still deeply moved by the moment. "He was so proud of what we had accomplished. He was so happy that I was carrying it on. At that point, all the risk and effort was worth it."

Initially it was Vic, Vic's mother, and Patty Fantegrossi, Jeanne's sister, who were running the store. It was still all in the family. As the clientele grew, they hired people for the first time. But with an expanding employee base, Vic, whose genius lies in dealing with customers and suppliers, found employee management overwhelming. This was 1989.

But synchronicity was in the making, and a convergence of events for Vic's wife, Jeanne, would lead her to join the family enterprise, and to take on, among many things, employee management. Prime Computer, where Jeanne was working as their international controller, was merging with Computer Vision to form a billion-dollar company. She was already feeling the strain from traveling around the world when Prime Computer asked her if she would relocate—they were thinking of moving their international headquarters to Munich, Germany. At the same time, and to Vic and Jeanne's great delight, Jeanne discovered she was pregnant. When Prime offered her a year's severance package, she knew the time was right to leave. She took the package, and started to spend little bits of time at the store that soon evolved to a full-time involvement.

This is how Jeanne, given her background in big business, described her initial involvement with the store: "I thought small business was simple—buy a little paint, sell a little paint, take a little inventory. How difficult could it be? Where's the challenge? And I like business challenges. I thought it would be easy. I thought I'd be bored. I soon found out it was totally different from corporate life, because in small businesses there are so many elements that you have to do yourself, which demands many different kinds of skills.

"When I first started getting involved with the store, I would say things like, 'Who do I call for a cleaning crew for the bathrooms?' And Vic would say, 'The bookkeeper does that.' If the computer broke down and I would call to get it fixed, I'd say, 'You mean, we have to pay for it out of our own money?' Also, having meetings in a small business is near impossible. It's like pulling teeth trying to get people together, because you have to meet on off hours. I'd try to get together with four people from the paint department, and then nobody would show up except me. That's a big difference from corporate life—we always had time to meet and discuss things. In retail, there's always just too much to do, with no time or money to do it, whereas in corporate life there are a lot more resources and a lot more cushion. It was quite an awakening for me. Our house is on the line for this business. You're out there with the business on a very personal level. But it also becomes more yours than any corporation could."

Jeanne's involvement led to transforming the wallpaper department into a decorating department. Several factors were involved. Being "a numbers person," as she describes herself, the ratios in that department kept telling her they had to get more sales—either beef it up or do something different. Wallpaper suppliers were beginning to send samples of matching fabrics with their coverings, and customers began asking for more fabrics. In 1990, driven by customer needs, the Babels hired Jean Goff, a designer, to head the department, which became, by 1994, a full-service, full-scale decorating center.

Although the presence of Home Quarters in their community was worrisome, Jeanne saw an opportunity to differentiate themselves. Big Boxes were geared toward volume, sameness, and self-service. The Babels decided they would compete at a level that Big Boxes couldn't, by offering a personalized decorating service and personal customer relationships. "Since we were smaller," explained Jeanne, "we could be innovative in our merchandising, we could offer the best, and find what's new and different. You could see from the customers that they thought our place was refreshing; they liked that the shopping environment was unique, and they liked the personal service. You can go in any Gap store in the world, for instance, and it's the same. What makes us different is that we have relationships with the customers, that our merchandising is new and different, and that our ideas come from our people who know what customers want." That year, 1994, Vic and Jeanne changed the store's name to Babel's Paint and Decorating Store.

Their responsiveness to customers led the Babels to create seminars that addressed their needs and interests: from how to hang wallpaper, to faux finishing, to stenciling. Although the new venture required lots of preparation and time, the Babels found that by offering these seminars, more product was being sold, more people were exposed to their store, their mailing list grew, and they were able to get more feedback as to what customers wanted. Today the decorating center is the fastest growing portion of their business, which has averaged 20 percent increases per year. The centers do commercial as well as residential decorating, and have five decorators, who average 75 percent of their time on the road, going to people's homes or businesses to give free decorating advice.

In 1990, the Babels' store was named the Business of the Year by the Neponset Chamber of Commerce, which encompasses fourteen towns in Massachusetts. In 1991, the Chamber named Vic Businessman of the Year.

With the success of the Norwood store, Vic and Jeanne started to feel confident that they could replicate their success elsewhere. They had a competent core of staff people and a computer system that had the capacity to run twenty stores. As Jeanne says, "From a business standpoint, you grow or die." Also, Vic, who was on the dealer council for Pratt and Lambert Paint and Benjamin Moore, began to get a sense that being a very successful one-store operation was no longer enough. He was right. His suppliers felt they couldn't deal with one store effectively anymore; they wanted regional operations. The time to expand again had arrived.

The term "growth spurt" is almost an understatement with the Babel enterprise. In 1996 they opened a store in the nearby town of Needham. In 1997, they learned that Paine Furniture Stores, which had been in business for 160 years, was looking for someone to do customized bedspreads for the beds they sold. The Babels brainstormed with the store's owners, and a joint venture resulted. They opened a four-thousand-square-foot, upscale display for custom window treatments, custom bedding, and the like in Natick, within one of Paine's four stores.

Momentum was building for the Babels. Where once they had to create opportunities, opportunities for growth were coming fast and furiously. And they went with it. As Jeanne says, "It's economies of scale. The more volume I can get, my fixed costs become a smaller percentage of the overall cost. People are a big part of the cost, but it is more profitable with bigger volume, and we can negotiate better deals with bigger volume." In 1998 the Babels opened their third store in Foxboro, and within a breath of that opening, Vic and Jeanne were looking to buy a warehouse for a separate paint sales operation to contractors. A business that had sustained itself as a four-hundred-square-foot store for thirty years suddenly burgeoned in size in two short years. Babel's Paint and Decorating Stores had grown to 22,000 square feet of retail.

As the Babels' business grew, they built a tower. They have made a name for themselves as the best in what they do. In 1997, they were named as one of the top ten retailers in the United States by Paint and Decorating Retailers. They are leaders in the industry, with Vic, who has attended every paint and decorating show for thirty years, being invited, out of 4,800 dealers, to join Benjamin Moore in helping them develop a new color system for the year 2000.

But the Babels have also entered a new world of increasing complexity. Where once they had one store running like a clock by family members, now they have four locations, and depend on other people to create the Babel spirit and uphold their standards. Where once they had intimate parties with staff, now they need to hire two buses for transporting people to their parties, and they wonder how to maintain a family feeling. Their economic web has become increasingly complex—interconnected and interdependent—with competitors, collaborators, suppliers, customers, employees, banks, the community, all vital dimensions of their world. This growing web of relationships demands a new vision that will provide a line of continuity in the midst of diversity, unpredictability, and a fluctuating economy. For the Babels, nothing less than creating a unified language for what it means to be a business will do.

Seeking a Common Language

From the business's nascent beginnings, a focus on people and relationships has been central to the Babels' philosophy for business success. Customer service has always been a primary issue for them. But paying attention to relationships with customers in one small, completely family-run store is not the same challenge as paying attention to the helix of relationships within the rapidly changing environment where the Babels now find themselves. Pressures of paperwork, paying bills, being strapped for money while trying to grow at the same time, daily maintenance of stocking shelves and upkeep of surroundings, all clamor to detract the Babels from what they see as essential. Seeing their world of retail left us with a profound regard for just how hard retail work is—the long hours, the constant demands, the economic precariousness; and we felt in awe that, although enmeshed in the day-to-day struggles, the Babels were focusing on a larger vision, and working toward a common language in their business world—the language of relationship.

What follows is the helix of their relational world and their efforts and challenges in bringing a shared value and meaning of good working relationships within their complex adaptive system. Vic and Jeanne are familiar with complexity principles, and you will see how these principles have helped them look at their world through different eyes, which has helped them be more adaptable. The relationships they spoke of were relationship to the customer, to employees, to suppliers, to other businesses, to the community, and to their economic web. In all these relationships, the Babels try to instill the value of relationship itself as the grounds for a common language.

Relationship to the Customer

Both Vic and Jeanne are unequivocal about the importance of developing good personal relationships with customers for business success. Unlike those who might simply espouse a similar sentiment, Vic's values are most apparent in his actions. As Vic put it to us: "I was talking to one of our new employees last week, telling them that I'd just spent a half-hour with a customer. The challenge is getting the employee to see that time spent talking with customers is valuable, because retail employees often come from authoritarian environments where they would be disciplined for spending time with customers. Of course, time with customers needs to be balanced, otherwise, you get into what I call 'being married to the customer.'

"I was telling this new employee that the half-hour I spent with the customer would never show up on the register. It wouldn't show up as a sale, because the customer had already bought what she needed. But after we talked she was happy, and that's important to me. She came in the next Saturday and told me she wasn't buying anything right then, but she just wanted to say that she had the greatest experience that time in the store. I know she'll tell three people who will tell more people, and that's how you build a business.

"When people come in, I know nothing about them, but in ten minutes I know a lot about their life and their personality. I feel that's my job, because then I can serve them better. After I've talked to people, they often say, 'Gee, I want you to tell the owner what a nice store he's got here.' I never tell them that I'm the owner; they haven't got a clue."

Jeanne is of a similar mind. "Customer service is about building relationships—to know as much as you can about their needs, take a genuine interest in the customer in terms of who they are and about their life. When our employees take a real interest in the customer, that's when our success is best.

Customers keep coming back when they feel that they are a person here, not just a consumer getting something off the shelf."

The challenge the Babels face is having all their employees share and value the customer relationship. For instance, during their growth spurt, when Vic and Jeanne's focus was on starting a new store, the atmosphere of the Norwood store began to change for the worse. The store was very busy, and the employees couldn't seem to handle the volume. As a result, customer relationships were neglected. One customer, whose grandfather had bought paint from Vic's father, called Jeanne and asked her what was going on. Where was that Babel family feeling? This kind of feedback, amplified by the generational dimension, "ruins my day," said Vic.

In particular, some of the men in the paint department posed the greatest difficulty. Technical skills for paint are easy to train, the Babels told us, but getting beyond that, getting the men to see that valuing the relationship to the customer is also important, is proving very hard to teach. They observed that often the people skills, which are so vital to retail, are lacking in male employees. Although the men are able to work with the contractor who wants to get in and out quickly, they have a problem when confronted with what Vic calls "Ralph Lauren women," who want paint guidance. The men don't have a clue as to how to help them or even think much about it. As Vic recounts, "There's this paint guy who doesn't have any use for yuppies. He's a towny and, at the end of the day, he wants to go to a bar or go fishing. The town is changing and it must be hard for him to see these yuppies come in with lots of money, and be more demanding. But he'd better have use for these yuppies, I told him, because that's a lot of who we serve in this store.

"It's hard to impress on them the importance of paying attention to the customer, and that can be a real problem, because how we treat people affects the atmosphere of the store. Although it's only about 30 percent of our people who aren't on board, it's enough to potentially have a poisoning effect. For example, we have this one guy, and no one likes him, because basically he's oblivious to relationships. He just doesn't get it in terms of customer service. He'll go off and get a cup of coffee when everyone else is frantic. You explain the thing about the coffee, and he says, 'What's wrong with getting coffee?' It's not the coffee, it's the whole thing. I tried to explain that each of us has an impact on the environment, and that kind of behavior can poison the feeling for everyone. But he just doesn't get it. He asked if I was going to fire him, and I said no. You can't exactly fire someone for not getting it." The "it" that Vic is referring to is about not only caring about customers, but also fellow employees.

Women, however, are better at "getting it," says Jeanne. "The women in the decorating department have great people skills and they are attentive. If they see a piece of paper on the floor, they'll stop and pick it up, whereas often the paint guys will step over it, not even see it or think it's important to pick it up. That says something about the level of care," Jeanne said.

Complexity principle: *Every small interaction has the potential for impacting the whole, for better and for worse.*

Relationship to Employees

Jeanne has taken over the task of developing employees and employee relationships because, as Vic admitted to us, "I'm not a good leader with employees, though they respect me. As Jeanne would say, I'm the most expensive stock boy in the world. I know I shouldn't be stocking, but I've been brought up in a small store to do that, and I still have a lot of the same feeling. It's automatic. If the shelves are empty, I stock them. The customers aren't being treated properly if the shelves are empty."

"The point is," Jeanne said to Vic, "that with four stores, you can't be in the basement, at the counter, planning, and everything else that needs to be done. We have to get things done through our people. You can't do it all yourself. You'll pick up a broom if the floor's dirty, and then come home fuming and exhausted because no one else is doing it. It's a vicious circle." To which Vic conceded, "It's true, it's done for the day, but the next day, it's the same problem." Linear may be faster at getting things done immediately, but not for the long run.

In an industry that can generate a 200 percent turnover in employees, the Babels still manage to keep their turnover low, at 10 percent, with most of their employees being long-term. This can be attributed largely to Jeanne's capabilities as a leader and her nonlinear management style: "The leader's job is to have strong values and to share those values with people and have them understand what they are. It's allowing the employees to translate those values into action for themselves. I don't have to tell them what those actions are."

What Jeanne values is a personal and a collective involvement from people, which, she believes, leads to satisfying work. "I think there's the potential in everybody to want to get excited about what they do, especially if they are spending forty-five to fifty hours a week doing it. I keep telling people that work here could be fun if they get involved, if they would come to work mentally every day, and not just come in with their body. It's not a performance issue; it's an involvement issue. The way I try to get people involved is I'll ask an employee what they would like to do, tell them that we have opportunities here, and that they have the power to change things around if they see something could work better. The women in decorating are always thinking of new things to do."

The way Jeanne imparts this value of self-efficacy is by setting up a few simple principles from which complex behaviors can emerge, which are: show up (not just your body), serve the customer, and maintain (stock the shelves, keep the store clean). "Of course, there are also those who say to me that they just want to come to work and then go home at the end of the day, and be told what to do in between," Jeanne told us. "In other words, 'Don't bother me with this stuff about work as fun.' That drives me crazy.

"I spend a lot of time talking to these people, trying to get them on board. I used to think that spending time talking with people wasn't work, that looking at numbers was work. Now I see it as fundamental if you want to create an innovative work environment and the sense of family that means so much to us. My dilemma is how much time I should spend helping those who don't get it. I probably spend too much time. If we had more money, we could hire more innovative people. Instead I'm faced with making it happen with the people we can afford. But for the most part it's happening. A woman who has worked for us for a while gave in her resignation the other day because of personal matters. And she was crying because she didn't want to leave, because she feels part of a family here. That's a measure of success for me."

Because of their company's continual growth, Vic and Jeanne are constantly interviewing and looking for the right people to hire. In the hiring process, the Babels are very clear about their work environment—that they are looking for people who have ideas, who can initiate change, who are not just followers, but also innovators, an unusual tally for a paint store job. And in addition, they now look more closely at interviewees' social skills. "We were interviewing this guy," Vic told us, "and I asked him how he handled one-on-one with people. He said he was famous for the 'walk and talk.' I said it was a busy store. He said, he gets people to go off with him for a few minutes, with a cup of coffee, and tells them what they're doing right or wrong. Nothing formal, no big deal and he does it constantly whenever there's a free moment. I like that."

In addition to trying to ignite a sense of personal involvement and passion for work in their employees, Jeanne also seeks a collective involvement, where people work together to generate innovative ideas that are the lifeblood of their survival and the blade that carves them a cutting edge. Jeanne works at breaking down the hierarchical barriers that stifle innovation by focusing on teams, and by cultivating a culture that encourages ideas.

"We want people to work together," Jeanne explained, "to foster dialogue, ideas, and change. Even our driver, who we hired to deliver items from store to store so that we can have an item within hours for our customers, we need his ideas on how things can work better for our success. We need people who want to be a part of it." But getting this philosophy across, which is not based on a boss/subordinate model, can initially meet with resistance. What Jeanne has confronted in introducing this approach is a mental obstacle where employees see the Babels as the owners, and therefore the boss, and thus the decision makers. Consequently, when Jeanne initially held meetings for generating ideas with the paint department, the response was "just tell us what you want us to do" as they looked at their watches. "I want them to stop thinking in terms of 'your' company, and instead to think of it as 'our' company."

Over the last ten years the Babels have been changing that mentality by creating a very open environment that invites ideas. Often in such businesses, a manager makes the decisions and directs what is to be done. The Babels found that when employees felt they weren't part of the decision making, they were less involved and cared less. Now the Babels create projects and open it up to their staff. "I started a customer service task force and put a memo out asking for volunteers. This way people who want to get involved, can," Jeanne said. "I tell our people this is not just our business, Vic's and mine, it's all of ours. I sincerely mean that. Now we've been meeting with the accountant to try to think of how to divide up the business, so we can give it out to our employees and people can feel a sense of ownership."

Complexity principle: *Build a critical mass by mass involvement.*

Relationship to Suppliers

The Babels develop relationships and partnerships with their suppliers that recognize their interdependence and that work toward mutually beneficial ends. This approach is particularly visible in how the Babels came to have their second store. They looked around for store space, but it was from a collaborative effort with Benjamin Moore, one of their paint suppliers, that the new store became a reality. The problem the Babels faced for expanding in their area was that Benjamin Moore protected the exclusivity of its product, and all the surrounding towns around Norwood were locked up. And the Babels wanted to continue to provide their line of paint. They learned from Benjamin Moore that a lumber company that sold their paint in Needham was steadily dropping in sales. That provided an opportunity. Vic and Jeanne showed Benjamin Moore their projections of how much paint they would sell compared to how much the current Needham dealer was selling, and they struck a deal. Benjamin Moore agreed no longer to guarantee a protected ten-mile radius. The Babels opened their second store in Needham within three miles of the lumber store.

Although interdependence links the Babels with Benjamin Moore, it is not a bond that binds. Complexity points to the power of diversity, and Vic values diversity of product in his store, as can be seen in the following incident with Benjamin Moore: "The dealer's council of Benjamin Moore, which I'm part of, meets twice a year. There are a core of stores that sell only Benjamin Moore paint, and these stores were asking for special privileges because they were loyal. I stood up and said I felt that I couldn't be a true leader in the industry selling just Benjamin Moore paint. My only reason for being in business is to be the best in my profession. My store is one of the best in the country and I can't do it with just their paint—we need diversity. And I said to the president of Benjamin Moore that I wasn't going to be loyal to Benjamin Moore just to be loyal to Benjamin Moore. That took care of the special privileges discussion."

Complexity principle: *Foster interdependence and diversity.*

Relationship to Other Businesses

The Babels are continually alert to developing relationships with competitors and complementors alike. Recently they joined together with competing paint stores for printing up advertising materials, which cut down the overall expense. Everyone benefitted.

Their Natick store, which is not a store per se, is an example of the Babels' venture coevolving with a complementor business. As we said earlier, the Babels set up an upscale display in a four-thousand-square-foot area in the Paine Furniture showroom for custom window treatment, custom bedding, high-end decorator fabrics, and the like. The intent was to sell these customized services within the showroom. As Jeanne put it, "We had it all laid out in our minds." The Babels spent $50,000 on setting up and construction, staffed the display, and put a sign outside saying Babel's Design Studio. It was their busiest time of year, November, and the new location was opened with much anticipation. And then nothing happened. In Norwood, the store was averaging two hundred paying customers a day; at Paine, it was three. The Babels discovered that Paine didn't have a high volume of customers: there's not a great rush of people looking for $10,000 beds.

Vic and Jeanne had to step back and reassess the situation. They started putting in lower-end, lower-cost materials to match more closely the customers of the store. But what turned the situation around was developing a relationship with the Paine staff. Initially, Vic and Jeanne decided they would stay separate from Paine employees, mostly because they didn't want to be part of the Paine culture, which, being based on leased employees on commissions, was very different from the Babel culture. But the Paine employees started talking to the Babel people. Pretty soon it was apparent that many of the Paine people had customers with whom they had worked for years and who had decorating needs. The Paine employees wanted the Babels to go out to their customers' homes to help them with their design needs. A partnership began between the Paine people and the Babels.

"Initially we said we wouldn't go out to people's homes," Jeanne told us, "and then we found out that's what people wanted. One woman wanted us to go out to Martha's Vineyard, and that one job turned out to be a $30,000 venture. Now we pay a commission to Paine employees when they bring us customers. The way we thought it was going to work just didn't work. I guess we were used to having our own control. It has turned out totally different from what we had expected. We had it priced wrong; people who have money still want a bargain. And now we're working with Paine people. The lesson here is realizing when you've made a mistake, and then acting quickly and being willing to let things be different than you expected. What comes into play for me here is that if you have an idea or a goal, and you have it so distinctly defined, and it doesn't turn out that way, you could quickly say that it's a failure. What I learned from complexity science is that you have to look at something, give it a chance to blossom or wilt. And see what is really happening. Our business here at Paine is not in isolation, as we thought. We are part of a system, and you have to be aware of what is happening in all parts of that system if you want to understand what the effects are on us."

Complexity principle: *Allow things to unfold, realize where and what the connections are, and expect the unexpected.*

Relationship to the Community

The community is not a separate reality but an integral part of the Babel business—the Babels have a strong sense of responsibility toward the communities where they do their business. For instance, Vic was at a meeting held at the YMCA, and he noticed that the walls were a shabby gray, littered with decals. He sought out the head of the YMCA and said, "We're going to do this place over for you. You supply the labor and we'll supply the paint." What, we asked, compels him to make such offers? "It makes me feel good. It makes them feel good. It's part of making a beautiful environment. We want our kids to be proud of who we are in our community. We'll probably get business out of it, it's good advertising, but that's not why we do it—it's about contributing to the whole. We focus a lot on helping the arts in the community as well. Unfortunately, when people know you contribute paint, paint hats, gift certificates, and such, you get lots of people asking. We got four calls today, and it's hard to say no sometimes. But if you don't, it can put you out of business."

The centrality of their presence in the community was most vivid to us when we stood at the checkout counter, watching Vic pick up the phone and hear him tell the person at the other end that the outdoor concert on the Common was starting at seven. People call the store, not just with paint and color questions, but with community questions.

Complexity principle: *The parts affect the whole and the whole affects the parts, creating a feedback loop.*

Relationship to the Economic Web

In Babylon, people were scattered and disconnected, which affected their ability to create, produce, and thrive. The Babels' economic web is also scattered, but it is also interconnected. "Business," says Jeanne, "is bigger than your own organization. Our business is the web of suppliers, customers, employees, the community, and other businesses we collaborate with. I feel we are an ecosystem full of different relationships—the relationships with other paint stores, where we have alliances; the relationships and partnerships with suppliers, where we are able to meet with them and say we have this idea and help us with this part of it; with the bankers, who come into the store and leave saying 'wow.' Employees are part of it, the industry is part of it, and even the Big Boxes are part of our ecosystem, because we need to know and be informed about what's happening in the rest of retail.

"The thing about the ecosystem is you have all these relationships entwined and working together, depending on each other. If the bank calls in our loan, that affects me, but it will also affect others in the ecosystem. Everything needs to be in harmony to make it work. Sometimes it feels like a house of cards—one little thing goes out of kilter and the whole thing can come tumbling down. That's where the fun is; that's where the stress is; that's where the paradox is. Sometimes I thrive; sometimes I feel like throwing up when I see one of those cards flickering. I go to the bookstore to buy books on business, and all I see are books on customer service. That's important but it's more than customer service. It's this whole system, and juggling all these balls in the air at the same time."

It sounds, we said to the Babels, like it's all held together by a fragile thread of commitment to these relationships. "Where's the security?" we asked. "There's no security," Jeanne answered. "All I know is that when Vic gets cut, he bleeds paint."

Chapter 11

The Industrial Society: Free to Achieve

Keep interested in your own career, however humble; it is a real possession in the changing fortunes of time. Exercise caution in your business affairs; for the world is full of trickery. But let this not blind you to what virtue there is; many persons strive for high ideals; and everywhere life is full of heroism.

On a wall in Old St. Paul's Church, Baltimore; dated 1692

"The Industrial Society promotes the fullest involvement of people in their work. Experience shows that increased involvement of individuals means greater efficiency, profitability and productivity for the organisation while resulting in greater satisfaction for the individual. This benefits the whole community in the creation of wealth."[1]

Such was the stated purpose of the Industrial Society as written in its first annual report in June 1919, in London, England. To define the nature of work in such a way reflects an extraordinary vision, and especially when one considers the work conditions of that time. Typically, work conditions during the First World War were indeed grim.

Vicar Robert Hyde, however, did not look dispassionately or with indifference at the existing work environment. In an effort to alleviate the appalling conditions Hyde witnessed, he opened the Boy's Welfare Association in 1918. With the support of Prince Albert, who later became King George VI, the Boy's Welfare Association quickly expanded its efforts to include *all* workers and, in 1919, became the Industrial Welfare Society. At the heart of the Society was a campaigning effort—to promote its objectives in communities and good practice in the workplace, to establish a pool of information, and to publicize its activities. Within several decades, it distanced itself from welfare, and the Industrial Society, as it henceforth was to be known, took on a larger scope and stressed the importance of people's participation at work and in the community.

Today, the Society is the largest independent developer of people at work in Europe. The Society continues to give direction and insight as to how to make work fulfilling for people—through learning programs, consultations, and information. Its vision of the workplace, where people are able to contribute their full potential, has remained steadfast over the years. Its leadership program is called Liberating Leadership, which emphasizes freeing people closest to the job to make their own decisions. The Society has its own publishing division, which in addition to books and periodicals also produces videos and CD-ROMs.

But like most organizations, the Society also faced difficult economic times, impelling them to change. It wasn't a choice really, a question of shall we change, or can we change fast enough? Rather, it was a matter of necessity—they either did or the Society would no longer exist. In 1994, it came uncomfortably close to imploding.

The Industrial Society story is a fractal story. An organization whose shared purpose is to improve the workplace for others, found itself on a journey to improve the Society's own workplace for its own people.

Uncertain Times

John Garnett, who was the Society's director from 1962 to 1986, is regarded as almost messiah-like within the Society. Under his leadership, the Society learned that they could improve the workplace, that they could, as their slogan said, "make it happen." But uncertain times befell the Society after John Garnett's departure. Certainly Garnett's charisma and ability to inspire others would be a hard act for anyone to follow. Between 1986 and 1994, two directors came and went. Both restructured the Society, and its people went through a lot of changes. After a massive reorganization in 1992, it became obvious that the Society needed to rebuild itself financially. Meanwhile, Britain was in a recession. Bill Beaver, marketing director at that time, recalls the state of the Society:

"For some, profit and sales were dirty words; selling sounded like prostitution, because we're a not-for-profit organization. Even though we were making money, we were spending more than we had. We were going down into bankruptcy at the speed of summer lightning. It was dreadful. And of course, there were those who harkened to the past and weren't thinking of the future."

As would happen in any organization, the fallout from too many changes, not enough security, and a lack of effective leadership was a tense and clandestine atmosphere.

Patrick Burns, communications director who has been at the Society since 1990, remembers those disheartened days. "By 1994, the cultural climate was appalling. Self-defeating, political, lots of cloak-and-dagger stuff, and a whole lot of destructive backstair conversations. People detached themselves from their colleagues and the organization and simply found their own corner and made alliances as and when they needed. The root of the crap was abysmal relationships."

The Society found itself sitting squarely in a contradiction: its people weren't practicing what they preached.

Navigator for Turbulent Seas

In 1994, Tony Morgan became the new CEO of the Industrial Society. A successful businessman and entrepreneur, among Tony's many accomplishments were forming an investment bank, directing the Youth at Risk program in Britain, and being the non–executive director and practitioner of Alexander Corporation, also in Britain. The corporation uses Socratic questioning as a method of coaching, which Tony immersed himself in and brought to the Society. When he had heard the Society was in trouble, he wasn't intimidated; instead it challenged him.

As he told us, "By the time I came on board, the mandate was: in six months, sort out the money, sort out the morale, and find a successor. When I told my wife, she said, 'It's only for six months, why don't you do it?' To take this on was probably a reflection of my arrogance.

"What happened was I fell in love with the people; they're such great people. And they were all sad and beaten and distrusting and all whipped, really. And these people come from the heart—they're a campaigning organization. They never discerned that you need money to campaign. In the first meetings, they said that I sounded like I wanted to make them into double glazing salesmen. They hadn't gotten that they were broke and that within six months they would be out of existence after eighty years! So many charities go straight down the tubes because they don't realize even as a charity you must make money. It's enormous what the Society is striving toward—changing the way people feel about the employment of women, ensuring there are opportunities for the disabled, creating fulfilling work for people in general. But, no money, no mission.

"By nature I'm a command and control type of person, very much so, but at that time I was getting a feeling that the command and control and linear thinking had a very limited life globally. So I approached the Society from a completely different angle. I was looking at how to change people from a structured organization to a nonstructured organization, and I did this blindly. I didn't do this by design, but by intuition. I had this consciousness of another way of working from what I learned when I lived in California, influenced by Fritjof Capra's holistic approach, Michael Rothschild's biological model of business, and Fernando Flores's model about the precision of language to gain access to action.

"From the start, I said we're going to live in chaos. That's such a daunting thing for people who've lived in a world of certain ways to behave, certain boxes to live in. It might be safe, but it's suppressing. The question was if we *could* live with chaos.

"This job has been the hardest job I've ever done in my life. Coming from a command and control existence, it was quite an adventure for me. But if I got it wrong, it would have been like me meddling with a national asset. If you don't think that I didn't wake up in the middle of the night and say 'this feels very uncontrolled,' you're greatly mistaken. I spent most nights thinking that. This is why this job has been more demanding than any other, because if you work within boxes, it's easy, because that's not about people. But this *is* about people, and that's much harder. People who work here aren't driven by monetary gain; they're driven because they want to make a contribution."

In relating the early days with Tony as CEO, Ann Jones, personnel officer, said, "When Tony came on, I think he reassured everybody. He said he wasn't going to make any more massive changes. We'd been through so many changes that people were exhausted with it. Instead, he said, we'll work with what we have. Rather than a concerted effort to change this structure and that hierarchy, it was more of an evolution.

"He forced us, really, to make commitments. You have a job description, he said. Right. I want more than that. I want you to commit to other things as part of your job that are over and above what you normally do. He raised the whole game. There was quite a lot of resistance to it—it was painful for people to change—but his strength of direction, in the end, has taken people along with him."

Tony was initially very tough with the Society, but it was his vision that compelled people to stick with it. As Yvonne Bennion, then director of research and development, recounts, "He walked into my office one day and said, 'Would you like to go on a journey?' I said yes. What it meant to me was that there was a different way of doing things. The point is that he didn't tell me *what* that different way of doing things was.

"His leadership is most marked by one statement—'keep your word.' Something about the simplicity of that statement—it's the easiest thing to say and the hardest thing to do—transcended everything we'd done. All in one phrase. Over the years we had been terribly concerned with titles, company cars. Keeping your word changes all that. I've seen Tony apologize openly to people, when he didn't keep his word, in a way most managers wouldn't. He was changing the conventional mind structure."

Bill Beaver expounded on Tony's efforts toward changing the mind-set: "The first thing he did was he came in and he listened. There was a problem with one of the senior directors whom he ended up dismissing. That was a clear signal to us that he was serious about trying to save the Society. But he also made it clear that he intended to draw the line there; he had no plan to fire more people. It was a great sigh of relief for everybody.

"He told us that he conducted business in a certain way, and his way was a breath of fresh air—things like, 'Don't lie to me; keep the messages you're telling me consistent.' He introduced the whole idea of developing us as a complex adaptive system, because he knew it would take longer any other way. He said if we were preaching about fulfilling work, we better be living it inside.

"Also, people liked him. He was accessible and available. He had a reputation—he was independently wealthy and he knew what the hell he was doing. When Tony decided the Society was a ship that could be saved, that led to an amazing outcome: the same people that were ruining the Society became the very same people who created the new Society. It was all the same people."

Saving a ship is not a metaphor lost on Tony, an Olympic silver medalist in sailing. In the Tokyo games of 1964, Tony sailed a Flying Dutchman, a two-man, nineteen-and-a-half-foot boat. After five races and one more to go, everyone felt his boat was nearly unbeatable; they could lose to only one other, New Zealand. Tony did lose that race, and instead of gold, he made the silver.

What is more important to Tony is *how* New Zealand won. "They did something wild because they had nothing to lose," Tony told us, "so they were able to take a big risk. It was absolutely brilliant. They tacked straight into the harbor against the good sense of every bloody nation. Every other nation in the world was tacking across. And they came out ahead of the game. Wonderful. Now that was a nonlinear, unexpected result."

Tony found himself in another race when he joined the Industrial Society. It truly was a sink-or-swim situation. Like the New Zealanders, the Society had nothing left to lose, and Tony was ready to take a big risk with them—to work with the complex adaptive system rather than the bureaucratic system, hoping for great nonlinear results.

But he did have to satisfy the needs of the structured core—the executive committee and council—in order to get the leverage he needed. After six months, Sir Robert Reid, chairman of the council, took Tony aside and said that he was really doing a good job. Could he reorganize his life and stay longer? Tony met with the executive committee, some twenty strong, who oversaw the Society's performance. Tony asked these high-powered people, who were senior executives of private and public organizations, "What is the purpose and the intended results of these meetings?" The response was, "To inform." Tony responded boldly, "Given all the information you've received the last eight years, you haven't done much with it."

There was a stunned silence—they weren't used to being confronted. Reid broke the silence to Tony's relief and asked, "What do you want?" Tony said, "I want a tiny executive committee—five of you and five of us. What do *you* want?" Tony asked the committee in return. They wanted to restore the reserves. Tony settled on getting a half a million pounds in the depleted reserves—which had a deficit of £600,000 ($960,000)—within a year. With the committee's terms for money satisfied, Tony found the latitude to do what he wanted.

Tony brought in a consultant, his Austrian friend of thirty years, Miki Walleczek, to coach him and to orchestrate three retreats called Klausurs, the German word for "retreat." Developed by Miki, these three-day retreats for reinventing the future are geared toward achieving seemingly impossible results, by changing the way people think. The Klausur process provides systematic ways for interpreting behaviors, actions, and speech, and for creating an open and honest operational environment, and greater adaptability as an organization.

Like Tony, Miki is an accomplished sportsman; he was the European champion in Formula V auto racing in 1966, is an expert skier, and a sailor himself. Like Tony, he, too, was an entrepreneur at an early age—taking over his mother's hand-weaving mill when he was nineteen, which developed into a very successful skiware company that he eventually sold to Kneissl ski company. Miki had a good track record as a consultant that included BMW, Siemens, and others.

And he has his own nautical metaphors for organizations. "I'm inquiring into what it takes to have people be in the same boat and row in the same direction," he says. "How can you design an organization so that everybody can contribute fully?" Bonded by a common love of adventure and a willingness to take high risks, Tony and Miki banded together to navigate the Society through turbulent waters. But the Society was a different kind of ship—one that neither of them had steered before.

Tony found himself captain to a female-dominated organization—70 percent women and with a history of campaigning for opportunities for women in the workplace. Neither Tony nor Miki had worked with a predominantly female organization before. "The Society is the first female culture I've worked in," Miki told us. "Not only is there a higher quantity of women, but it is a female culture; it's shaped in a female paradigm. It's very different dealing with a male, engineering-type culture, which is obviously linear, to a female culture that has nonlinear qualities from the beginning. Women are more open to nonlinear ways of doing things and there are greater possibilities for talking about purpose and meaning at the workplace, rather than just about profitability, like you find in male cultures. In the linear field, people think that the universe consists of things which exist independent of each other. If you look at life as having nonlinear dynamics, then everything exists only in relationship with each other."

Although there were powerful women in high positions, their potential had not been realized under previous leadership. Rather than empowered, the women were demoralized in a culture that was critical, where theoretical models were imposed on them, and their power stripped away. Tony's strategy for unleashing the potential in the Society that he knew was there was to focus on relationships. "Relationships are the most important thing for creating nonlinear processes," says Tony. "If you don't have this, none of it will work. People are either trying to look good or trying to make other people look bad. It's not about blame; it's about integrity. It's about being observant of yourself when you're inauthentic. When you confront someone and say they're a liar, it's great when they get that they're a liar. You become more aware of behaviors in relationships that lead to positive rather than negative outcomes.

"What I set out to do was to actually get rid of this negativity that was killing them and lead them toward a consciousness of another way of working. We started tearing down the structure, by allowing people to speak up and to talk honestly. I started this process by speaking very directly and straight in ways that were totally unexpected to them. Once I took the lid off, they all did it. I didn't do anything really. I've just allowed. It's creating a space for people, which sounds simple, but it's painful for them and scary for me. It's a major responsibility for me."

In the course of this unplanned and unknown journey, Tony found that addressing relationships would indeed unleash enormous and unimaginable potential, for this strategy of relationships struck an inner chord—it is in the world of relationships that most women live.

Given the opportunity, many women with huge potential were able to get to where they should be. Tony set sails that caught the winds of their capabilities and ambitions. And he himself would change and unexpectedly find himself in a different relationship to his organization. The anchor of his command and control disposition would begin to lift with the release of this potential, and he would find himself afforded opportunities in this feminine environment for creating another way of being for himself: to be free—to sail beloved as a man, not just as an executive director, within the Society.

Shifting Tides—From Chaos to Clarity and Cash

Tony began his journey in dark waters. "I started with the management team and directors, who weren't talking to each other," said Tony. "It was all about establishing relationships, team-building exercises. It released so much energy, energy all over the place, just spewing out."

He took them away on Klausurs where management worked arduously to clarify the existing dysfunctional personal relationships, and to forge new relationships that had not existed with each other and with the organization.

In one of the Klausurs, Tony reminisces, "We were pushing for really bold unattainable goals, for nonlinear thinking. We asked what was the craziest thing that we could do in five sectors of the company for generating income—

in-house, membership, public courses, sponsorships, and publications. Out of that, champions emerged, and this was dominantly women. It was wonderful to see so many powerful women that haven't been allowed to be powerful stand tall. People would stand up and say, 'Yes, this is what I can do.' The executive committee told me I was clearly very wrong in what I was doing because, 'What would happen when they didn't get there?' Out of these totally stupid, outrageous goals, because that's what they looked like, after a year and a half, these people had achieved almost everything they said they would."

From these retreats, the management team found solidarity in a shared effort and desire to save the sinking-ship Society. In this process, people transformed—their management styles would change from directing to servicing the people in their area. They found direction by creating projects and setting impossible goals. These projects were open to everyone and anyone who wanted to participate. This led to self-managing teams and to portfolio roles— a mix and match of traditional business tasks blended with high-risk projects. Job titles were often hard to define because roles fluctuated.

Ultimately, the projects changed people's relationship to the organization as they became engaged in reinventing it. The culture became more democratic, open, fluid, and dynamic. And the Society did become financially successful.

Following are stories of people's experience as they undertook the daunting task of reinventing themselves—which did result in clarity and cash.

Patrick Burns: Reinventing Work Relationships

"There was an intensive and extremely painful phase we went through as we were trying to get all the stuff that had been buried for a long, long time onto the table. Why A hated B and didn't talk to C; why we kept selling something when it was garbage. When you get that stuff out on the table, it completely changes the nature of the discussion. Once stated, it has to be addressed. There were distressing conversations, very uncomfortable hatchets to be buried. But it was very enthralling and stimulating to be a part of it as well.

"There was a great effort on the part of managers to take that experience out to their part of the organization—a kind of cascade principle. We wanted to change how we dealt with our own teams. I realized that I thought I was quite smart at involving the people who worked with me. Actually I wasn't good at it. Although I thought I was being quite liberating in the amount of responsibility I was giving to people on the team, I wasn't giving nearly enough. If you want to have magnificent people on your team, you don't coach them, you let them do it. The thing I picked up was that you've got to make sure people can go *miles* with things, without you continually chipping in and effectively retaining control of it.

"For example, a woman, Julie Kibblewhite, who worked as an assistant in our group, decided that the organization was lacking a large comprehensive guide for its own staff—what everyone does, what their qualifications are, what languages they speak, information on products. Nobody asked her to do that. No one said it was needed. She just decided it was needed and she made it happen. She got the right number of people together, delegated the right amount of work, got me involved as a collaborator. You can replicate that kind of story all over the organization.

"In a short time, we pulled back from financial catastrophe—that's very good for people's morale. It would have been completely impossible if the management team hadn't been welded together very quickly to a reasonably united force. Even though we might have had ideas about turning the organization around before, they wouldn't have worked. Reinventing isn't just about ideas; it's about relationships. Without the proper environment, ideas don't get anywhere. It's about the safety to err and the opportunity to say it, and not being afraid that an idea might sound stupid.

"The best ideas came after we worked on the relationships. I think generally those ideas were a result of an environment in which views would come up in a completely unstructured way, and we would bang them around and then the *great* idea would emerge. Creating that environment for ideas is more important than most things, and we're not quite with it yet, but when we do get that going, it's phenomenal. Ideas in a command and control environment, by contrast, can often survive from beginning to end and never be bashed about or tested before they get out. That can be very dangerous."

Bill Beaver: A Personal Reinvention

"For me, working at the Society resulted in a personal transformation. It was a big leap with very, very, little steps in between. I thought at the time that I was going to get fired, because I thought they expected me to come in and save the ship, and it wasn't happening. Tony did a 360-degree appraisal on me and I found out it wasn't about me not saving the ship. The problem, he pointed out, was that people just didn't like working with me. I had some idea about that, but it was dreadful to hear it.

"Because I had worked before for a company that did not behave well, I did not behave well. I was a real command and control freak. I was really not a very nice guy to be around. I'd shout at people, slightly out of control. I just figured they were weak, mealymouthed civilian types who couldn't get their act together. I saw them as comforted by the Society and that they wouldn't last three and a half seconds outside in the real world. I expected loyalty and they were going to give it to me just because I was director of marketing. And when they didn't, I would get a bit cross, especially as I could see we were failing and they knew we were failing.

"So Tony coached me to get my relationship to people straightened out. He was very supportive. At the same time, the atmosphere was getting exciting, because some of these new projects were coming on board. That meant that the people that I hadn't valued that much were on projects that I said I was going to service. So this meant I had to service these twenty-two-year-old teeny-boppers that I hadn't been very nice to. And they were going out and doing incredible things.

"Once I realized that every time I walked in the room people thought, well, maybe this guy will bring something to the party, that became my goal. When I realized that I was part of the team and that I had a responsibility and talents to make the thing work, we started to shift as a team. I never took risks before; I didn't think it was sensible, until I saw these kids. The teenyboppers were the ones taking the real risks and doing fantastic things in the name of the marketing department. They were committing to producing eighty, ninety thousand pounds and were coming back and doing it. And I made sure all the backup they needed was there for them.

"And to think that I used to be upset because they didn't let me come and play and be a big group leader. I learned through this process that we could actually accomplish a hell of a lot more if we worked together."

Mandi Harris: Reinventing Work

"We're completely project-focused here. Anybody can get involved in any of the projects. Before Tony came along, you had to be a certain person to be on a project. My job as a personal assistant, who minds somebody's diary and things like that, would be too boring if not for the fact that I am doing projects. I've been here for eleven years. I've done six different jobs since I've been here and moved across a lot, as opposed to being stuck in the old hierarchical ladder. I like to do different things for the experience as opposed to just getting paid for a job. Right now we have this huge information technology project and I want to get involved with the Internet aspect. And I can do that because the Society allows us to do that.

"Working together this way, people really learn to care about each other. On many occasions, when you've hit rock bottom and you're thinking, I can't go on any longer, there's somebody who will come and pick you up and help you. It's not the fact that you have to tell somebody—somebody will notice. For example, someone needs help, and I'll say that I'll give her two days over the next four weeks or something, and we'll sort it out from there. It's part of the job. It's not groaning about having something more to do; it's more that, we need to do this and we'll divide the work and figure out the logistics for how to do it. And another thing, we have great parties together. We do that very well."

Sheridan McGuire: Reinventing Teams

"We have this notion that came from the director of human resources called jelly in a box. The organization is like a rectangle and all the jobs are traditionally square-shaped. So you try to squeeze people, who are more like jelly, into their box and, of course, bits stick out of the boxes. But maybe Jane might like this bit that is sticking out of that box. And maybe Fred wants that bit. Maybe they could be reshaped. So you shape the jobs to fit the jellies, rather than squeezing the jellies into the box.

"We did this in our publishing group very successfully. We were accommodating the way people were in the world, a little bit more. As a result, they became more productive because, now they were saying, 'Great, this is what I can do. I hate to do accounts. I can go and do some platform work though.' Whereas another person might love figures, but couldn't do accounts before, because it wasn't in her job. Of course, you're going to get bits that nobody wants to do like photocopying, but then you have a conversation to resolve that."

Chrissie Wright: Reinventing the Organization

"In the second Klausur, we were asked to find a target to achieve that would be stretching us but also realistic, and that we would be accountable for it. We were in a big group, deciding what we could do and it was fun and exciting. I'm responsible for public course income; money generated from 130 courses that we run for our members. I said I would raise a million pounds over and above what we had already budgeted, which itself was already beyond what we had been doing. A million pounds would create a half-million-pound surplus. Now, that was a far reach, but my department had a record of success, unlike others who were taking on projects against all odds.

"I was willing to take that risk because it felt safe. I didn't feel I would be shoved out the door if I didn't achieve it, but I also felt that it was achievable. I might have thought it was achievable before, but I wasn't prepared to take the risk. What Tony did was create a context for risk, by legitimizing it and saying it was valid, rather than a mad thing to do. It was very liberating. Of course, afterward, you get the backlash of, 'Oh God, what if I don't achieve it?'

"Day to day, year to year, it's very important for me to achieve targets that are set. Somehow, this target seemed to exist in a different space. Value was placed not on the goal, but on the attempt. And even if we didn't achieve the goal, it was bound to take us further than we were.

"What was more frightening than making the commitment was throughout the year we had to present our progress to the executive committee, who met every two months. We, the directors, had to stand up and be counted on several occasions—which is to be expected—but it was a strain. If we weren't exactly where we said we'd be, we felt vulnerable.

"Part of the problem was that the people we were presenting to had not been involved in the program that led up to these projects. Their way of thinking was very bottom-line and very linear. We had to adapt our way of working, our vision to what they needed to hear, and put it in a language they could understand. It was very difficult to put nonlinear thinking into a linear language—it sounded a bit unreal in their terms. The difficulty is in getting an understanding between different mind-sets. People who are more analytical and use clear structures have more difficulty living with what is perceived as a lack of structure. At the end of the year, though, I did achieve my target."

Tony Morgan: Reinventing the Executive Core

"This moment, when we had presented our results to the executive committee, saddens me. The executive committee are all wonderful people, but they didn't acknowledge what had happened. I had five key champions telling them what they had done and the committee was saying, 'Thank you very much.' The champions all marched to the door and I said 'STOP.' They stopped and I turned to the committee and said, 'I don't think you know the definition of heroines and heroes. These are people who established goals for themselves without any idea of how to get there and just committed to it. Look at these nonlinear results.' The committee members burst into applause. Bob Reid told me later he wished he had thought of saying that. Eventually one or two members came and experienced the program firsthand—they came to see what we were doing. So it's about acknowledgment, open and honest communication, integrity."

Free to Achieve

Within three years, Tony had fulfilled his objectives: the money was there (currently a £4 million surplus, or $6.4 million), the morale was up, and the membership was increasing. It was a different and a successful Society. Effectively, a focus on projects that involved people widely enabled the Society to be agile and to react quickly to the changing environment, and thus able to escape any further financial crises.

Being successful can, however, have its problems as well. Tony explained it this way: "It's difficult because you have to be continually interactive; you have to keep working at it. Otherwise complacency sets in: 'Oh, we know that, why do we need to do that anymore?' And that's a disaster, because complacency moves us into a safe place, and then we're no longer on the edge.

"You have to keep working at creating productive relationships. I can't conceive of myself as a leader without the burden of responsibility to create powerful relationships—where people can speak to me openly all the time, throughout the organization, and that's really difficult. I slipped up in the last four months and people have stopped being open and honest with me. Complex systems work on feedback loops; the feedback stopped. Why? Because they said I shouted at them. What shows up is 'Tony's not walking the talk.' I stopped behaving authentically, and people shut down. The Society is a living organism."

Complacency was not the only developing undercurrent. There was a growing discontent with the performance rewards system. Performance commitments are seemingly impossible goals people make for themselves. The problem people were feeling with performance commitments, which are often difficult to measure, was that they were tied to financial rewards. The reward system tended to divide individuals from individuals, to pit team against team. Also, there was no way for rewarding people for *being* great.

In addition, with success there emerged an identity crisis. As Patrick Burns told us: "We've been set up as a campaigning organization and have discovered on the way that we can make a mint of money in training. The questions coming up are, 'Will we or will we not seriously become a campaigning organization around principles that have stayed reasonably constant?' Right now we don't have a campaign. We're perceived as a training and learning body, which isn't the same as a campaigning organization."

It was this mixed broth of emotions—growing complacency, an identity crisis, discontent with performance commitments—that preceded the three-day event called Free to Achieve that took place in September 1997. A huge financial investment, the entire Society was invited to go away for three days, expenses paid. It was Tony's next nonlinear leap.

Some people regarded the event with suspicion. Even though people were told they didn't have to attend, many felt they had no real choice when the invitation was coming down from the top. Even though they were told this would not be a Klausur, people were skeptical, and resistance was growing against Miki's continued involvement because people felt they were capable of managing organizational changes on their own. In spite of or perhaps because of these undercurrents, the event would ultimately set the Society on a new course.

In the course of the three days, people spoke of three pivotal events. One was Yvonne Bennion's talk about values, the second was guest speaker David Whyte, a poet and business consultant, and the third was Tony leading the discussion on the last day.

Yvonne Bennion:

A generally reserved and soft-spoken woman, Yvonne is someone widely respected in the Society, having been there a long time. The personal nature of her talk moved many, at a time when the sense of the group was beginning to splinter. This is how Yvonne experienced it:

"Early on the morning of the day I was to speak, Tony talked to a group of us about the role of values as being the foundation for what we are as an organization. I thought, actually, all I can do is talk about values from my own experience and in my own way. And it's what I wanted to do. It wasn't going to be 'Yvonne the director.' It was just going to have to be 'Yvonne.'

"I wanted to tell people that I felt the Industrial Society had a higher purpose and that sometimes we forget because we spend so much time in practical activity. For me, the Society manifests what democracy is in the workplace, which for me has always been tremendously important. I wanted to acknowledge that I'd been part of a time when I think we did come close, and I certainly had come very close, to losing those values in the battle for the Society's financial survival. I told them how I had gone to Belfast and saw the difficult and tense circumstances under which some of our people were working, and it was extraordinary. It very much brought me home to myself.

"When I said I believed that the values have always been there with us, there was a palpable movement, a feeling that the audience was being moved and aligning with what I said. I asked people to be quiet and still for a few minutes, to contemplate, and then I asked them to talk to the person next to them. There was an explosion of conversation. Miki and the design team felt they could not go on with their intended plan after that. The necessary space had been created and it needed to be held in a very delicate way and nurtured."

David Whyte:

David Whyte was a guest speaker at the event. In his resonant voice, he improvised his talk, using rich imagery and beautiful poetry, and he invited the Society to rediscover what the soul means for an organization. As the event took place shortly after the death of Diana, Princess of Wales, he made reference to her in his talk. Listening to him, people began to see that the Society wasn't just about money—that maybe it was unique; maybe they could help change the world; maybe there was a better world out there to be discovered. This is how David saw it:

"I was working with the whole threshold I felt was very apparent in Britain after the death of Diana. It wasn't just the death of Diana, it was the election of the new government and the collective weariness of that old decaying government that was there. And the death of Diana just catalyzed something whereby I think people realized that they were collectively tired of their institutions as they were presently constituted. They wanted much more of an adult-adult relationship with the world and with their work. And they wanted an adult-adult relationship with themselves. I tried to work with a sense of both the magnificence and fear that is right there now—that we're both emboldened to claiming our lives back from our institutions and we're also fearful at the same time.

"I used a lot of images, the applause rippling back from the streets in London into the center of the Abbey during the funeral. And the image of the swan out of water, moving toward the river. It looks tremendously awkward while walking along the river bank, then the moment when it touches the element it belongs in, it takes on this grace and this effortless movement. I related this to campaigning; that it's not the hard charge ahead to seek, but rather a rested confidence in one's own belonging."

Tony Morgan:

Following is an excerpt from a transcript of dialogue that took place at the event. For many, this time with Tony was the most powerful turning point of all. Tony is speaking to the audience.

Tony: Someone earlier said something about performance commitments. Shall we have a crack at that one? Is that all right? I have a responsibility for performance commitments. I used them in the Alexander method and they work very well. What I intended to create was something that served us. What I'm hearing is that it doesn't serve you. What would make performance doable? We can't enter into something that might propel us back to where we were before. You can all remember what it was like to be short of money. So, what would make performance doable?

Voice: Take the money out of the equation.

Tony: What else? I need something I can rely on, a metric.

Miki says to Tony: Don't judge.

Tony: I'm not judging.

Voice: The only thing you need a metric for is to measure. Why do you need to measure? So you can make a judgment about me?

Miki: Don't judge.

Tony: So, a performance commitment that doesn't judge?

Voice: To be free, we need to serve each other. In terms of being free to achieve, charity starts at home. We need to look at the way we work with each other, the way we help each other. (Applause)

Voice: I feel strongly about personal commitments, but after eighteen years in sales, I'm used to being targeted, measured, monitored, and made to perform in a variety of ways. (Laughter) I have a completely different feeling about working with the Industrial Society. The commitment comes from here, the heart, and is devalued by putting it down on a piece of paper.

The topic gets tossed around for a while, suggestions are made. Tony commits himself to sorting the performance commitment out. They take a break. After the break, Tony speaks.

Tony: I know the conversation before the break made a number of you unhappy and distressed. I just want you to understand that my commitment to you is complete. That when that happens, your hurt just crucifies me. We screwed up a bit. I want to recover the space where we were. One of the interpretations was that Miki's intervention with me demeaned me. What you couldn't know was that all the directors made a request, myself included, that he would intervene and coach when appropriate. . . . I have a serious face; it doesn't mean there isn't enormous affection and commitment to each and every one of you here. So has everybody got that? That if you are upset, I am really distressed myself. (Tony is visibly moved)

This is how Tony experienced those moments:

"It was a terrifying moment. One minute I had the Society all with me, and the next I lost them completely. And I thought, 'This is three and a half years of work down the tubes.' And then I lost it on the platform. I've been brought up in a school where big boys don't cry. So, that was very difficult for me. The tension during the break, two hours before the whole event was to end, was palpable. Directors were coming in and saying things like, 'There were eight people in the corridor crying.' I knew that that was my mistake.

"The group had been asked to do an exercise on identifying blocks to their dreams and I asked which one they would like to discuss and that I'd tell them what I can do—action-focused language. I had been previously listening to their upset about performance summaries, and was responding to it, but to the rest of the people, this was irrelevant compared to the huge dreams they'd been expressing. Yes, performance commitments limited them, it created fear, but this wasn't what they wanted to talk about. I knew my response was greatly upsetting things dear to their hearts, and totally inappropriate. People went out thinking we were back to crossing t's and dotting i's when they've had this great dream.

"After the break, I acknowledged that I heard that people were in a major upset. My hurt came absolutely from their hurt. Just acknowledging that, got it back on track."

A Realignment

Like any event, the three-day retreat received mixed reviews. Some people were disappointed because they hoped to have a strategy and a business plan, which was not there. But for the most part, people found it to be very positive with enormous benefit. Ann Jones's story captures the feeling that they had, indeed, moved to another place. "I had a conversation with a consultant who is very cynical and has been quite damning about things for a long time. I asked him how he felt about the event, given that he was going to retire soon. 'Oh, no,' he said, 'I'm not retiring. Now I've got too much to do. After these three days, I am really here; I'm in it.' It was a complete change."

The Society did change its performance commitments. They became authentically generated commitments—commitments emerging from what really excited the individual, and that were in line with the Society's goals. In other words, as an organization, they fully embraced the responsibility of making work fulfilling for people. That performance commitments did actually change also showed people that they could, indeed, impact the organization as a whole.

Many lessons were learned from observing Tony. The people in the Society spoke with awe at seeing their leader inviting completely uncensored feedback about the business. They appreciated the courage it took for Tony to do that. They appreciated that they were genuinely allowed to say what they wanted and needed to say.

In the face of Miki's challenges, they saw Tony as someone who was able to accept criticism publicly, in front of colleagues and subordinates, someone who was open to learning and listening. They saw someone who could admit he didn't know it all; that he, like they, was engaged in a learning process. But they were also uneasy with seeing him publicly criticized or compromised, and felt very protective of him.

They saw Tony as someone who wanted to make a difference in people's working lives, knowing as they did that he himself did not have to work. They saw his commitment to lead them to the next place, his commitment to carry on the legacy of John Garnett, and they wanted to be involved and be a part of that.

But perhaps the most powerful of all, they saw someone speaking from the heart, and they in turn responded with their heart. They spoke of him as someone they could talk to; they saw a human being. He presented another role model for what was possible in their organization—openness, vulnerability, conviction. And with this insight, the Society's relationship to Tony realigned.

Over the years, the Society had watched and empathized with Tony's struggle to reel in his command and control style, his struggle to really listen to things he might not want to hear, just as Tony had watched them struggle to achieve their potential. It was a mutual relationship, and the people wanted this mutuality and mutual need recognized. People at the event had expressed a desire for Miki to go, but this was more about Tony than Miki. The Society recognized that Miki had done a lot to prepare them for this moment—this moment of being ready and capable of going forward on their own. It was no longer appropriate for Miki to set the agenda. And the Society's people, whose business it is to impart information, are strong individuals with a tendency to do things on their own. They wanted Tony to know that they now could be there for him, and for each other. They were one organization again—they could go forward with the same goal and work toward it as a real team. They had outgrown a need for outside help. And they could do this because a shared purpose had emerged.

The shared purpose emerged in the midst of 265 people in one room over three days. Separate departments were now visible as one whole. People who were voices over the phone now had faces. And in these faces, people in the Society recognized themselves—as caring for people, caring for the same values. From this recognition, a collective powerful emotion emerged, what Patrick Burns called "a palpable sense of humanity" and Sheridan McGuire called "a group touch."

The shared purpose emerged in recognizing that most of them had been carrying campaigning in their hearts, and that what was closest to their hearts had not been shared. They had lost sight of their hearts while on a treadmill of numbers. As senior staff in the publishing division Suzanne Hyde notes, "I was surprised that campaigning was so welcomed, because I have always felt that it was sidelined. I think it was such a boost to feel that it was being acknowledged—it had a profound effect on people that have been carrying this silently. The Society reestablishing campaigning as our heart was very powerful and moving for me. My husband is the grandson of the founder of the Society and they kept bringing Robert Hyde up, and that was lovely. For me, I feel more in line with my integrity, because my deepest beliefs have been acknowledged."

The shared purpose also emerged in recognizing that, although campaigning had become dormant in the collective consciousness, it had, in fact, not stopped for individuals who carried its messages in their everyday work. As Jenny Davenport, a senior staff in the training division, says, "It's what I think I do every day. When I see secretaries who took a course of ours go out the door with a view of themselves they wouldn't have had before—a bit more self-confident, a few more skills—that itself is a campaigning activity. You're doing as much campaigning with them, for instance, as when you're doing a pre-recruitment campaigning for minorities to get into police work."

The Free to Achieve event had unearthed a shared desire that catalyzed a realignment within the Society—eyes, once turned inward and introspective, turned outward, wanting to make a difference in the world. Freedom, where the Society people could act on their own behalf, and on the behalf of others, had been released. And with this uncovering of the collective purpose came a surge of activity throughout the Society that would protect and nurture what was dearest to their hearts—putting into place the framework of principles, processes, and practices that would underpin and sustain the Free to Achieve culture that had emerged and that would ensure its continuing development. They had reached a milestone in their continuing journey, which they recognize is long and difficult, that is, to ensure that the Society and each of its people would truly be free to achieve their shared purpose.

Chapter 12

Monsanto: Transformation of a Chemical Giant

We are all in the gutter, but some of us are looking at the stars.
Oscar Wilde, *Lady Windermere's Fan*

Founded in 1901, Monsanto Company became one of the world's leading chemical concerns, building its economic clout with products such as saccharin, aspirin, phenol, acrylic fibers, ammonium nitrate fertilizer, and Roundup, the world's biggest-selling herbicide. In 1997, with a workforce of 22,000 people in a hundred countries around the world, Monsanto had sales of $7.5 billion and a market capitalization of $28.7 billion. But what many people are unaware of is that Monsanto is no longer the chemical company it once was. In September 1997, in a culmination of a profound process of transformation that had been under way for two years, the chemical operations were spun off as a separate and independent company, Solutia Inc. This change left the new Monsanto to concentrate on three historically separate but increasingly coherent business operations, those of agriculture, food ingredients, and pharmaceuticals. Today's Monsanto describes itself as a life sciences business, based on advanced bioscience and with a professed goal of helping people around the world "to lead longer, healthier lives, at costs that they and their nations can afford, and without continued environmental degradation."[1]

Given the company's former reputation, shared with other large chemical concerns, of having a negative impact on the environment, through pollution of the air and water and spreading harmful chemicals on the land, Monsanto's ongoing commercial shift and professed lofty goals are dramatic indeed. Dramatic in itself, but dramatic in other ways, too, which are less visible to the public eye. Namely, inspired by CEO Bob Shapiro, the company has transmuted the way it works as an organization, as it wrested itself free of a traditional mechanistic management style and embraced a much more flexible, more organic mode of operation that in many ways follows the principles of complexity science. Monsanto's new personality is credited with being central to creating a company that can be as innovative and adaptive as it needs to be if it is to survive and thrive in its new environment. That environment is the increasingly fast-changing business sector that is driven by revolutionary discoveries in biotechnology. In many ways, the life sciences industry finds itself in the late 1990s in a position where the computer and communications industry was three decades ago; that is, poised for explosive growth, burgeoning innovation, and an ever-changing and unpredictable business environment.

A lawyer by education, Shapiro joined the Monsanto fold in 1985, when Monsanto acquired G.D. Searle, a pharmaceutical company made famous for developing the artificial food sweetener NutraSweet, whose commercial success Shapiro had shepherded. In 1990 Shapiro became head of Monsanto's Agricultural Group, whose operating style he transformed by introducing the notion of self-organization, which replaced the more traditional command and control structure. Five years later Shapiro became Monsanto's CEO, in which position he embarked on a similar process of transformation, company-wide. Under the new regime, the company's share price doubled in a two-year period, in part due to an enhanced spirit of experimentation and creativity that had emerged cogently in the company's people. Shapiro talks here about what in complexity science appeals to his style of management; about the transformation of Monsanto and what inspired it; about the emerging nature of the company and what he values in it; and about his vision for the future.[2]

Business Through the Lens of Complexity Science

I first learned about complexity science when I came across a book by Mitchell Waldrop about half a dozen years ago.[3] It talked about work going on at the Santa Fe Institute, and people like Brian Arthur, John Holland, Stuart Kauffman, and others. What struck me most powerfully was that there is a defined mathematical realm in complex adaptive systems that is very creative, very adaptive. It's the realm between order, which isn't very fertile; and chaos, which is also not very fertile. The realm in between, the edge of chaos as it's called, is where everything interesting happens. It struck a chord with me because it was very like something I'd been thinking about for years, but in a different context.

Back in the 1960s I'd found myself teaching law students at the University of Wisconsin in Madison, and one of the courses I gave them was about cities. The organizing model of urban planning at the time came out of an engineering mentality, a very inorganic way of viewing a city. A city consisted of parts, it was said; it consisted of buildings; it consisted of roads and traffic flows; it consisted of utilities' infrastructure. Architects who followed this model said that if you could tear down the slums and build these tall tower blocks, and have green space around them, life would get better. As we all know, it was a disaster, and caused enormous human misery and degradation of the urban environment. For me, an alternative organizing paradigm, which came from the work of Jane Jacobs, was much more attractive, because it was very organic and paid attention to what really happens in cities. Specifically, she paid attention to people.

Jacobs's first book was called *Death and Life of Great American Cities,* and it was revolutionary.[4] It changed the way everybody talks and thinks about cities. She began understanding neighborhoods in terms of very subtle, micro interactions. It wasn't just about things like ten thousand cars coming in through this corridor; it was about questions like, "Do people sit on the steps of their buildings and watch the streets?" Because if they do, certain things happen, and if they don't, certain other things would happen. Her work was very thorough, and she said that the life of cities was the collective result of many such small behaviors. It became very clear to me and to other people that something very subtle, very complicated was emerging out of a set of individual decisions that in themselves seem trivial from the perspective of those grandiose urban plans. Traditional urban planners simply had no idea of the complexity of the systems they were dealing with, because of their mechanistic mind-set. Cities are more like ecosystems than they are like machines.

It's the same kind of thing in the business world. Intuitively I felt that the mechanistic mind-set wasn't going to get you to where you wanted to be, where you *needed* to be. What I had been groping with was a transition from a mechanistic way of viewing business organizations to an ecological way of viewing them. And when I read about complexity, it fit very nicely with an ecological notion of the way interesting and important things worked, including in business.

The Creative Power of Diversity in Business

Although I had never really planned to be a businessperson, I ended up doing the thing that overprivileged Jewish boys often do, and that is I went to work for my father's company, General Instrument Corporation, a Fortune 500 company. I joined as general counsel, and to my surprise I discovered I loved business. What I first fell in love with was that this was a wonderful, interesting, complicated game. I enjoy games, and so that aspect of business appealed to me. Then there was the discovery not long afterward that, yes, but this is a game about *real* things, about *people,* in very powerful ways. I began to see some possibility that if I got lucky, maybe I could have some influence that would be benign and useful in the business world, and I spent ten years trying to persuade somebody to let me run a business.

As a child I'd thought a lot about issues such as how to reconcile power and justice, perhaps because I grew up in a family environment in which those two were not always aligned. So it was always a dream of mine, which I despaired of because I always thought it wasn't realizable, of working in a just system, in a *human* system. Running a business myself would give me an opportunity to create that. However, I don't think I would have articulated it like that at the time. It was more, "Gee, if those morons can run a company, I sure can. And, wouldn't that be fun. Gee, think of the things we could do!"

I got extremely lucky because my first chance to run a business was when I was with G.D. Searle. I was head of their NutraSweet operation, which was made an independent unit. That was an amazing experience, because we had a chance to create an organization from scratch. We went from six people to fifteen hundred in three years. I basically was saying that "there is something powerful and good going on here. There are a lot of resources, and we just have to get them into the soup somehow, and it will sort itself out." That really was true, because for a period of time there was almost nothing we could do that wouldn't work. Two reasons: first, because of the quality of the product itself; second, because the need for the product was so strong that almost any activity would produce good results. But it was also because of the way we worked, which was quite different. We had many people who, like me, were just stretched way beyond anything they had ever done before. We made our share of mistakes, but we did many things that were fun, interesting, and novel.

In the early days, we'd get everyone together in a room every week or so, and we'd go through things, like, "How are we doing on capacity expansion?" We'd have a few who knew something about manufacturing, of course, but the rest of us didn't. But everyone pitched in, making suggestions like, "What would happen if we tried this," and so on. People were always coming up with the most creative ideas, even in areas where they lacked experience, or maybe *because* they lacked experience. You have to have a rich mix of the two, a diversity of experience among your people.

We looked very hard for parallels for what we were trying to do, places that had been through a similar experience, but we never found anything that was very apt. We didn't know about complexity science at the time—it was still being developed—but had we known, we'd have seen that diversity promotes creativity in complex adaptive systems, something we came to intuitively. As it was, we had this very conscious sense that we are making this up as we went along, and that we are doing this together, and there is some risk. But it is fun.

The creativity that flows from diversity is about surprise, coming up with things that aren't obvious, things you haven't done before. Diversity is what it takes to get enough creativity in the organization for something surprising to happen. The thing about old companies and about machines is that they are totally predictable. You know exactly what they are going to do. They had been designed to take surprise out of it. The classic old-line business manager would say, "No surprises. That's my motto around here. Everything is going to be as controlled as it can be. If you see something out of the ordinary happening, you'd better let me know way in advance. I don't like surprises." All of us who were in business in the 1970s heard a lot of people give that speech. It was the orthodoxy, and it stultified creativity.

I see diversity as *the* key to creativity and adaptability in an organization. But it is more than that; it is also about creating an *anticipatory* organization. The trick here isn't just adaptation. It has to be either very fast adaptation, or anticipation, because all systems adapt, or die. The advantage comes in adapting before others sense that the environment is changing. For this to happen you have to have a lot of different kinds of people. That is the difference fundamentally between a machine and an ecosystem. A machine is designed to do a certain job, and it does that job superbly well. You cannot design an ecosystem that will do a particular thing better than you could design a machine to do it. But the difference is that when the world changes around it, the machine doesn't have any mechanism for doing things differently, while ecosystems can and do respond to changes in their environment. Like machines, businesses that operate on mechanistic models are also unable to respond to changes in their environment. They want to keep doing the thing they've been doing. That's not a bad thing to do, if you can get away with it. But you aren't likely to be able to get away with it for very long, particularly these days, and certainly not in the kind of business environment that Monsanto is in.

Having promoted the power of diversity, I have to admit that it's not easy getting diversity in a company like Monsanto. The tendency is for people to want to surround themselves with people who make them comfortable, and the people who make you comfortable often are people a lot like you. The old Monsanto was designed around that because, as a chemical company, what it was looking for more than anything else was reliability. And reliability essentially calls for similarity, so that people will arrive at the same answers under similar circumstances. The system was designed so that by the time anyone got any real power, they had been through a set of experiences that would acculturate them, so that they would decide things the way the generation before had decided them. The system was designed to weed out those folks who didn't do that. That was probably an appropriate system, given the objectives of the system.

The new Monsanto is in a different business. We are not about reliability, although we do need to be able to manufacture things with some consistency. We are more about invention, and invention is a different mind-set. It requires different types of people, different systems. The model I suggested some years back is that what you want is that every meeting should look like the United Colors of Benneton; you want to have the world. It's easy to say, and it's a good idea, but doing it isn't so easy.

The Transformation of Monsanto

There were two reasons why I felt transformation was necessary. The first was the internal culture of the company, which I didn't feel comfortable with. The second was the external business environment: it was changing dramatically, and if the company didn't change, too, it would be in trouble.

I remember when I moved from NutraSweet in Chicago to St. Louis to run the agriculture business, in 1990. They processed me through the new-person thing. I don't think they literally fingerprinted me, but it sure felt like it. I remember walking around the Monsanto campus, which is large and peaceful, physically very impressive. It was as though I could hear Monsanto speaking to me through the architecture and through the process, and the fundamental, underlying message was, "We are very big, you are very small." And the corollary of that was, "Obey orders and no one will get hurt." That's what it felt like, and that didn't seem to me to call out the best in me, and I didn't think it called out the best in other people either. The sort of place I wanted to create was one that says to people, "If you're really great—and there are many ways of being great; we don't all have to be great the same way—and if you have some abilities that can help us, let's figure out what it is you're going to do around here, because it is you and people like you who are going to make the difference around here, not the system."

At that time, Monsanto had the most successful agriculture operation in the industry. It had grown out of an ag-chemical orientation, and yet it was clear to anyone who thought about it for very long that the basic set of assumptions on which it was predicated were heading for some rocky times ahead, either for environmental reasons, for economic reasons, for changes in the way government was subsidizing agriculture. But most fundamentally because of changes in the technology. Monsanto was leading in exploring the application of biotechnology to agriculture. I thought that would have radical implications for the industry and for the way we would have to work.

The challenge was, how do you create radical change in a very proud, successful institution? The old literature about how you change an institution is very leader-centered. The charismatic leader comes in and says, "There are three things I want you to remember; say them when you get up in the morning; say them on every possible occasion." And then people will change the organization. There are many wonderful business leaders doing that kind of thing, but as a matter of style and personality, it didn't seem right for me, or for Monsanto. I didn't want people to come to certain conclusions because they were ordered to. I wanted them to come to those conclusions themselves because they *believed* them.

I decided that the only way to make that happen in a successful organization was to make it unsuccessful. I don't mean unsuccessful in the marketplace, or unsuccessful financially. I wanted to break the organization down internally, break old habits and old ways of doing things, by giving people challenges that they couldn't handle by doing things the way they always had. The problem with making changes in big, complicated organizations is that, at any particular time, all the parts have to fit together. They may fit in a dysfunctional way for a system as a whole, but they do fit. If you try to change any single part in isolation, it wouldn't fit with the rest. It would be rejected. So you can't take any single part out, redesign it and plug it back into the system and make it work. You have to redesign all the parts at once. But no one is smart enough to do that, because it is too big and too complicated for any single person to see it as a whole. You have to get *everyone* working on *all* of it. You have to have enough interconnections among people who are doing that, so that they can see someone making a certain change in one part of the organization that might have implications for their part. It's an experiment on every part of the organization all the time. I can't prioritize that. I can't say one part is more important than another, because they are all part of the same thing. They all have to work together.

The way we pushed the organization into this grand experiment, into becoming internally unsuccessful, was by overloading it, by demanding much more of the system than its linkages as they were structured, which were very rigid and very vertical, could handle. In the language of complexity science you could say we pushed the organization into a state of chaos as a way of finding new, more adaptable, creative ways of operating in the new environment. I didn't know that language at the time; I just felt intuitively it was the way to go, even though I wasn't certain it would succeed. I did know it would be hard. I used to get people lining up outside my door, saying, "Bob, you've got to tell me; I've got five different things I have to do here. What's your priority? You have to prioritize these things for me." And I'd say, "Well, you'd agree we have to do this one; and you'd agree we have to do this one, too." And so on through the list. I'd say, "We have to do them all, and you are going to have to figure out how to do that." I knew that the minute I would prioritize it, we'd be back into the old model, of the boss having the answers and telling people what to do. But the truth was I couldn't prioritize the list, because we *did* have to do them more or less all at once.

I predicted that there would be certain people who would love this way of working, and there would be others who would start tearing their hair out and start looking for early retirement. We brought some early retirement programs in to help them. But many people were comfortable with a very ambitious set of demands and an environment that was changing under their feet, the cultural air which was changing its composition, and they liked that. The astonishing thing about the whole process was how fast it went—just a couple of years. Very soon people were self-organizing, posting proposals for a project they cared about, inviting others to join in. E-mail is the vehicle that makes it all possible, because it just rips through hierarchy. People started forming cells. They'd get reinforcement from places that had nothing to do with how the formal organizational chart worked; they just found each other, mostly through internal e-mail.

The reason this works is because it's what people really *want*. We're not trying to extort more work out of them. We're giving them an opportunity to grow and do things they *want* to do. There's a negotiation about that, of course; you can't *just* do the things you want to do. But if you do enough of that, so that this is worth caring about, it taps into a whole different level of involvement, commitment, creativity, and achievement.

What I wanted people to understand about this process was that if we have the right people, and we have a basic shared understanding of the kinds of things we wanted to happen in a generalized way, then you can allow people to organize themselves around their purposes. I was recently quoted as saying that what I really want to do for the budget process, for example, was have nobody sitting at the top saying "This is what we are spending on this." Instead, my hope is that someone will have an idea, and people will say, "Yes, I'd like to be part of that," and they'll do that if they think it would be fun and interesting, and help us accomplish our purpose. Let everybody do that, and that's the budget. The budget is collectively who is attracted to doing what, not just based on whim but on shared purpose.

This is a very idealized version, I know. But I would trust the process more than I trust a system that is operating on archaic information, on what we used to know when we were actually doing something, making a set of decisions you don't know much about, rather than letting the people who are engaged in that set of activities make those decisions. I don't know whether I would trust them individually any more than I trust myself as one individual to always optimize everything, but I'm prepared to trust some kind of collective placing of bets, if you have the right people and the right information available. It depends heavily on creating a very information-rich environment.

The Challenge of Teams

The first thing is to acknowledge to each other that this way of working is hard, for everybody. Fun, but hard. Second, unless you have people being authentic and caring, you won't achieve as much as you could otherwise. There was a study of successful teams versus less successful teams at Hewlett-Packard, and it showed that the key difference was that people in successful teams were *authentic* and they *cared.* That feels exactly right to me, from my own experience.

Years ago, when I was a young lawyer, I used to hang around the office late at night, trying to look good. That wasn't being authentic. We ought to be adult enough to get past that one, and trust that other people will judge us on our merit, not on the basis of how good we look. One of the first speeches I gave to the old Monsanto management was, "Hey, can we just stop trying to look good, can we just let go of that? It's a waste of everybody's time and energy. Just do it." Mixed results. But I feel very strongly about this. It's much harder to be something you aren't than to be something you are. It takes more effort, you have to be on guard all the time, you don't want to let that mask fall. I know this myself, when at times I felt myself in an environment where I didn't think people would value me for who I was, but wanted me to be something else. That's hard work, tiring, and I don't do it as well. I do me better than I do someone else. Inauthenticity diverts energy and makes us tired at the end of the day, so it's an efficiency as well as a mental health issue.

On the issue of caring, it's obvious that people behave differently when they are doing something they care about. They are more committed to their work, more willing to put in extra effort when the pressure is on. That's one of the advantages that Monsanto has over some companies, because the stuff we are doing is stuff that's easy to care about. It does matter, enormously, because we are trying to help people generate more food. We are trying to discover things that help people live longer and healthier lives. If I were making office supplies for example, I could do it, but it wouldn't be the same, I wouldn't *feel* the same. And when you are working with others on something you all care deeply about, it can be very powerful, both for productivity and in personal ways, too.

One of the dreams I have, and I think most people have, is to have a workplace in which you not only love your work, you also love the people you work with. The notion that commitment to each other at a deep level—not just a commitment because you are instrumental in accomplishing the task that I want accomplished, but because you in yourself are important—is a very powerful form of social organization. The question is how you create this on a scale larger than kinship, but I think it does in fact happen, at least sometimes. It's a fact of the workplace that you often end up loving the people you work with, but most people are understandably reluctant to talk about it. It's a taboo subject.

If you are working with people who really care about each other, they have an interest in your being healthy, in your being whole. They don't want you to be here every night until eleven o'clock. Doing that for long periods of time, it's not going to work for you. And if they care about you—not they as a company, this isn't an HR policy; I don't think we need to have a department of mental health—then they will support you and look out for your best interests. That's part of trying to have some justice in the workplace. Part of justice is to be seen for who you are, and be valued for who you are.

If we get authenticity and if we get caring in the workplace, then we've got something very important. The rest will fall into place. But I'm not being idealistic about it. My predecessor, Dick Mahoney, used to tell a story of one of the great puzzles he dealt with. He said, if you go around the company and talk to people, and ask them what was the best experience they had here, they would all talk about some kind of crisis, some sort of emergency mode when the flood was coming or the customer demanded something that we couldn't possibly do, and we'd lose the order, shut down the plant, or something. For some period of time everybody forgot all the stuff that they had learned as part of the job, and just did what they had to do, coming up with the unexpected, and enjoying it. Everyone would tell stories later about how some lowly person in the hierarchy came up with the idea that saved the day. They'd forget the clock and do miracles. Whether or not they win or lose, whether the flood wins or they win, is less important than that they had this peak experience.

Dick would then ask, "When this was all over, what did you do?" "Oh, we went back to the way it was before." That was the mystery. Why did that happen? How do you sustain that quality of peak experience? There's that William James phrase, the moral equivalent of war, trying to find that crisis mentality that pulls out the heroic in people. I don't know that you want everyone to operate in a mode of continuing crisis. That would be hard on the endocrine system, but I think everyone knows they can do a lot better than they have done. As we have found, it doesn't take much to make those improvements, and we are now doing a lot better than we were.

I said that this way of working—of self-organizing teams—is hard, and it's true, partly because it means the freedom that comes with it also means accepting uncertainty and responsibility. I've heard it suggested that because people have become used to being told what to do under the command and control model of management, they find freedom threatening or frightening in some way. I'm sure that can happen, but I haven't found that to be a big issue at Monsanto. I'd say that it isn't freedom they are afraid of. It is the possibility that you might be conning them, that you are giving them an *illusion* of freedom, but that if they exercise their freedom, you are going to slam them down. I haven't found a lot of examples of people being led out of their dungeons and dazzled by the light in a way that makes them incapable of acting. But what I *have* found is that they are afraid of being thrown back into the dungeon. You have to find a way of convincing them that this new way is *real,* that we are not going back to the old way, no matter what. I think people can handle freedom.

The Challenge of Leadership

I know that many business leaders are appalled at the prospect of letting go of control and of trusting the collective wisdom of their people. That hasn't been an issue for me. I said this recently, and it attracted some funny looks, because it is so distant from the traditional role of the CEO, but it's true. But that's not to say the whole process was easy, either. I went through an awful lot of self-doubt about this at the beginning of the transformation, because I didn't know whether it was going to work. I knew I was taking a big risk with a very successful agriculture business, and then with a very successful corporation, so I was nervous about it.

I had become chairman in April of 1995, and in June I had what was clearly going to be my signature meeting. I'd asked five hundred people from around the world to get together, some chosen on a hierarchical basis, some chosen as representatives of various populations around the company. I stood up at the end of each morning's activities, paced around on the platform, and talked about things on my mind that seemed to relate to the themes of that day, all very casual, spur-of-the-moment musings. You have to put that in the context of the kinds of meetings we and other corporations would typically have, where someone reads a lecture, all very formal. We didn't wear suits and ties, which was a big deal back then. The whole event brought up a lot of childhood fears for me of, "Gee, they're not going to like me. There are going to be a lot of people out there who will see this as threatening or weird in some way." The third day was about environmental sustainability, about why this was an important issue for Monsanto and why we had to have a special relationship to that issue. When I finished, I knew we were together on this. I knew we were on the right track, and that they would go with me; I could sense it physically. It was a very emotional moment. It's still emotional for me when I think about it now.

In the first year I was CEO, I really thought I ran the place. I was trying to change something, and I felt I was there pretty much by myself, but with a few people I had worked with in the Agriculture Group and who understood what we needed to do. But we were pushing against this enormous system. By midway into my second year, I realized I wasn't running it, that we had the right people, at least in a lot of places, and that *they* were doing it. I understood what they were doing, I understood where we were going. I understood what they were trying to accomplish, and I liked it. It felt good. By my third year, a lot of the time I didn't even understand it. And it felt wonderful. As is perfectly appropriate, it felt as if the place was outgrowing me.

The potential that is released this way took the organization further than I could *ever* have taken it as an act of will or an act of individual cognition. There's that line from Lao Tzu, to the effect that of the best leaders it is said, the people do not know they exist; and when the job is done, the people say, "We did it ourselves." I really believe that. Obviously if I think something is going off course, I've got to involve myself, but I try to do it in a way that explores the possibility that I'm right about it, and also explores the possibility that I'm wrong. I have to keep the leadership of the company fresh, so that we don't start falling into a new orthodoxy that's as maladaptive as the old one. And I have to try to influence the systems to keep them open. It's at a very abstract systems level that it seems to me I have to operate at. I have to identify places where there are constrictions or blindnesses, where there are denials, and try to help that out. But I don't then have to tell people what to do. If we have the right folks, and by and large we do, it's just going to work.

My role as CEO therefore becomes more and more one of trying to see us in the context of a broad world. My specialization is generalization. That's something I can do from where I sit that most other people can't do, because they don't get the same view.

The New Business Environment: Economic Webs

The key characteristic of the business environment of the life sciences industry is its pace of change. What's happening in agriculture, for instance, is phenomenal. The earth is shifting in a ten-thousand-year-old industry. Agriculture has changed radically in recent times, but by a series of relatively slow evolutionary steps. Agriculture of twenty-five years ago was very different from the agriculture a hundred years earlier, for example. But the pace of innovation is now accelerating, and decisions have to be made in months, not in decades. What's driving this is principally to do with what you can do with genetic modification, producing plants that are resistant to certain insects, for example, through inserting genes into the germ plasm of seeds. This is just the beginning, but it is changing the basic working stuff of agriculture. It's an information industry now, a knowledge industry. The same is true in the pharmaceutical industry, and we believe it will soon be true in the field of human nutrition.

Many people are aware of Moore's Law of semiconductor technology. In 1965 Gordon Moore, who later became a co-founder of Intel Corporation, noted that the number of transistors that could be put on a silicon chip was doubling every eighteen to twenty-four months. He said that this trend would drive exponential growth in computing power, which turned out to be one of the best long-term predictions in history. Not long ago I sensed that something similar was happening in the life sciences industry. The understanding of gene sequences and functions was burgeoning, driven by new technologies, making procedures faster and cheaper. For instance, in 1974 the cost to find the DNA sequence of a single gene was $2.5 million, and it took many months. In 1998 the cost is about $150, and it can be done in a few days. I wanted to back up my intuition about the pace of change, and so I went out and got some data, and it turned out to support the intuition. I therefore coined what I call Monsanto's Law: "The amount of genetic information used in practical applications will double every year or two."

The life sciences business environment is therefore very different from that of the traditional chemical or agriculture business. Fundamentally, the chemical business doesn't have the same growth and change characteristics as the life sciences sector. It was hard to run what is an essentially defensive, slow-growth, slow-to-decline business in the same place you are trying to run an explosive growth business. The tempo is different. The kinds of people these businesses attract are different. Maybe it could be done if we built enough walls between them. But there's a cost to building and maintaining walls, a financial cost and a psychic cost. But from the standpoint of the life sciences it created needs to compromise and sub-optimize what we were doing. The same was true from the perspective of the chemical business. We were not devoting the passion to that business that it deserved. Culturally there is a big difference between a place that's based on constant innovation and speed to market on one hand, and a place based on reliability, predictability, customer service on the other. So we decided to separate them last year as part of the transformation we've been going through: the newly created Solutia Inc. continues much of the traditional chemical business of the old Monsanto; and the newly transformed Monsanto Company has become exclusively a life sciences company.

If you want to know about the business environment of the life sciences industry, the computer industry is a good model for what is and what lies ahead. A few years ago I joined the board of Silicon Graphics, largely because I admired what they had accomplished and wanted to understand how that high-speed culture worked. And now I feel that we are as evolved as they are. It's happened very fast. One issue is how you deal with information. You want to protect proprietary information, but some of the traditional ways of doing that can slow you down. The opposite model is to put everything you learn on the Internet, and count on being able to get to the market faster than anybody else. The notion that you don't want to treat this intellectual treasure as gold bars you put in the vault of a bank, with Swiss guards outside, but that you treat this as a world of abundant information, with more than enough out there to keep us all busy, is intriguing to me. We're still trying to find that balance.

We've seen that in this kind of business environment, high-tech companies form alliances with each other that are constantly shifting as partners' needs and interests change. This has led to the formation of very dynamic economic webs that have many of the characteristics of biological ecosystems. The same thing is already happening in the life sciences industry.

When you are dealing with large, complex systems, you cannot internally develop or buy or own all the capabilities you need in order to make the system create competitive advantage, either for you as a separate firm or for the domain in which you are engaged. You have to become part of a network of companies whose interests overlap and whose interactions bring greater value to the network as a whole. It's like creating a meta-organization, and it gets very complex, like an ecosystem. I don't view what we are doing as simply an increasing-returns kind of model, in which one system or technology will dominate a particular market; it is more interesting and more subtle than that. It's about developing a standard, developing the best network, the best system, and that will tend to attract the best technologies and the best new participants. But it's all evolving and changing, and the roles of individual participants keep evolving and changing.

We are trying to do some very large things with global agriculture, which is a trillion-dollar system. Obviously, no one can own or dominate a system that big and complicated and adaptive. If one company or network owned it they'd screw it up. That's the lesson of the Soviet Union. The way we see it has some connection to the concept of diversity. The idea of having independent actors who express their perspectives as part of a decision-making process that can't be hierarchical gives you a better opportunity of hearing more and learning more, and coming up with new ways to understand what you are seeing.

We are in new territory here, with these alliance networks, and trying to figure out what the rules of engagement are in that network is very tricky. I truly don't know how this will work out. I mean, what are the obligations that you undertake when you form these relationships? One side of it says that because speed and trust are directly correlated, I have to behave in a way that is far beyond legal obligations, that really treats my collaborators as part of my family. What I know, they know, and what they know, I know. That requires a level of consciousness and a level of shared commitment I'm not sure is always present. But to the extent I allow the trust to be eroded, I'm undercutting the very thing for which I entered into the relationship.

It's also not clear what the obligations are, in the sense of optimizing the value of the network. Who do you share what with? How many people? How do you get coordination? Everybody says, "Yes, I'm prepared to enter collaboration, as long as I'm at the center of the web, so I have a series of one-on-one relationships, but I'm the only place where all the relationships come together; I'm the integrator of the system, and I get all the value of the system." Nice work if you can get it. People won't want to enter into exploitative relationships—at least not for very long. So, the rules of a network evolve, and probably represent a new form of legal and economic organization. There's no charter for it. If I were able to say, here are the ground rules that we will all follow—here's what we share, here's how we resolve disputes—that would be useful. But it doesn't exist.

To what extent can we shape the environment in which the rules for networks emerge? Somebody has to lead, I think, but the form of that leadership and the nature of it are unclear.

The New Business Environment: Ecological Webs

About four years ago we got a group of our people together and asked them to think about what was happening in the world and the implications for Monsanto. Out of that emerged an awareness of human impact on the environment, and the prospect of human and ecological disaster. And around *that* coalesced a commitment to sustainable development, which you might describe as finding ways to continue economic growth while not negatively impacting the environment—even *improving* the environment, because that is going to be necessary.

Being aware of the environment is part of our times, of course. But we really have no choice if we want our descendants to live with the kind of quality of life some of us enjoy today. Demographers tell us that in thirty or forty years from now, the global population will have doubled, to around ten to twelve billion people. It's obvious that, with the technology we have, we will be facing a Malthusian crash of population or an ecological catastrophe. Probably both. I don't know how much time we have. I don't think anyone does. My assumption, for what it's worth, is that we are unlikely to do anything that's fundamentally irredeemable over, say, the next twenty years. And by that time we will either be mostly operating on a more constructive paradigm, or we'll be running out of time to change. It's already happening in biodiversity. We are causing species to go extinct at much too rapid a rate, and we have no idea what the consequences of that might be, but we know that they are likely to be very dangerous. Our world's ecological webs cannot indefinitely resist our impact on them.

So what is our responsibility here? The model that most of us were pursuing until a few years ago was, "We don't want to be cast as the villains. We know we are putting stuff out into the air and into the water; we'll clean it up." You have to do that. But moving from the concept of an awareness of pollution to the concept of sustainability is a huge step. It broadens the inquiry, and it takes blame out of the equation. It is not about, "You're a bad guy." It's about, "We don't have technologies or systems that enable us to produce enough wealth to support people of this world in ways that can last. We just don't know how to do it." If you phrase the issue that way, it is less a matter of good guy and bad guy. It is, "We have a very big, very tough problem here."

The problem is more about technology than about anything else. It is about political systems as well, of course. It is also about justice. But it is fundamentally about technology, because right now, if you had ideal political systems, everyone operating out of the good part of their hearts, you could not produce a decent life for even six billion people, let alone ten or twelve, using the technologies we have, without destroying the biological systems we all depend on. Companies like ours are good at finding and developing new technologies. We just need to find a new criterion for the technologies we work on: they have to be more sustainable than the ones they replace. We're working in at least one of the technologies that we believe can help the world move toward sustainability. That's biotechnology. With biotechnology it will be possible to produce plants that have reduced needs for added chemicals, and can grow more efficiently; and perhaps even produce some of the chemicals themselves that today we get from the chemical industry. All of this reduces the impact on the environment, and leads to ways of producing more food than we can now. I don't know how we are going to get there, but I *think* we can, and I *know* we have to. Not striving for sustainable development is simply not an option.

One Path, Many Paths

Sometimes people at other companies think they should imitate what we're doing. The first thing I'd say is, "Stop looking to us. We followed our path, it has to do with *our* history and *our* business." I don't think we are a model for anybody, although I know there are companies who are using us as a model. If we'd had a model, I don't think we would have done as well as we have, because we might have felt constrained to do things in a certain way that didn't fit us. The most important thing is that this is an experiment, an experiment still in progress. We like to think we function differently from everyone else, and in some respects it's probably true that we are a little further out than most companies are; but in other respects we are probably a little more traditional than we'd like to believe. Our behavior and our rhetoric still aren't fully in sync, especially when we get scared. When we are anxious about something we regress to less interesting models. But we do keep trying.

Because we are in times of unprecedented change, unprecedented discontinuity, you need to keep enough flexibility so that if you face something surprising you can take advantage of it, or recoil from it, whatever is appropriate. I think, because of the way we work, we can do this a lot better than in the past. And my guess is that most organizations would know how to do all this, too. If they took people off to a mountain and sat there for a couple of days, they'd come to the same kinds of conclusions we have. People can see lots of things that they know aren't productive, things that are demeaning to people, things that slow them down and restrict them. We all know we aren't achieving our best potential, and it doesn't take too much thought to recognize why. I think most people would come to the same kinds of conclusions we have. It's part of being human and trying to do work in a way you can feel good about it. For most people, the hard part is translating those sentiments from the mountain to the workplace. But it *can* be done.

Chapter 13

Alchemists: Changing of the Guardian

Every corporate giant says it wants to change. Few can do it. *Every young company starts as a natural force for change.* Few can sustain it. *Every organization has people who think they want to be agents of change.* Few can survive it.[1]

In organizations that are high on efficiency, stability, compliance, and organizational mandates, where title, entitlement, and position are important, initiating change can be a daunting task. In such organizations, high value is often placed on loyalty, dependability, and a strong work ethic, and on preserving tradition and heritage—all admirable qualities. Too often, however, such organizations also display an overreliance on past corporate experiences—"this is how we've always done things"—which ossifies thinking, and, in turn, can stifle innovation and creativity. In their book *Please Understand Me,* Marilyn Bates and David Keirsey describe this collective mind-set as the "Guardian temperament."[2]

Change efforts often fail in Guardian organizations because, by its nature, change challenges and threatens the organization's fundamental desire to attain and maintain stability and control, bound as they are to established modes of doing things. As Peter Senge notes, "The harder you push, the harder the system pushes back."[3] Often, such organizations will initiate change efforts, but insist on controlling the effort, which effectively prevents change from happening. For those members who were skeptical about the effort in the first place, they create a self-fulfilling prophecy. What it boils down to is that you can't have it both ways—you can't change and maintain the status quo at the same time.

How to introduce new ways of thinking and new ways of working, how to deal with resistance in Guardian organizations, are among the initial challenges that change agents face. It requires a kind of alchemy. Alchemists were those who could "transform something common into something special." The alchemy of change agents is to create novelty out of the status quo. Recognizing what change already exists in normal conditions of the organization can instigate the alchemy of changing of the Guardian. Does the organization *acknowledge* the need for change? Does the organization *recognize* what is already changing? These are some of the questions that change agents who think in complexity terms ask, which give an entrance into working organically with the organization as a complex adaptive system.

Change agents who try to introduce complexity thinking face even greater obstacles than normal. Complexity by its nature is polychronic, that is, simultaneous, nonlinear, system-oriented, and multidimensional. In a context where the mentality is scheduling, compartmentalizing, doing one thing at a time, implementing change then needs to be fashioned into a linear, step-by-step method. This linear approach to change flies in the face of complexity's intrinsic nonlinearity. Change agents who try to introduce complexity thinking in this context are fraught with contradictions. Needing to provide concrete facts and a step-by-step method for implementing change in order to be taken seriously, and as a way of engaging the Guardian, change agents end up perpetuating linear thinking, the very thing they are trying to change. In defense of themselves, complexity thinkers often revert to a reductionistic argument to make a point that others are thinking linearly—another contradiction. Not surrendering to linear demands for specific goals, predictable steps, and defined outcomes is not only difficult but frustrating. It is entering, at best, murky waters where two different minds juxtapose, and, at worst, a stone wall of irreconcilable difference.

Although difficult, it is, however, not impossible. According to Keirsey and Bates, in order to implement change successfully, the change agent's approach must be sensitive to the traditions, values, and beliefs of the organization. Approaches that are not inclusive of the existing culture, such as subverting, dismissing, or imposing ideas, will ultimately fail. It is about working with and immersing in what *is,* with the way the organization currently functions, and finding value in that, rather than just valuing what it ought to be. From a complexity perspective, the change agent needs to hold a paradox—valuing both the tradition of the organization and a nonlinear view—knowing that from this tension something new will emerge.

Veteran change agent Mark Maletz, who created a school for change for industry giant Siemens Nixdorf (SNI), developed a model for effective change: "Each candidate in the change agent school must have a strong project, clearly linked to one of the company's strategic goals, and supported by a senior executive."[4] Maletz believes it's the change agent's job to create tension rather than balance. "Ambiguity defines the work of the change agent: not a comfortable balance, but a dynamic tension between opposing poles."[5] In other words, the change agent finds the edge of chaos, the zone of creative adaptability in the organization. The place of tension and ambiguity common to Guardian organizations today, the junction for potential change, is found between the desire to preserve tradition and the desire to exist in a business environment that *is* change, and where most organizations have been taken over by change.

David Clark, who heads the information technology team at W.I. Gore & Associates, the maker of Gore-Tex, adds that the informal network is the change agent's source of influence. "People have to trust you, and networking becomes the way you build trust. Once you have it, you can initiate change. There are no top-down edicts here. It's all informal, based on building your network."[6] From a complexity perspective, it's working with organizations organically, entering the culture, and rather than seeking a 100 percent change effort, it's making small changes that can lead to big effects.

Such are guidelines for the alchemist who strives to change the Guardian organization toward a nonlinear way of thinking. Many people who embrace complexity principles try to bring these ideas to their organizations. Everyone can be a change agent in their organization. But, as you will see in the following stories, this is usually easier said than done.

Three Stories

The three stories that follow are testimonies of people who attempted to change organizational thinking in line with complexity ideas. Lily's and Laura's stories illustrate attempts that ultimately failed to change their organizations but led them personally to other horizons. Both women, you will see, were acutely aware of the dark side of the Guardian. You will see that Lily, a designated change agent in the organization, lacked a strong project. Her task was to help the organization build a team-based structure, a project that was linked to the company's strategic goals, but the task was vague. Her approach to team building was based on the self-organizing principle of complexity, which was not supported by senior executives and resisted by the team itself. And overall, creating teams was undermined because the organization didn't recognize its impact on the community of which it was a part.

Laura, on the other hand, a self-appointed change agent in her organization, had none of the three in place—no project, no strategic connection, and no support. Neither Lily nor Laura had a strong informal network. Without these supports in place, the walls of tradition became impervious to their efforts for change. The fire in their struggle toward a different way of being and doing within their organizations was extinguished by a lack of influence, and collapsed into ashes of helplessness and resignation.

Curt's story, on the other hand, confirms that real change is possible, and that complexity ideas can grow in organizations. Curt, a leader in his organization, is effectively a change agent. He is a change leader who both leads with vision and follows the needs of the groups. You will see that most of the elements for effective change are present in his story—a strong informal network and executive support. In addition, he introduced new ideas while still respecting the history and tradition of the organization. By the nature of his position as a leader, he didn't have a strong proximal project but rather a strong purpose.

All three change agents do have something in common. Whether the organizations changed or not, one thing is certain—the change agents themselves did change.

Lily: The Masked Marvel

Lily, a change agent at a large timber company and a big advocate of complexity and self-organizing, tried to apply these principles as her organization experimented with creating a team-based structure. As you will see, she recognizes that imposing teams onto people doesn't always develop into a spirit of teamwork. Generally, she has a brilliance for seeing the subtext of the organization—what is really going on rather than what is said.

Similarly, imposing, rather than cultivating, an environment for a model of self-organization for creating teams can be problematic. In her heroic David and Goliath–like attempts to introduce a complexity way of working, she countered the existing hierarchical structures by not imposing structures on her team, with hopes that a structure would emerge from the group itself. In doing so, Lily neglected to recognize clearly enough the paradox of self-organization—the need for both structure and no structure. Without structure, the team became chaotic. With structure only, they became regimented into a hierarchical way of working with separate tasks. Although Lily's heart was clearly in the right place—her efforts rose from genuine care and her strategies and advice were sound and potentially powerful—it was ultimately not enough to influence the existing culture. Lily (a pseudonym) recounts her struggle in her own words.[7]

Change in a Traumatized Community

In the timber industry that I worked for, senior management wanted the workplace to shift to a more self-organizing approach. They want to shift from a hierarchical structure to a team-based structure that they called "high-performance work teams." My job as a change agent was to create and implement that process, and to develop leadership.

As a pilot project, management wanted to take one of the units and make it into a team system that would exist within the traditional hierarchical organization. Before this began, they took the planning department of 150 employees and changed the technology, which took away tasks from people, and eliminated eighty jobs. Now you have to realize that this plant was in a small rural town of a thousand people, and the company had recently closed one facility, eliminating over two hundred jobs. At that facility, the average time people had worked there was twenty-seven years. Some people were laid off after working there forty years. When we closed the plant, families would weep, crying, "How could the organization do this to our families?" These folks had been working the land for generations and had been supported by the timber industry forever. It was all they knew, and now it was taken away from them.

I was involved in closing this mill. Management said they had to close it because of environmental reasons. It was my job to say to those who were fired, "Hey, look, we have this nifty training benefit package and you can go to the community college and take some courses!" Maybe 30 percent took advantage of it; the rest resorted to alcohol or abuse. They just weren't prepared to go out into the market; they weren't able to keep up with the change and the new demands. Many were illiterate. I mean these people lived in one town and ran one machine for their whole life, and the thought of going to college was overwhelming.

The remaining staff were supposed to move toward teamwork, and were told that they all have the power to make decisions, while eighty of their former co-workers, who are probably their neighbors, were out of work. Management didn't see the irony in what they were saying. Here's how the scenario went. They said to the employees, "Okay so we laid everyone off," but of course management wouldn't talk about *that*. They said, "You're here though," which meant you should be grateful. Management wanted teamwork, they said, but we knew it wasn't because they cared about people working together. It was because management heard that it would make employees more productive. And women especially will be exploited, because they care. "So let's get to work!" management said, as if they could be trusted, despite what had happened.

Change That Doesn't Change

The employees were really used as tools; they *felt* like tools; they *knew* they were interchangeable parts; that this bullshit that "Employees are our greatest resources" was just that, bullshit. In reality, the workers knew they couldn't make mistakes, even though they were told they could. And they knew they couldn't complain because they'd be replaced. With plenty of people waiting for jobs, they'd be ousted pretty easily.

The employees see and live with hypocrisy. A team leader, the "chosen one," is handpicked, and has the spotlight shining on him. Everyone knows that the chosen one is in a very precarious position. It's a fact of life that he or she can sink at any moment. He might last a day, a month, a year. So the employees' response is, "Okay, he's the chosen one and we'll be quiet and work hard and wait it out, or get drunk." In order for a leader to hold on to the light for a month to several years, it requires silence and denial, because he is expected to always shine and never ever have a dissenting voice. One leader called me and said he just wanted to talk to me about what was really going on. All these clandestine conversations. What happens is things start falling through the cracks and they can't keep up, but they also can't say anything either.

When team-based units were introduced, the supervisor's title was changed to team leader, but their behavior didn't change. They were still supervisors saying how it had to be and the employees were saying, "Whatever." The employees weren't fooled: "You call this team-based? Fine, but we know you call the shots." The internal structure is command and control—do as you're told—and people on the floor know that. In reality, they'd rather have management say they're going to tell them what to do, because that's what's really happening. That would be more honest. They're really offended by the empty notion of empowerment. Use the word and you can see the rage in their face. They don't like pretense.

The problem with changing to a team-based system is that if you're working within a structure where the dominant power doesn't recognize the role of power and oppression, then you can't make real changes. When management is unaware of the shadow system; when they don't know the impact of their decisions; and when they blame the employees for not producing; then changing hierarchy to teamwork becomes impossible. Without a discussion of how the dominant culture functions, or an understanding of it, there's no way to address it and change it. Change was limited to the external structure, and if those structures didn't work, it was said to be the employees' fault.

The best way to develop a team-based way of working is to just find out what the employees do best and make sure they're aligned with the vision. Are their needs being met and part of the flow? Are the employees valued? Instead what happened was that management tried to create teams by saying, "We're going to work as a team and this is how it's going to look. You all have to communicate well, make decisions together, be multiskilled, and then you can be a *more* interchangeable part in the system. This is how it is, you've got to like it and enjoy it; you've got to do it, and be cheerful when you're doing it!"

Change—Wanting It and Not Wanting It

So as a change agent, I was supposed to do this with the accounting department. I worked with them for a year. The department consisted of fourteen people—two bosses, accountants, and assistant accountants. Accounting people are in this profession because they like to work with numbers rather than with people, and they prefer to be solitary. And now they're being told to become part of this team-based thing, and that they have to know each other's jobs. They're still being treated like machines, even though it's under the guise of team policy. And they didn't *want* to become a team.

So when I came on board they were worried—"She's going to drop a bomb; she's going to make us into a team. Oh, no!" At the start, I brought in a facilitator to address the individual differences in the group. One of the things that came out was that this department felt very oppressed by the high-performance work system. They experienced it as a concrete image. The image was of a hovercraft—they couldn't see it, they didn't know when it would land, but it was above them, hanging, a shadow over them, constantly threatening. I knew that to force them into a team shouldn't be a goal. Instead, the goal, as I saw it, should be to improve the way individuals work together, to attend to the issues they had raised and the complaints they brought to management, and to make it easier to work in the current environment. Rather than saying, "You're going to look like a team," I wanted them to self-organize.

The hovercraft represented their lack of trust. They had seen enough failures in their department, in strategies, and approaches, to know they would have to go through pain. There was a collective sigh of relief when I told them we weren't going to do this team thing *to* them. Two surveys that had been done on this department showed that employees needed consistent leadership and consistent messages. I took that seriously.

My grand scheme was to focus on Melinda, a woman brought into the leadership position because management needed a woman, like they needed an African-American on another project. Now this is a woman who had spent her whole life working independently, auditing people, not managing them. She wanted the leadership position, the title, the pay, but she didn't want the responsibility—she hated it. It was hell for her. Melinda had so many gaps in her interpersonal skills, she knew she shouldn't be doing this kind of work. I told her there wasn't any shame in finding work that played on her strengths, rather than her weaknesses. That wasn't an acceptable option for her because she felt compelled to go through with it, being the first woman in a position of leadership in the history of what seemed to be all of humankind! I watched her struggle, and she told me she could develop her interpersonal skills. I thought it unlikely. Melinda was a very shy, introverted person, very skilled technically, but hated group interaction and hated dealing with people!

Melinda has a great heart and wanted to trust and be trustworthy. She wanted it intellectually, but in reality, letting go wasn't possible for her. Her whole job as an auditor had been to find the flaws in a system and to control them. Even her title had been controller! Being team leader required a whole new set of skills, and failing at it took a toll on her self-esteem. Her weaknesses were pecked at all the time, and her strengths weren't being recognized or valued. You could see her confidence in interactions deteriorating over time.

I said to Melinda that her most challenging role would be to stand back and allow the group to come up with recommendations, to support them, and get the resources they needed. If she started vetoing what her team brought forward, I felt everything would be lost. I said her role as leader was to support, provide, and trust. And to know that along the way, she would make mistakes, and that this was going to be a messy process.

To the group, I posed the questions of how they wanted to work and how they wanted to make decisions. Some wanted to facilitate this discussion, and this attempt at claiming power uncorked a lot of emotions. For several sessions, they vented; they stated the abuses. I knew they had to come to this point of getting it out. Mostly the harm done to them was in management not walking the talk, saying one thing and doing another; and in the employees being told that they all can have a say in the process and finding out they really didn't. They had been burned over and over again by this hypocrisy. So when new strategies were imposed on them, like the team-based system—the flavor of the month—they responded cynically. Instead of efficacy, what they had developed was learned helplessness.

I recognized I was in treacherous waters, because if the accountants didn't come to have an effect on how they worked together, then I would be seen as someone who just perpetuated what was. So I said "Screw the change agent role; I'll just try to make a difference individually." I saw my sole role as protecting and honoring what they came up with to change the climate of work. And that their agreement with Melinda, that their suggestions were not only heard but could be implemented, was intact.

The first thing they came up with was that they felt their information was so sensitive that they wanted a facilitator from outside. They didn't want anyone who knew Melinda or the big boss, Henry. It was tough to hear that. I kept thinking, "God, what have they got to say?" I said "Okay," instead of saying "No, you need me." I felt my part of the deal was to respond to what they wanted. I amazed them every time by coming through with my word. That's the healing process—coming through with your word. It was about my trusting them, which was a way to try to reestablish their trust in the company.

The downside of this was a lot of uncertainty—what were they going to come up with in terms of working together? Here are these accountants who work with certainty and numbers, and now they were faced with not knowing from one day to the next how they would look. Sometimes they turned on me: "What kind of facilitator are you?" they'd say when I refused to tell them what to do. They wanted a road map, perfectly laid out. On the other hand, they wanted trust and respect. Which was it to be for me? To provide or not to provide a road map for them? They couldn't believe that I didn't have a master plan. It was worse for them that a master plan *didn't* happen rather than that one did! They wanted a plan because there's safety in it, or at least an illusion of safety.

The way I dealt with their insecurity was to say that it was a normal part of the process, which pissed them off. "Oh right," they would say, "it's normal. Thanks a lot! See if you like feeling this way! Just tell us what we're supposed to be doing." I told them to listen to what they were asking for—hierarchy. They were trapped in a paradox: they feared that things *wouldn't* change; and they feared that they *would*.

My continued vigilance about not enforcing a solution, allowing the uncomfortableness and not trying to fix it, was dangerous for me and for Melinda, because externally the implicit demand on us was to make changes without making any waves. The system was saying, "Change but don't change." So we went along and I was thinking that this openness I was creating, this struggle we were experiencing was great. And they looked at me like I was an alien, and told me I was out of touch with reality. They wanted structure.

A three-ring-binder person eventually took my place, someone who played by the rules, played it safe. She adopted a method rewarded by the organization—that is, work with specific models for moving into a team base. Back to imposing a model, the same old thing: "Let's do teamwork without really incorporating it." It's just a Band-Aid, and the accounting group were crying out for it. They were caught in a contradiction of "I don't like the old way; give me back the old way."

I'm hoping they've had enough taste of freedom from when I was working with them that there is no going back. That was the case for me. I left the company soon after that and started my own consultancy.

Laura Odell: Agent 007

We met Laura at a complexity conference on self-organization at Santa Fe in April 1997. Laura, a special event meeting planner for the Coca-Cola Company, had tried, like a secret agent, to affect the company's bureaucratic system because she saw it stifling people and limiting their potential. On her own initiative, she challenged the co-workers, managers, and eventually the president to think differently, to see the organization through a lens of complexity, to see it as a whole rather than working parts, to expand the vision of what people and the organization could be. Her brilliance in this endeavor rests in her provocative questions and illuminating metaphors that consistently cut to the heart of the matter. However, being outside her realm of jurisdiction, the task proved to be too daunting for one person. But although her efforts ultimately failed, it is surprising just how far commitment, vision, and passion took her—on a journey of seeing in a different way. Laura's story follows in her own words.[8]

Seeing Limitations

For me, the whole thing began with a team-building effort. The company had a couple of excellent programs, looking at how we can get our people to work together for the same purpose. An excellent concept. They put fifteen or twenty of us out in the woods for two and a half days, at a small inn in the north Georgia mountains. Through the process of many exercises—such as running an imaginary company and outward-bound stuff—we all learned a lot. I know I did.

For instance, I realized that job titles are limiting, because they give people beliefs about who they are and how their relationships can be. Managers play it safe behind their titles and are afraid to go beyond them. Each of us is limited to our title. I'm limited by my boss as to what I can do; he's limited by his. We learn that from our parents, from authority figures. We come to believe that we can't go beyond their authority, which limits our potential. But what if we got rid of all that, got rid of that frame of reference of how we should be?

When we dropped our roles in this training, we saw each other for the first time. We came to be ourselves. People spoke out; some cried; we saw exactly where people were. What mattered was not what someone's title was, but who they were as a person. We came to understand each other better; our strengths, our weaknesses. But we also came to see that when we went beyond the sacred cow of roles, we were limitless. We could do incredible things. We became aware of how powerful we were, not just as individuals but as a group.

Seeing the System

We went back to work and tried to sustain what we'd learned. We wanted to have projects together and work on them together. That's when I began to see the system—the hierarchy, the bureaucracy that people can hide behind. It's the order imposed on the organization, which makes people have to be something in particular, which limits what they can and can't do. We tried for a while to sustain this sense of cooperation and sharing knowledge we'd achieved, but it didn't take long for the system to say, "You don't have time for that; you've got other things to do." Our new way of being had to cease to exist. And it wasn't just the system; we did it to ourselves. We went back to our titles and roles, and became a part and a function of the system again. I'd say it was fear: "This is my role and if I don't play my role, they won't need me anymore, and I won't have a job."

It came back to being limited again. You say to yourself, "If I'm not limited by my boss, then what is he? He's supposed to manage me. What if I start working on something that he can't control, then where will he be?" And his boss has the same thing imposed on him: "I put you there to manage her, why aren't you doing that?" What they're saying is, "This is all you are; this is all you can be." It's like having your back to the future. It's perpetuating the past, perpetuating the same: "Let's keep it the way it is because we've succeeded at this." Once you do that, the organization turns inward and you have to keep it alive, which gets into maintenance, and that creates procedures. Now you need people to follow procedures, to keep the system going, and people become fuel: "Let's keep this in place because if we don't we might fail." Now we're doomed to succeed in the same old way.

But what if we see beyond that, beyond the familiar, the assumed, the expected? Now we're not stuck, but evolving. And with that comes renewal, possibility, and pure potential. Take, for example, a fish. The fish lives in an aquarium. It has its little plants, rocks, artificial light, and its boundaries. It can't go beyond the glass. Now we have another fish who lives in a river. This one is going to bump into new areas of challenge, see things differently. This one sees day and night. It becomes part of the river itself. This fish is growing, adapting. It can grow to its full potential while the other one is limited to the tank. Certainly there are more risks and dangers in the river, but the fish in the tank has its dangers, too—its biorhythms probably get messed up being in artificial light all the time.

The same thing with organizations. They say, "Don't go beyond the glass; play your part, and don't go beyond that part because it doesn't help the whole." When actually it's the other way around. It's the whole, the system, that needs help. How are we going to find that river of potential instead of using people as fuel to feed and perpetuate the system? There are passages in the Bible of the beasts that devour humanity. Humanity can't be itself and reach its potential when people are being used as fuel for the system and when the system is more important than the people in it.

Now what does that have to do with the Coca-Cola Company? What if we look at it as a whole and feel part of that whole? What if it wasn't just about a drink? What if it was about customers, people, education, a part of humanity? No telling what I can bring to it and, equally, everyone else. If only it could value people instead of just profits. I mean, it's the most recognized trademark in the world.

Seeing Barriers

I started seeing the system for what it was; this was new for me, to really see it. I observed how it operated, saw what it did to people. I was watching, not ridiculing. That's when I saw the barrier to ideas. What if I have a vision to share? How do I get it in the system? They can't see me seeing anything because I'm in a part of the system that shouldn't be seeing. I can't act on ideas because it's a closed system and only certain people are privy to act upon them. I started seeing the people as puppets in a play; they would do anything to keep the same reality—their titles, their money, all the things the system gives them to keep them in their place. I saw brilliant people—the best educated, the most talented. I saw the younger ones being invited more readily into the system because they were easily programmable. I saw their vitality and life, and then I watched the system stifle that—their disappointment when a great idea of theirs was put aside because they weren't supposed to have something to say about that, because it wasn't their job.

The bureaucratic system is based on fear and control. It doesn't allow openness; it doesn't really allow people to truly work together. But what if people transcend the system and they become something else?

Seeing Yourself

When you're participating in the system, you can't see it because you're in it; going by the rules and staying within the rules. I was dutiful. I gave myself over. I was intimidated. It's nobody's fault. It was me that gave myself over. It was really about my courage to *be*. From this vantage point of reclaiming myself, I began to see authority differently—the way they are, which led me to making different choices through that awareness. Reclaiming myself was really a process of taking back my authority through self-reflection. Why do I feel this way? Why do I let it happen? Why look at authority as authority? What is sacred? And it's getting rid of it. I'm the authority. It's my life; I have one life to live. I'm it and you're not responsible for my life.

Each of us decides if we want to participate in the system or not. And we decide whether we want to share what we're seeing with people. There were pockets of people who would secretly talk to me, but not openly. They would get all excited about an idea. I'd see the light in them, and I'd ask, "Why don't we go tell them?" And they'd say, "Oh, no, that's not what they want us to do." I would ask, "How do you know? And who's *they* anyway?" I'd watch them get to a point, and then back off. It's like Chuck Yeager, who was the first pilot to break through the sound barrier. Before he broke through the barrier, the plane was shaking so badly, he pulled back. And he said, "Oh man, this isn't working." But he went back up and did it again. He went up several times. Then one time, when again it seemed like his plane was falling apart, nuts and bolts flying everywhere, and he thinks that he can't do it—he goes for it and pushes the throttle. The plane almost completely falls apart. And then he breaks through the sound barrier, and it was so smooth and so beautifully silent, he thought he had died and gone to heaven. He did it; he broke through the barrier.

The people in the system are at that same edge—they can't break through their barrier. They keep backing off. As long as they back off, it is what it is. By not breaking through their barriers, they perpetuate it as it is. Keeping people from creating new ideas and from making connections with other people—which is what's going to create something else—if you keep people from that, then they're only parts that continue to do their job. All that does is perpetuate their existence and creates nothing new for Coca-Cola. But what if Coca-Cola's managers had a belief in people, in ideas, an openness to seeing where we can all go, and be willing to play? It might be a little risky, but the possibilities are greater, like the river. The aquarium is safe, you get fed every day, but guess what? You can be replaced; you can float to the top and they'll just throw someone else in.

Seeing Others

There's this Face to Face forum that happens regularly, where the organization can talk to the president of the company. At one of these meetings, after the president talked about this new knowledge system, I stood up and said that I understood what he was saying, how he wanted to capture knowledge in the system, but I wanted to know, "What if I had a new idea; how would I get it in that system?" He made a joke of it, he objectified me, saying something like, "Did I have an idea about changing the formula of Coke?" Everybody laughed, and I just looked at him. And then he said that what I was talking about was communication, and if I had an idea I should tell my manager, and he would tell his, and it needed to go through the proper channels. Hearing that, I thought I had a better chance at winning the lottery than I did for having a new idea that might become something. I knew it would be stopped before it ever got anywhere.

My manager thought I was crazy. He said he'd had a dozen people come up to him and tell him they couldn't believe I stood up to ask that question. And I said, "What's a Face to Face for, if not to ask questions?" Then I asked him if he knew what my question was. He said he didn't. Then I asked him, "How can you tell me what you think of it?" He didn't say anything. I had a lot of people say to me that if I didn't like how things were going, I should leave. Fair enough. They didn't see that I loved this organization and my faith in its enormous potential for humanity.

I did start having a conversation with the president. He came to understand that I was talking about a state of being and creativity. He asked me what he should *do*. I told him that complexity doesn't work that way. I told him I couldn't tell him what to *do*. The hows would emerge from the purpose, and the whys. He said he wanted tactics. And I said the tactics would emerge from the vision. If the vision was to go outside the aquarium, then the tactics would emerge from that. I ended up making a deal. I would give him seven steps if he would be open, have a dialogue with me, so that together we could figure it out. I suggested that we spend a couple of days working on this. He told me he couldn't get away for a whole day, but he'd give me an hour. I was instructed to get on his calendar, to call his secretary. I knew exactly what he was doing. He thought that just giving me the time of day was cool. That's where he was. "Okay, I'll get on your calendar."

We had many conversations. If he wanted to unleash the potential in people, it couldn't happen within the system. The system was too strong and powerful; it would kill the initiative. I told him that. "We can get a team of people out of the system, let them start from scratch, create a purpose and a vision, and watch how fast they will grow." At first he was open, and then he became fearful. I think he was afraid of losing his position; it seemed to me that his having control and a title became more important to him than valuing people, even if it was for the betterment of the whole. He couldn't do it from where he was. You can't get there from here. I tried riding two horses for a while, but you can't be *you* when you give yourself up to a system and become fuel.

I made a video, and sent it to the senior executives because I wanted to share what I knew was going on in the company. It was about the mainstream franchise bottlers who were getting squeezed out by Coca-Cola, a company strategy to try to make mega-bottlers so they could have control over mega-profits. The video was in reverence to these bottlers, the very people who made the company grow and succeed for the last one hundred years. Instead of letting the bottlers evolve, Coca-Cola was stifling them and buying them out. I wrote on the video: "Caution, contains confidential information about the Secret Formula." Of course, management never responded to the video. There seemed nothing else that I could do. I was bored to death; there was no growth, no way to get things moving in Coca-Cola. I was dying actually—felt it physically, emotionally, mentally, intellectually. I wanted to feel and be a part of something growing. The only way I could expand was to leave. So I did.

Curt Lindberg: Johnny Appleseed

VHA Inc., formerly the Voluntary Hospitals of America, is a network of independent, nonprofit community hospitals, involving about fourteen hundred health care centers across the United States. VHA functions as a cooperative: hospitals come together to help each other out, from buying large quantities of drugs and equipment together in order to get a better price; to developing information systems and data that enable them to compare their performance against other hospitals; to supporting new approaches to community health improvement; to a variety of leadership learning initiatives.

Curt Lindberg started working as president of VHA of New Jersey in 1986. His was an unusual job in that his sole directive was to help the member hospitals of VHA in his region improve. This objective led him to a path of learning—tracking down new ideas and seeking wild notions that held the potential for helping hospitals advance the way they worked. In 1994 he came across the science of complexity, and it fully grasped his attention and would ultimately define his course.

Curt became a planter of complexity-related ideas, and, like Johnny Appleseed, spread seeds of learning in VHA. Starting locally with his own members in New Jersey, it was at first a tentative journey, with Curt not knowing what would grow from these seeds, whether they would flourish as trees or just become weeds. His efforts, however, spread to other regional VHA organizations, and included people outside the health care family. In 1996 an executive vice president of VHA, Curtis Nonomaque, having heard about the promising things happening in New Jersey, asked a remarkable question of Curt: "What do you really want to do with the next part of your career? If you could create your dream job in VHA, what would it be?" Curt is now senior consultant of complexity management for VHA nationally.

Unlike Lily and Laura, Curt succeeded in nurturing a new way of thinking and working in health care. By starting small, by developing support bit by bit, by creating opportunities to share personal experiences and to discuss ideas, Curt created a vibrant, interactive web of learning connections. These learning connections, stimulated by ideas and enriched by personal interactions, ultimately moved the participating members to a new way of thinking about the workplace, and Curt's endeavors continue to attract many others into this collective exploration.

Curt's story shows an unconscious brilliance on his part in fostering connections between many and diverse people; his ability to create emotional and personal connections with many; his gift in creating a safe, supportive, and re-sourceful environment, an oasis really, for health care people to discover an-other way of working and being together. But most of all, his story shows that an earnest commitment, a steadfast humility, a deep desire to serve, and un-equivocal care can produce an enormous and profound impact on many peo-ple, one that harbors the possibility for radically changing the health care industry itself. We attended several of the VHA conferences, and it was obvi-ous to us that the seeds of learning that Curt planted were germinating into a deeper understanding of complexity, a different way of working. Trees of knowledge were sprouting, nourished by an atmosphere that can only be de-scribed as love.

Curt tells his story in his own words.[9]

Learning Through Ideas

Health care was moving into a period of rapid change, entering an age of re-structuring and new ideas, and I saw a lot of attention being given to informa-tion systems, to mergers, to buying physician practices. But I saw very little attention being given to the nature of organizations themselves. It seemed to me that the most fundamental capability needed in times of great uncertainty and change was the ability to adapt, to create, to be nimble, as opposed to structural fixes and technological solutions. I've always been interested in new ideas in general, and so I wanted to know what was out there about leadership, about systems of all sorts, and how they change.

I saw a lot of traditional management ideas and practices that we all grew up with weren't working well, or as we expected. Our hopes for change weren't being fully realized. Before I joined VHA I was vice president of Eliz-abeth General Medical Center, and one of the things I was supposedly respon-sible for was planning. When I would look back after the planning process, I'd find that many of the things that made the most difference to that organization weren't planned. They weren't in the documents that we prepared. They seemed to happen on their own.

I first learned about complexity science in 1994, prompted by Jim Webber, a colleague of many years, and a man keenly sensitive to emerging new ideas. We jointly engaged in a reading frenzy, looking to see what was new in eco-nomics, math, psychology, biology. We started coming across some books like

Mitchell Waldrop's *Complexity,* Kevin Kelly's *Out of Control,* and Edward Wilson's *Diversity of Life.* The work of the Santa Fe Institute kept cropping up in things we read and heard, so in the summer of 1995 I visited the Institute for the first time. I went back four or five more times. I remember returning from one trip, where Jim and I helped organize a workshop on strategy and complexity. It was 5:30 in the morning as I was driving down to Albuquerque. I was filled with a rush of ideas and feelings, trying to take notes as I was driving; probably going off the road!

I saw that complexity is all about how systems really are, how they adapt, create, and live. When I realized that this new science is helping us understand healthy systems, a light bulb went off: "If hospitals, nurses, and physicians can become 'healthier' systems, wouldn't they naturally be better paths to health and well-being?" I became convinced that complexity had to find its way somehow into how we think about organizations and health. When I got to the airport, at about 7:00 A.M., I called my wife in New Jersey, and said "How about moving to Santa Fe?" She said, "What's going on with you?" I scared the wits out of her. It was then that I decided to devote the next part of my life to bringing complexity more to life in health care organizations.

Jim and I learned that a few academics in business schools were thinking about complexity science in business, such as Ralph Stacey, at the University of Hertfordshire in England, and Gareth Morgan and Brenda Zimmerman, who are both at York University in Toronto. They became important people for us in our initial efforts to introduce complexity-related concepts into health care organizations. It was a period of many conversations, a way of exploring a new landscape of ideas. We also made contact with Tom Petzinger, who writes the *Front Lines* column in the *Wall Street Journal.* He's a wonderful person, and he, too, had recognized the importance of complexity science in organizations and put us in touch with other like-minded people. Tom wrote about complexity science in business in one of his columns, and I was intrigued to hear that he got more responses to that column from people in health care than from any other sector. Through Tom I got to know Frank Karel at the Robert Wood Johnson Foundation, a big health care foundation that is interested in social change and health. Our network of connections was slowly growing.

What we were doing was really about developing new ideas through relationships. It's not about trying to plan your way into the future; it's about developing a network of relationships with people who have different ideas, but generally care about the same things, and having confidence that something constructive will emerge. I grew up in the little world of hospital administration and hadn't had much opportunity to interact with people outside the health care family, so this has been a wonderful journey for me. Complexity has had a powerful impact on me—it validated some of my thinking and it guides my approach.

Learning Together

In early 1995 I asked ten or fifteen hospital people that I had come to know over the years to start exploring complexity with me. I felt distinctly uneasy, because I didn't have the grounding or the confidence in complexity ideas yet. Also, as president of VHA of New Jersey, which was a small, fragile organization, I felt vulnerable—what if this initiative failed? People weren't asking for this. I was just doing it because I had a hunch it was important. I felt I was really out there in a way I had never been before. I had no idea how they would react.

I had a belief, though, and it's getting stronger all the time, that these ideas could really make a difference in health care in this country. And that it could help these organizations become healthier places, and help them do their work with people better. There are so many wonderful people in health care, and they are really dedicated to helping people and communities to better lives. I saw this as a chance to work together with them, to learn how to recognize and follow life's natural processes, to figure out how to reduce some of the structures and barriers that can get in the way of those processes.

And at the same time, I wanted to honor where we came from and not denigrate the more traditional, conventional organizational and health care ideas, because some of them are very important, too. It was about uncovering what is better in the new ways, but also rediscovering old ways that make a difference.

You could say I gathered friends, really, people I could feel safe with, who would give me space to fumble around in. Even so, I was afraid and worried that they would think I was a loony tune, that they'd say, "Curt has really lost it this time!" But I also knew that this initial nexus of people were searching for new ways of leading and providing health care. They were open to new ways of thinking, and they had a reputation of being able to tolerate uncertainty, ambiguity, and unfinishedness. I thought complexity would come a little easier for them, that they could take it further than people who are more wedded to traditional management thinking. I effectively said to them, "Let's figure this out together." They said, "Okay, let's do it." They trusted me.

I was bent on uncovering more health care people who might be interested, and started organizing ways to find them. I got the word out in the VHA management structure, and would ask them if they could give me four names from their part of the country of people who do new things sooner, who could embrace new ideas. Others came because they heard on the grapevine what we were up to. As a result, in 1996, we formed an experimental group of health care leaders from across the country; that gave birth to two more groups. We now have four learning networks devoted to learning about complexity.

As part of VHA's national leadership conference in April of 1996 we offered an introduction to complexity. We expected eighty people to come, but in the end three hundred turned up, which told me there was an interest out there. We tell people who come to these complexity networks to bring whomever they want to from their organizations. That way they can start creating their own group in their hospital, and they can expand and build a local community. That's one of the reasons Muhlenberg Medical Center, in New Jersey [see Chapter 5], has gone the furthest with complexity, because they brought more people in early. When people learn together and are able to talk about possibilities together, more connections happen sooner, more action is spurred.

The science was telling me to create conditions—connections, differences, some tension—and hopefully something good would happen. It's about creating conditions so things may be more likely to jell, appreciating when those things do emerge, listening to that, and then going down that path. You can do something to create conditions, but you can also recognize when they're already there and let them work.

One reason I think these learning networks are so important is because it's a safe place for people to come together who have a common interest; it's a place where they will be stimulated by new ideas, and have an opportunity to help each other out. When they're together, these folks are forever thinking and talking about the new science, and then they go back to their jobs and do a little more, try something different. They use these learning experiences to create a difference in their own organization, and then bring those experiences, and lessons learned, back to their network colleagues. We started to organize learning materials, resources on complexity, and applications to meet their needs.

Learning Through Stories

Now that we have some grounding in the science, we're turning the corner to trying to understand how complexity concepts can be used and appreciated in these organizations. One of the early ideas for building understanding was to have people look back at their experience through a complexity lens. We found that everyone was able to come up with a wonderful little vignette, and when we would look through the complexity lens, we would really see something different.

For example, the medical director at Maine Medical Center, Steve Larned, told us about a big storm that cut off the water supply in the hospital. Water is pretty important in a hospital, so it was a real crisis. He said he could look at that situation and appreciate that what *really* happened was self-organization. People took control and did what they had to do, guided by some simple rules. They created all sorts of wonderful quick solutions, from toilets, to surgery, to waste treatment. They kept functioning without the main water supply. He thought that the place was functioning better than it ever had! So then we explored how we could learn from this unplanned experience, and what it told us about how to make organizations better and more creative.

Listening to people tell their stories in small groups, and seeing how those stories built fortitude and courage for others to take action, led us to seeing their importance, their value, their power. We can learn from stories, by reflecting, sharing, and using them in organizations as resources and learning experiences. Stories help people become more equipped to face the challenges before them. We soon came to appreciate the need for written stories, to capture them and therefore be able to share them with others, instead of just having them told one time. Now we're offering as a resource stories and principles that we have published and written up and put on our Web site.[10]

Learning Through Action

We were trying to get the knowledge, courage, and energy to consciously behave differently. Health care organizations tend to be conservative, because looseness and experimentation can have deadly consequences. And so health care organizations need structure, but they also need to spawn new ideas for programs. I've watched this group of people rethink who they are, what they do, and how they view their organization. I've watched them begin to experiment, begin to let go, and give themselves permission to try something different.

For example, Linda Rusch, the vice president of patient care at Hunterdon Medical Center in New Jersey, started saying that she needed to change the context for how her hospital thought about community. She just started talking, opened a discussion with some of her nursing colleagues about connecting in a different way with the community around health issues. As a result, the operating room nurses decided to organize a program that would make operations and surgery less threatening to people, by having a day for community people to come to the hospital and see surgical instruments and have them explained to them. Some of the pediatric nurses started up a program for battered women. And that's only the beginning of it.

It didn't happen from a design perspective. It was simply Linda saying "We ought to do more," and then letting her people do what they felt was needed, giving them encouragement and freedom to connect around things they cared about and thought might be useful. And the nurses just got up and did it! It's a very different relationship. Linda organized some meetings with the community leaders to talk about community and health issues, and the group wanted to come up with a plan. She said to them, "Can't we find new things we can just start doing, just get some things going? We don't have to all agree. We don't have to wait for consensus, as if there's only one way that it can be done. Let's experiment." She is an incredible leader, and her group has accomplished amazing things. And on top of that, that bunch of people are really close and genuinely care about each other. And it shows in the patient satisfaction ratings—they're at the top of the list for New Jersey hospitals.

One of Gareth Morgan's contributions was to say to the learning network members that a small action around an area of tension or paradox can make a big difference. Find a paradox—if you think it's significant, it will likely relate to other paradoxes that may be in the larger organization. There may be little areas that embody the whole. It was a powerful directive; the group just suddenly switched gears and was ready to act. I can remember Rick Weinberg saying to me, "I've got it! I know what I'm going to do when I get home." Rick is a physician responsible for creating a network of doctors for a growing health care system in New Jersey called Atlantic, and he was involved in trying to get two physician groups to merge. He gave up trying to "engineer" the merger and instead worked to expose the real areas of tension, increase the dialogue around these issues, and articulate their central expectations. Rick told me later that one day it went Bang! Both groups flipped from being enemies to deciding to become partners.

Jim Taylor, one of the finest hospital CEOs I've met, was president of the Medical Center in Vermont when it merged with another hospital and a large physician practice that used traditional management ideas. You know, "We will control this, we will plan for it." He helped to make that merger happen, and ultimately stepped aside voluntarily, because he thought a physician needed to head the new system in order for it to really come together. Now he's at another hospital and his board wanted to pay half a million dollars to a big consulting firm to do a long-range plan for the hospital, and he said, "That's ridiculous. We know what the issues are. Won't we learn more by going to work on those issues ourselves?"

Jim was working on developing a regional cancer network with three hospitals that were competitors. It didn't go as far or as fast as he hoped. He recognized that it wasn't going to happen, and that there were a lot of reasons for that. Instead of feeling that he failed, because he had known what he wanted and it didn't work, he was able to ask what did they learn from that effort, what was it telling them about the relationships among these organizations, and what was possible. He was able to let go and move on to other things. He also noticed that the complexity-inspired approaches he introduced on the cancer project were being used in other corporate endeavors between the three hospitals. Jim is very important to the people in these learning networks because he sees the situation from the outside and the inside. When he talks about his experience he exposes himself, his vulnerability, his anxiety—things all of us know but are usually hesitant to share.

People struggle with how to act on these ideas. Often they feel they have to go the traditional route—do a presentation to senior management or get the board on board. In many cases, that's not directly possible. I say, "Why don't you just find the people in your organization who are interested. I know they're there. Get something going with them, a little experiment." Like one time after one of our meetings, people from Muhlenberg went back to their hospital and formed a voluntary group—whoever in the hospital wanted to talk about complexity, show up on Thursday morning. It's about acting within a sphere of influence.

At a VHA management meeting I was asked how I was going to measure the results. How will I know if I'm making a difference? I said that a measure for me is whether interest is growing. Are more people coming? Is it reproducing? Are people saying it helps them? Most of the people in our complexity learning networks would say that they are approaching tough issues more effectively. They're getting new things off the ground that take hold quicker. They think they're better at their jobs because they're helping groups they work with become more creative; they are finding new ways to go about truly merging organizations. They are feeling better about their work. They've given up the burden of believing they should be able to control their organizations and their futures, and feeling more hopeful about helping their organizations discover a good future. It's quite liberating for folks.

Learning About Mystery

I've become very close to this group of people, and I have felt responsible for this group—for learning together and for knowing what to do next. At first I approached the formation and work of these networks from a scientific standpoint, complexity science especially. "Pay attention to diversity," "simple rules," "boundaries," "create safe places," I told myself. Then I began to see the wisdom hidden in the human process when such concepts are in the mix. The process itself speaks. The group knows what it needs next, develops a higher level of functioning. Scientists might call it self-organization. It's just magical to me. Al Hertzog, a psychiatrist, once said to our group that "It was happening because we were now able to hold open an issue, to tolerate unease, that we've learned to trust it." Hearing him say that was very emotional for us.

I just think something wants to happen; it feels like that. And it *is* happening. Why are some of these connections just blossoming? Why are all these odd things clicking? People are saying this is the most important thing they do in their organization. I know they're going to make a difference somehow. There's something more within us all. All of us can do more, and *be* more, and contribute more, and help each other more. I think I can help a little bit; I can do more connecting. It's got me thinking about who I am. I'm not me; I'm these relationships. It's these social, human interactions that define me and make me. I mean, *you* are *me*.

PART THREE

The World of Relationships

Chapter 14

The Buttercup Effect

We do not see One in the form of many because the empirical mind sees the single one which is a numerical unit. One plant is not the One plant.

Henri Bortoft, *The Wholeness of Being*

In the stories you have read, you have seen a struggle—a constant struggle—to create a different way of working together. From this struggle, a radical change occurred in the culture of each of these organizations, which made them more creative and adaptable, and led them to financial success, or, in the case of Muhlenberg Medical Center, to increased patient satisfaction. These businesses think, as we do, that they are forging a more effective way of working for the twenty-first century. We see them as nothing less than part of a movement that has the potential to revolutionize the workplace.

We saw in these organizations common patterns in their way of being, which affected the way things were done—for leaders, for teams, and for sustaining constructive relationships across the organization, in their economic web, and in their communities. These ways of *being* cultivated conditions for constructive emergence, that is, for business efficacy, for innovative ideas, and for a sense of community within their organizations. A sense of community is not a minor issue for business success. When people felt part of a community and felt that they belonged, they said they were more willing to adapt and to be flexible, which in turn affected the overall adaptability and flexibility of the organization. Counterintuitively, a nontraditional approach led to business success in traditional bottom-line terms.

We identified three common practices among these organizations for a different way of working and being: *paradoxical leadership,* a way of leading change in organizations as complex adaptive systems; *emergent teams,* a dynamic way of working together that keeps organizations on the edge; and *relational practice,* a way of being with co-workers, customers, suppliers, and other businesses in your economic web, which develops strong and rich connections and has the potential for creating a sense of community. We will describe these three practices separately in the following three chapters, which, collectively, will offer guidance for how, on a personal level, leaders can think differently about their work, and can navigate their organization through change and nurture a culture that accepts change better; how managers and teams can maintain their organization at the creative edge; and how everyone can develop constructive relationships within and outside the system that create strong interconnections and keep the organization robust.

In this chapter we will show the commonalities in how these companies jump-started their way into a different way of working, which can be regarded as an overall strategy for engaging your organization and guiding it most effectively as a complex adaptive system.

Different, but the Same

How, you might ask, can you, as a leader, create change in your organization that better enables it to take on the challenges ahead, and better prepares you personally? How might you as a worker be more engaged at work, improve how you work, and find ways to make work more satisfying? How do you find the soul in your work and in the workplace? Each organization followed its own unique path, guided by its history and its business, and, as Bob Shapiro of Monsanto said, and rightly so, "Don't look at us. Find your own way." But when we look at this collection of stories, common patterns emerge in how they changed their organizations. It was, as the philosopher Henri Bortoft might say, the very same buttercup.

In his book on Goethe, Bortoft evokes the image of the creeping buttercup, a plant that sends creeping runners along the ground.[1] Where the tip of the runner touches the ground, it grows, and a new buttercup plant shoots up and flowers. Organically, the "new" plant is the very same One, part of the same whole. But each is also different. If you see the wholeness, you therefore cannot say that all the buttercups are the same, says Bortoft, but you can say that each is "the very same buttercup," because they have a common root and a common essence of "buttercup-ness." It is the same with the organizations whose stories we told: each is different, but all share the same deep root, and a common essence.

Like the buttercup, certain behaviors and ways of thinking took root, grew, and spread within these organizations. Even though the companies themselves were very different and their behaviors were qualitatively different, they all came to a similar order and gave rise to a particular quality of culture. It was the very same buttercup in all these companies.

These behaviors afforded them opportunities to tap into the same generative source—a wellspring of productivity, creativity, adaptability, and goodwill. Not every day; not everyone, but enough to alter the workplace environment so that new possibilities coexisted as well as collided with old habits, enough that a different and better way of working manifested. Because we see the same patterns of behaviors emerge in these companies of very different size and very different economic sectors, we infer that we are seeing something fundamental that applies to organizations in general. They are all complex adaptive systems that frequently operate in a state of creative adaptability because of the style of management of their leaders and people's way of working.

Valuing Relationships

The organizing principle for all these organizations was placing value on relationships; we heard it over and over again. As complex adaptive systems, organizations generate emergent novelty from the interactions among the elements in the system—that is, in human systems, the relationships among people within the organization. For an organization to enhance its adaptability as a system, it needs to engage with nonlinear processes of that system. Traditionally, most organizations are founded on a linear structure of a hierarchy and bureaucracy, which impedes their agility and flexibility, qualities so needed in these times of unprecedented change. The most effective way to change a linear structure to a nonlinear process that can lead to the fluctuating zone of creative adaptability is to attend to the nonlinear world of relationships.

Feedback loops exist in complex systems, and through their dynamics the system evolves over time. In order to have positive outcomes, you need positive and constructive relationships to feed into those loops, and you need lots of interconnection among people to enrich the loops. As Patrick Burns of the Industrial Society said, the root of organizational problems is often "abysmal relationships," which create negative energy and limit what the organization can achieve. It is, however, not sufficient to just leave linear thinking behind in favor of embracing nonlinear processes without addressing the quality of existing relationships. If the relationships within the organization are not positive or if there is chronic disconnection, the potential creativity of the system will be blocked. As Hatim Tyabji of VeriFone told us, it was strong, positive relationships that maintained his organization at a high level of creativity and adaptability. We heard how good relationships gave these organizations an edge in the market. As Will Pape put it, VeriFone's success was through "people not technology." Similarly, the Babels' competitive edge over Big Boxes was in personal relationships with their customers.

Most of these organizations did not have a *design* for working with nonlinear processes. Rather than a concerted effort to deliberately change the hierarchy and structure in a particular way, they attended to the existing relationships, and then allowed the organization to evolve from there. They did, however, share common patterns, again qualitatively different, in how they began to work with these relationships and with their organizations as complex adaptive systems. The outcome of this shift in focus was the creation of a safe environment, within which people had freedom to experiment—to find solutions to problems and to explore innovative paths—and to self-organize. And this in turn made them more creative and adaptable as organizations.

You may have seen some of these strategies in some form or other in business theories. The difference here is that these organizations came to these choices intuitively or knowing about complexity science, and approached their organizations in an *organic* way. When they looked at their organizations organically, that meant looking at the whole organization more as a living organism rather than a machine, and employees not as cogs in the machine but as complex humans, as part of an organism. This perspective led them into the world of relationships, a world where they were all just finding their way without a road map. And they all ended up in similar places.

They found the very same buttercup.

Unleashing Potential

We said that valuing relationships was the central organizing principle. Paying attention to this dimension in an organization, we have seen, creates an opportunity for unleashing enormous potential in people. When we think back on these stories, what is evident is a concerted effort to engage people, not in a superficial way, but fully, the whole person—their feelings, their thoughts, their aspirations—and to get them on board on an uncertain journey that would be difficult but also fun and full of hope and possibility. Leaders in these stories began to see the workplace as an *experiment in progress,* and were explicit about the fact with their people.

In order to fully engage in this experiment, people needed a degree of trust in the organization and in each other, which led leaders, counterintuitively, to *creating chaos* in varying degrees. This allowed for all the dark shadows of the organization to surface—the rigid behaviors, the festering emotions, the disconnections—and be dispersed. This process of briefly entering a period of chaos encouraged the interaction between the formal and informal systems of the organization, from which something new could emerge. To guide the organization through these difficult times, people had a *strong ethical foundation of care,* which provided consistency in a climate of no constancy and much uncertainty. And these organizations began to fully address people as people, and explored ways to *cultivate* them. The bottom line here is that to unleash potential, leaders recognized that they had to *cultivate* conditions for the organization to change, rather than *direct* change. Rather than turning the organization *around*, they turned *to* the organization.

An Experiment in Progress

The leaders in these stories decided to do something different in their organizations; for many it was a matter of *having* to do something different in order to survive and thrive. They essentially embraced their organizations as complex adaptive systems by accepting a process of unfolding and unpredictable nonlinear results. Not knowing where this experiment would lead them, they displayed a strength of conviction to embrace this new direction, no matter how rough the journey got, and, as you saw, there were plenty of rough times.

As John Kopicki of Muhlenberg Medical Center said, "You have to keep try-ing, and be prepared to get things wrong." By taking a risk, they created a con-text for risk within the organization by evoking the imaginative. Since there was no longer a right way of doing things, trying crazy things was no longer crazy in unpredictable and disorienting times. Rather, trying things became a journey of discovering ways to better adapt to the environment.

That commitment to change and to take risks was graphically visible in St. Luke's advertising agency, and symbolic for all these organizations, when Andy Law drew a line across the floor and asked those who wanted to join on this uncertain journey to step over the line. Stepping over the line, they had committed themselves to an experiment in progress.

Creating Chaos

To break down old, dysfunctional habits, and to forge new connections where disconnections existed, these leaders created chaos in some way or other in their organizations, but in a safe context. Tony Morgan of the Industrial Soci-ety created chaos and broke down old habits by simply allowing people to speak up and talk honestly about what was really going on in their minds, and he started with himself. He, like others, opened up a psychological space that allowed people to be more themselves, and he worked with people from where they were rather than from where he might hope them to be. He created safety by reassuring people they wouldn't get fired. John Kopicki, at Muhlenberg Medical Center, did the same, and, in a more immediate sense, created safety by accepting silence in meetings early in the process, waiting both frantically and patiently for people to feel safe enough to speak. Bob Shapiro brought Monsanto to chaos by overloading the system with impossible demands, so that people had to discover for themselves another way of working together and to self-organize around the most immediate problems. He created safety by hanging in there with them as they found their way. St. Luke's went into chaos when they confronted the task of inventing their dream company, and found safety in Andy and David's conviction that it would work, even though they didn't know what the "it" would turn out to be.

All faced a discomforting period of extreme anxiety and fear with people pleading, "Where are we going? What are we doing?" From these painful transitions there were a few who couldn't stomach it. But mostly people stayed on and, surprisingly in these organizations, they became the very same people who would create a new work environment. Massive firings were not necessary in these cases to create change. And those who stayed learned to better accept uncertainty, since it is inherent in nonlinear processes.

It took time to break down the established norms of working and thinking, the "shoulds" of bureaucracy, the "oughts" of hierarchy in these organizations. In retrospect, the time of transformation was relatively short, given the magnitude of change that had occurred—from nine months in DuPont's Belle plant of a thousand people, to two years in Monsanto's 22,000 people. We saw that changing from hierarchy to the zone of creativity is both scary and fun; and it often involved a continuous struggle to not fall back to old structures. But as complexity science promises, out of chaos order will eventually emerge, even though its form is largely unpredictable. Whether that order would be constructive depended on the kind of interactions people had, which in these stories was guided by a code of ethics.

Ethical Foundation

The cultures in these organizations could be characterized as most people being well connected to and caring for each other and their organizations. In part this can be attributed to a strong ethical foundation of shared values and principles. They had seriously taken on the question, How do we live and work together? They had a shared sense of how to be together and how to behave with each other. In VeriFone it manifested in the little blue book, in DuPont's Belle plant it was the Treatment of People Principles. These organizations placed value on caring in a context where largely, as Andy Law of St. Luke's said, "business has no formal code of ethics," and strove toward living by a code of ethics of their own making. For Hatim Tyabji, success was not measured only by financial parameters but by an ethical standard as to how caring and connected the culture was within itself and to its customers.

Generally, there was a sense of a higher purpose, beyond the monetary bottom line, a conversation shifting from profitability to purpose, from performance to involvement, such as the Industrial Society rediscovered in its three-day event. They all struggled with a balance between financial realities and creative and ethical ideals. It was sticky, but they all felt it was worth it. The Babels needed to make money, but that's not why they were in business—they were there to serve and bring beauty to people's lives. As Andy Law put it, "Profits are like breathing. You need it to live, but it's not what you live *for*."

Being human, people had their failings and flaws, such as when Katherine Beall overheard people at VeriFone complaining that VeriFone didn't live up to its principles. As she put it, at least they knew there were principles, and they felt free enough to voice their dissent, rather than repress it. A strong ethical foundation, that is, values, provided continuity for people, and, as Dick Knowles of the DuPont Belle plant put it, it is "like the poles you hold on to in a crowded, jostling subway car so you don't fall." In his case, the plant people were involved in developing the ethical principles and were able to challenge management when they weren't walking the talk. Because they defined and acted on these values, people felt the principles were more their own rather than something imposed on them.

Cultivating People

We said earlier that organizations are like ecosystems. But they are really more like gardens, because ecosystems don't need cultivating; they just are. The difference here is that, unlike ecosystems, human systems have intent and foresight. Humans have more than instinct; they have conscious choices and deliberate actions, which influences the system's evolution.

In our research, we consistently saw an intent to cultivate. A gardener doesn't grow buttercups; he or she creates conditions so that buttercups can grow.[2] Just as a gardener gives water and fertilizer to a plant, which encourages it to grow, flower, and spread runners, leaders at all levels cultivated their organizations, replenished them, and, when necessary, pruned. "Cultivate," taken from the Latin, means to take care of, to cherish.

As with tending a garden, cultivating your organization is a daily practice. You don't cultivate a garden and then walk away from it. When a garden is left unattended, it gets overgrown with weeds, plants bolt, others die; it becomes chaotic. Similarly when people are unattended, organizations get overgrown with resentments, people become complacent, creativity suffers, as was the case in Lily's alchemist story at the lumber company. But when people are cultivated, like a well-loved flowing garden, they begin to blossom, which extends itself and influences others, and in turn affects the whole garden. Remember Muhlenberg Medical Center, in which the culture of care and connection spilled out into the community, and created a new relationship between the two?

As you read, many people said they were growing and learning, and they were doing it together. Others mentioned the importance of having fun. People want fun places to work; a place they look forward to going to, as Gerry Wentworth at VeriFone stated. Play and learning go together, it's natural—look at children, engaged in play, and experiencing a huge learning curve. A playful environment lightens the inevitable existence of stress and, as these stories show, promotes productivity. Without hierarchical ladders to climb, people need learning and experiential goals to keep them engaged. As Andy Law said about the people at St. Luke's, they were "growth-driven by a thirst for experience more than cash." Mandi Harris, who had six different jobs during her time at the Industrial Society, concurs in her statement, "I like to do different things for the experience as opposed to just getting paid for a job." Generally these organizations had a low turnover, indicating that these work environments engendered loyalty in people for their organizations.

These organizations respected the individual and what they could bring to the table. As Andy Law put it: "Everyone is brilliant." It's a matter of finding their place, of allowing them to reach their potential. But with seeing people as brilliant comes a responsibility for the organization. Andy's sentiment holds true with the rest of the companies in our book, in that he sees that a company's responsibility is in fulfilling its people. In hiring people at Monsanto, this value is clear from the start—they ask, "What excites you, and how can this contribute to something that is important to us?" Similarly, Jeanne Babel asks her people what they would like to do, and tells them that they have opportunities, and that they have the power to change things. At the Industrial Society, Tony Morgan asked, "What more can you do?" In essence, this approach reaches and connects to a higher self in people, knowing this is where the best work comes from.

These organizations cultivated people by creating conditions (which we will discuss in greater depth in the chapter "Emergent Teams") that allowed people to grow as they needed on their own terms, as long as those needs were aligned with the organization's goals and purpose. And they believed wholeheartedly that, given the opportunity, people know what they need to do and will do it, because they have come to their own conclusions and believe in it rather than being told it. We also saw how difficult this path was because of psychological barriers—people indoctrinated into trying to look good rather than taking responsibility, as at DuPont's Belle plant, and being used to being told what to do rather than initiate, as some felt in the Babels' store.

These leaders worked to cultivate a sense that their people could influence the company, were able to affect its direction, by creating opportunities for them. These leaders know full well that when people don't feel part of the process, they are less invested, less involved, and care less. These businesses actively engaged in reimagining how their people could be with each other in the workplace: how to replace suspicion with trust, guardedness with openness, recalcitrance with cooperation. The source of this change is in the being. "The being is the cause; everything else is a manifestation of that being," Hatim Tyabji said. "And the being is care."

A Different Way of Working

If we need highly motivated people to face the upcoming challenges of the twenty-first century, then we need a different way of working. Looking at a different way of working through a nonlinear lens shifts the focus from getting the job done to *how* the job gets done. This leads us to change the questions we ask. Rather than ask "What can I get out of this," it becomes "How can I contribute?" "How can I do it faster?" becomes "How can I do it better?" "What can I demand?" becomes "How can I engage others?" "How can we make people be more creative and productive?" becomes "How can I nurture a culture that fosters creativity and productivity?" "What should I do?" becomes "What is dear and important to my heart?" "What did we achieve this year?" becomes "What are we doing differently this year?"

The answers to these questions can't be found only in the rational mind. "The answers are here," says Hatim Tyabji, "here in the heart." As Antoine de Saint-Exupéry said in *The Little Prince,* "It is only with the heart that one can see slightly; what is essential is invisible to the eye."

Chapter 15

Paradoxical Leadership

A leader is best
when the people are hardly aware of his existence,
not so good when people stand in fear,
worse, when people are contemptuous.
Fail to honor people, and they will fail to honor you.
But of a good leader who speaks little,
when his task is accomplished, his work done!
The people say, "we did it ourselves."

Lao Tzu

Letting Go of the Old

Leaders in complex adaptive systems lead change. For leaders coming from a command and control tradition, leading change requires an expansion of skills. But it's not just skills, as you will see, it's a different way of *being* a leader. You can't command or control change—a linear approach doesn't work with something essentially nonlinear. It requires something more organic—rather than *doing to,* it's a *working with* and *for* people. To change how people work begins with changing how you lead, as we saw in these stories, which then sends runners of influence throughout the organization, like the buttercup.

It starts with you. It starts with you in a very personal way—who you are, where you place value, what you do, and how you relate to people, all of which has more influence on the organization than what you say. It starts with you creating a new understanding of yourself. It entails a reflection of yourself; placing aside ego-driven needs and instead finding gratification and satisfaction in cultivating others; it's embracing the leader as servant.[1] It's turning *to* the organization in a personal way as a way of changing the culture to one that accepts change.

It involves a reassessment of yourself; finding what is most important to you and taking a stand. It involves a reassessment of others—a trust and faith in people—and embracing democratic processes of self-governance. It begins, as it did for the leaders in the stories, with nothing short of a personal conversion, that is, a difficult and often painful process of learning to let go of the illusion of control.

Before we explore paradoxical leadership in the context of the companies' stories you've read, we'd like to step back for a moment and remind you of a story that many of you may know—one that illustrates this transition from a command and control style to a more organic style of leadership needed for leading in complex systems—a classic American story, *The Wizard of Oz.* It is rich with metaphors and archetypal characters, and offers many insights into organizational life, such as can be found in *The Oz Principle,* a book that uses the story as a way of exploring victimization and accountability in organizations.[2] We have a different focus; we'll focus on the Wizard (as portrayed in the book, not the film), a leader whose way of being lends itself to a deeper understanding of the world of the leader in a command and control culture and his quandary of control—both controlling and being controlled by the illusion of omniscience.

CEOs and Wizards

As you may recall, Dorothy found herself in a strange land, and wanted to go home. She was told by the Good Witch of the North to see the all mighty and powerful Wizard of Oz, who would surely be able to find a way to send her back to Kansas. Along the way she gathered three companions who also wanted help from Oz—the Scarecrow, the Tin Man, and the Lion. After many adventures, they found themselves in the audience of Oz, who, in a display of plumes of fire and a thundering voice, proceeded to terrify them and, instead of helping them, ordered them to kill the Wicked Witch of the West. Only when her broomstick was in his hand would he help them out, he proclaimed. Against all odds, Dorothy and her companions managed to do just that. Dorothy was furious when, on her return to the Emerald City, the Wizard dissembled and failed to keep his promise. The Lion roared, to frighten the Wizard. The roar had more effect on Toto, Dorothy's dog, though, who jumped in fright, and knocked down a screen, exposing a little old man standing behind it, maneuvering levers.

"Who are you," they asked incredulously. "I am Oz, the Great and Terrible," he said in a trembling voice, "but don't strike me—please don't—and I'll do anything you want me to do." Dorothy and her friends were shocked, having believed him to be a great Head, a terrible Beast, a ball of Fire. "No, you are all wrong," said the little man meekly. "I have been making believe. I'm just a common man." And so we learn that among his tricks was ventriloquism, which enabled him to throw his voice onto the illusions he created.

This moment of personal conversion, when a person steps out from behind the screen of illusion, when apparitions of power are dispelled (by none other than a dog, which archetypally symbolizes intuition), and a common man is revealed, is perhaps every leader's dream and nightmare. But how did the Wizard find himself behind a screen of illusion in the first place? And why is it so frightening for him to reveal himself as a common man? The Wizard of Oz, as CEO, gives rich insight into the complex dynamics and collusion that occur in a command and control culture.

Like Dorothy, Oz also landed in this strange land by accident, ending up, like many CEOs, where he never expected. Seeing Oz descend from the clouds in his balloon, the people of this strange land thought he must be a great wizard. And, of course, he let them think that, tantalized by the privileges associated with power. Because the people were afraid of him and would do anything he wished, he ordered them to build a city and a palace. In this way, he became the CEO of Emerald City. He ruled with a fearsome and arrogant hand, a true command and control type. But his story of leadership is not that simple, for Oz is an ambiguous, paradoxical character: he is both a perpetrator and a victim of control.

To be idealized by your people can be very seductive to a leader, especially if they are insecure in themselves. To be idealized is to be adored/feared, but not *seen*—the paradox of enormous visibility as an image and simultaneous invisibility as a person. Oz's high visibility was captured across the land in the myth of his omniscient powers. On the other hand, his invisibility was quite literal. Once the people built him the palace, he shut himself up in it and would not see anybody. And he did this for reasons no one would have imagined— out of fear: fearful that the witches would discover that he was not more pow- erful than they, and afraid that they would surely destroy him. And he feared that if he went out of the palace, his people would discover he was not the wiz- ard that they thought he was. As he says, "then they would be vexed with me for having deceived them. And so I have to stay shut up in the rooms all day, and it gets tiresome." In this way, Oz controls and is controlled by his position. And so we have the portrait of a leader who projects a power he does not gen- uinely feel, who is inaccessible out of fear of being found out, who is isolated and out of touch with his people, who lives a lonely life. And he is also some- one who has become somewhat comfortable with the illusion; as Oz states, "I have fooled everyone so long that I thought I should never be found out."

But, not surprisingly, Oz is found out. And the discovery of his true identity exposes a collusion between Oz and his people. *Both* propagate his illusion of power. His people need him to be omniscient, which perpetuates a parent- child relationship. In every organization there are people who just want to be told what to do; who need to think there is someone more powerful than them- selves, who wish for another to take care of everything. They attribute powers to their leader that the leader does not possess. And they project their own longing for power onto him. And, like Oz, there are leaders who allow it. Still, there is a vulnerability with this type of power; as Oz despairingly notes, "How can I help being a humbug when all these people make me do things that everybody knows can't be done?" What we see is how debilitating pro- jected power can be for a leader.

Even when Oz acknowledges his failings and admits he can't keep the promises he made to the foursome, they in a sense don't allow him to stand on grounds of mutuality. He points out to them that they don't really need what they are asking for, such as the Scarecrow not needing brains and instead needing experience, which he already had. But the Scarecrow and his friends insist that the Wizard bestow these traits on them anyway. And so he ceremo- niously gives them what they already have, and always have had.

Why do some people in organizations when given authority and power, as Dorothy and crew were, resist it, refuse it, retreat from it? In part, what we en- counter in these behaviors is the psychological residue of people used to being controlled. When people work in an environment day in and day out, where they are used to being told what to do, are rarely asked what they think, are used to perceiving themselves as weaker, used to a parental type of relationship with their leaders, it has its effect. It undermines striving and encourages settling for less. It instills an insecurity which blinds them to their own capabilities. Ingrained behavior doesn't just disappear. It takes time, patience, and guidance.

The transition from a command and control culture to a culture of change and adaptation requires a dual conversion and an adjustment of expectation, for the leader and for the people of the organization. Both engage in a process of parting veils of illusion—that the leader has complete control and has all the answers, and that people in the organization, especially front-line people, don't have answers to organizational problems. After all, it was Dorothy who killed the Witch. The role of the leader is not to be superhuman, like a wizard, but to be an "ordinary human being," as Peter Drucker has so adroitly pointed out. Finding this ground of mutuality, based on a common humanity and a shared purpose, generates an adult-adult relationship. For Dorothy and Oz, the moment of mutuality occurs when Dorothy, realizing that her expectations would remain unfulfilled, says to the Wizard, "I think you are a very bad man." "Oh, no, my dear," Oz responded, "I'm really a very good man; but I'm a very bad Wizard, I must admit."

Dispelling Myths

Leading in complex adaptive systems that, by their nature, can't be controlled dispels three myths propagated by the command and control world. Parting these veils of illusion leads to greater clarity for seeing the organization as a complex system and seeing oneself as *part of* the whole rather than *apart from*.

No. 1: Myth of Autonomy

Adam Bryant's comment in a *New York Times* article about teamwork, "In the age of the celebrity CEO—the lone ranger who can ride into any troubled company and turn things around, reaping outsized rewards compared with the 'team' that helps him,"[3] underscores a denial common among many CEOs and their organizations. The CEO is never a lone ranger; there are always many behind his or her success.

In other words, as part of a complex adaptive system, you don't live in a vacuum. Everything you do depends on others, and it always has, whether you admit it or not. You are interdependent, and how you behave has far-reaching effects in the connected web of complex systems. And you can't do it alone, nor is that the wisest choice. It's too complex. The Industrial Society's board members saw Tony Morgan as the Society's savior, but Tony insisted that they recognize the achievements of the people who had actually wrought the economic miracles that saved the Society, calling *them* heroes and heroines.

No. 2: Myth of Control

When the complexity-guided leader gives up the illusion of control, it's both liberating and terrifying. It's liberating because many leaders, as Muhlenberg's John Kopicki pointed out, feel burdened by the expectation that they have to provide the answers, when in fact they know that much in their world of work is beyond their, or anyone's, control.

It's terrifying, for two reasons. First, control is often viewed as power, and many traditionally oriented leaders find it hard, if not impossible, to give up this veil of power. It's terrifying to discover that old modes of leading just don't work anymore. As AlliedSignal's CEO Lawrence Bossidy puts it, "The day when you would yell and scream and beat people into good performance is over."[4] Remember how even though the Industrial Society's Tony Morgan recognized the limits of control in the modern business environment, he still woke up in the middle of the night, fearing the Society was out of his control? Or Dick Knowles, at DuPont's Belle plant, who felt he "had to struggle with the temptation to fall back to what seemed like the safety of the old command and control structures," when things were not going as he hoped? And John Kopicki, at Muhlenberg Medical Center, gritting his teeth to keep from shouting out, "Who authorized that?"

Second, it requires a different confidence—not just in yourself but in your people. It's coming to terms with the fact that what emerges from the efforts of your people will be at least as good as what one leader can come up with, as Mary Anne Keyes at Muhlenberg put it.

Giving up control is the toughest thing to do for a leader, all the leaders in the stories admit. But in their efforts to let go, they learned something else—flexibility and patience, apt qualities for our complex times.

No. 3: Myth of Omniscience

You don't have all the answers. It's impossible to have and know all the answers. To recognize this is a strength. Pretending you do have all the answers is a weakness. It's giving up a demigod status and, instead, opting to join the human race. Leaders who burden themselves with having to have all the answers are easier to find; it is more unusual to see a leader, like John Kopicki or Andy Law in their staff meetings, being forthright with the staff, and willing to show themselves as not knowing, and also as needing others. That in itself is a sad commentary about the dehumanizing repercussions that a command and control approach can have on leaders.

In the stories, many leaders spoke of uncertainty as they embarked on their journey, knowing they didn't have the answers in hand, which makes these leaders very human. Hatim Tyabji made a very clear distinction about his role as leader, which allowed him to be a strong leader and a human being. "Doubt has to do with whether you're going to go forward or whether you're not. There is no clarity of direction. I have no doubt, but I do have uncertainty. Uncertainty is accepting the fact that you may or may not succeed." Recognizing uncertainty is not a weakness, but a strength, because uncertainty is the hallmark of nonlinear processes and their unexpected results.

Although uncertain, people still need to feel some security. Security, in a linear world, is often associated with having control and achieving specific linear goals. In a nonlinear world, security is found in people's commitment and involvement, which creates a well-connected system that can move forward, adapt, and innovate. That means leaders need to be involved and closely connected to the people and the realities of the workplace. As professor of management at McGill University Henry Mintzburg puts it, "We may need great visionaries to create a great organization. But after the organization is created, we don't need heroes, just competent, devoted, and generous leaders who know what's going on and exude the spirit [of the organization]."[5]

As you heard in the stories, there were plenty of devoted and caring leaders, qualities that provided continuity in their organizations. What you didn't see was that during the interviews with each and every one of the CEOs of these organizations, there was a time when the CEO referred to "my people" and was visibly moved during the recollection. And this was reciprocal when we talked to people in their organizations. Many showed an emotional connection, a care and concern, for their CEO. Not a bad trade-off for omniscience.

Leadership and Clarity

An initial step that leaders in our stories took in shifting from a command and control culture toward one of change and adaptability was to see their authority in a different way. Rather than seeing themselves as the ultimate authority, with all the answers, their authority rested in their ability to see the wholeness of the organization and potential of the people in their organizations. We saw how John Kopicki, Jeanne Babel, Andy Law at St. Luke's, and Bob Shapiro strove to extricate themselves from, rather than foster, people's dependence on their expertise. "Experts and specialists are a dime a dozen," says Robert E. Lee (yes, that's his name), the Marines' top trainer, who applies complexity principles in his training. "What the world needs is someone who can grasp the workings of the entire organization, understand people, and motivate them."[6]

What organizations need are leaders who can see the complexity of their organizations, a *clarity* at both the macro and micro levels that informs their choices about direction. At the macro level, that translates into seeing the wholeness of the organization—recognizing patterns, anticipating the larger picture, being aware of external influences affecting the system, and envisioning what the new possibilities are, what new story they can create of their organization. For VeriFone, the wholeness was global where there wasn't a VeriFone Spain, a VeriFone France—only one VeriFone. Seeing one VeriFone made the system robust because a shared purpose linked a decentralized company together and created strong connections among the people all over the world in their shared identity as VeriFoners. For the Babels, it was recognizing that business was not just *their* business but their business was defined by the economic web of which they were a part. Seeing the wholeness of their business shifted their focus and strategy to forging positive connections in their multidimensional world. For Monsanto, it was forging alliances with other companies, forming an economic web that enhanced value for all members, engaged as they are in a global economy. At the macro level, a leader's work is paradoxical; as Bob Shapiro stated, "My specialization is generalization."

At the micro level, it's seeing the connections and disconnections within the system. At a personal level for the leader this means seeing oneself as in relationship to people, and cultivating strong relationships and connections within the system and outside it. As Fran Hulse of Muhlenberg observed, "It's John's way of being in relationship to people that defines him as a leader, not his position."

At the organizational level of seeing connections, the leader's role then becomes one of identifying where the blindness, denials, disconnections, constrictions are in the organization, and cultivating connections for a more robust system. Tony Morgan began his journey by addressing the disconnections among senior staff, which resulted in revitalizing the organization and led them to a shared purpose. Andy Law addressed the blindness in the domain of ethics in advertising from which another company emerged.

At the heart of leadership, what drives the leader and the organization is a clarity of values. The leaders in these stories were very clear about their values and they made it their business to create, uncover, and articulate them. But these were not just espoused values; these leaders *embodied the values* of the organization—the purpose, the ethics, the vision—and were diligent at staying true to them. As Roger Bertman of VeriFone said, "The soul element of the business is what Hatim is."

These leaders embodied these values by living them, by walking the talk and admitting when they didn't. For example, Tony Morgan, who valued keeping one's word, didn't hesitate to publicly apologize when he didn't keep his own. The leader, most of all, embodies the values of the company for others to see and emulate. And, you can be sure, your people are watching—closely.

Practice of Paradoxical Leadership

Paradoxical leadership is a way of leading the wholeness of an organization and cultivating connections in the system toward greater creative adaptability. What emerges from these leaders is a different way of being that leads to a different way of doing. They share a characteristic in their style of leadership—paradoxes. From a complexity perspective, paradoxes aren't problematic and need to be solved. Instead paradoxes create a tension from which creative solutions can emerge. Paradoxes are something to embrace, to contain. These leaders lived with paradox knowing, as Heraclitus said, "nothing endures but change." Seeing paradoxes in their leadership is an indicator that these leaders are leading from the edge.

We said complexity science doesn't *replace* traditional models but, instead, *expands* them. Such is also the case with leadership. It's not about throwing away everything you know and do as a leader, but rather augmenting and encompassing different skills and placing those skills in a wider context of a new understanding of business. Paradoxical leadership fluctuates at the edge of a mechanistic and organic style of leadership, between structure and less structure, and in the world of complexity, fluctuation is healthy. Paradoxical leadership incorporates both the need for a leader to be strong, in terms of a strong sense of direction, a clear sense of self, and definitive values, and also an ability to let go, be open-ended, and to allow the organization to evolve, to respect that development, and let it take its own course. Both guidance and open-endedness are needed to lead in complex adaptive systems. It's not enough to just sit back and let things unfold. Then you enter chaos. It's not enough to have an iron grip. Then you enter stasis. The trick is, and it's a challenging one, to find a way to dance in between. As Tony Morgan pointed out, it's probably the hardest thing you'll ever do, but also potentially the most rewarding. The fundamental paradox in this leadership style is being *leaders by not leading*.

We intentionally use the word "practice" to capture the sense of *striving toward* rather than *achievement of* a goal, because human beings aren't perfect, their behavior fluctuates, they're messy really, and often find themselves off track, falling back into old behaviors. A practice provides guidelines, a point of reference, so that getting off track only means to start again and get back on. There's always another chance. As we said in the first chapter, it's not the falling down that's important, it's the getting up.

A practice also dispels any illusions of idealization; these practices, although essentially simple, are very hard to do. The most profound truths are the simplest and the most difficult; and, in the end, the most worthy. One thing that's obvious from these stories is that there's no getting *there* because *there* is always changing. But there is a different way of being there.

Following are the three practices, the three "A's" of paradoxical leadership—*allowing, accessible, attuned*—that cultivate conditions for change and adaptability in organizations.

Allowing

Allow things to emerge

Allow solutions to unfold rather than push answers too quickly. It's refraining from what Piaget called "la question americaine." Americans would always ask him how they could hasten and make growth happen faster. This perplexed him, because growth happens naturally and in its own time. Growing and getting bigger are two different agendas, as Andy Law pointed out. He wanted his company to grow, not get bigger, in such a way that they could continue to work in the way that they did. Paradoxical leaders both grow their organizations and let things unfold.

Hearing this line of argument, leaders often have a knee-jerk reaction, "What, you mean just let everything go, complete chaos, hoping something good will happen!" This is not what we are saying; we do not advocate continuous chaos. In order to be adaptable, people need to have freedom for maximum flexibility, but with freedom comes a need for an even stronger sense of direction. The leader's role as was demonstrated by many in these stories is to give vision and provide values to guide the direction he or she feels is right. And then get out of the way. As Jeanne Babel put it, once people understand the values, allow *them* to translate those values into actions.

But as we said, freedom requires strong leadership, and there are times when the leader has to follow what they feel strongly about, such as when Andy Law insisted on no assignment of personal desks, even though his people pleaded to have them.

The leader allows things to unfold by creating a psychological structure that will nurture people and foster many connections and help them grow. Dick Knowles's image of the bowl is a very useful metaphor in that the bowl is a safe container that gives people freedom to experiment, to create improvements, which gives order and freedom at the same time. To create this bowl, which has permeable walls that allow outside influence, is to involve many people in a conversation about the values, the mission, principles, standards, and expectations for the organization, from which a collective vision emerges and is constructed and reconstructed over time. As Dick said, "Most people know what to do if they have a good sense of the bowl."

Allow paradox, ambiguity, contradictions, uncertainty, redundancies
This is the critical mass, or more appropriately "mess," from which novelty emerges, from which change occurs. One common paradox among these organizations, which they were conscious of, was that they were very caring companies, and at the same time their people were often working extremely hard and were left to themselves to find a balance between work and home.

At the Industrial Society, by addressing and containing rather than ignoring the contradiction where they were helping to improve the workplace and needing help to improve their own workplace, a shared purpose emerged.

Allow experimentation

We'll talk more about this in the next chapter on emergent teams, but suffice it to say, experimentation keeps the organization at the creative edge, and that in complex adaptive systems small changes can have huge effects, as was the case in developing express admissions at Muhlenberg Medical Center.

Allow failures

Failures may be an unwanted result, but from a complexity perspective it's not just failure—period. Failures are points of learning, opportunities for generating greater adaptability in the organization in that they indicate what needs to change. As Jeanne Babel saw in the endeavor with Paine Furniture, it was a failure in that the custom design boutique didn't generate money, but it did lead to an unexpected and profitable result, where, facilitated by forming an alliance with Paine staff, designers went to people's homes. Chrissie Wright, project manager at the Industrial Society, said failures might not get you to where you want to go, but they can take you further along in your endeavors.

Allow mistakes

Leaders who cultivate don't avoid, deny, or punish mistakes, they transform them into learning experiences. Consider the following response to a "mistake" by Mike Ockendon, CEO of Barclays Home Finance, England. Mike, who works with complexity principles, describes what happened:

"I was sitting at my desk, and it was 2:30 on a Friday afternoon. The computer system went down. It's the weekend before a bank holiday, and so it's a big completion day for mortgages. So you immediately think, 'Oh God.' The lads from the IT department were in my office in five minutes. 'All right,' I say, 'I can see that the computer system isn't working. So you know what I want to hear next is not to worry—all the payments have been made or if they haven't been made, we've got a contingency.' Instead, they say, 'Wait a second, we know who did it and we're going to go and take care of him. Here we go.' And I say, 'I'll take care of this one personally.' You could almost see the glee on their faces at the prospect of a public execution.

"I went straight downstairs with them to the IT department, and was taken to this guy's desk. He was actually shaking with apprehension. I said, 'Please stand up. What's your name?' He said, 'John.' I said, 'John, I'd like to shake your hand and thank you for showing us the biggest system weakness that we have in this business. Now that we know it, we can fix it and none of our borrowers will ever suffer again. So thanks very much, John. I'll never forget your face. I'll never forget your name. Please sit down. Now you all can go and work out if all our customers are going to be able to move into their houses this weekend, please.'

"I mean there is no way you can crash a whole computer system from one guy's desk. And they did fix it. And all the borrowers moved in that weekend, and it went okay. I think that helped us a lot with the blame thing. If you make a mistake, then it's a learning experience. It's an opportunity; use it. Don't shy away from it. Don't be frightened to say it. Make it available to the whole business. If you do it two times, ask yourself why you did it the second time. If you do it three times, that's dumb. That event became a mini-legend in the company, and it's a kind of a joke around here. You know, a good way to get noticed around here—hey, I made a mistake, too."

Consider vice president of patient care at Hunterdon Medical Center in New Jersey, Linda Rusch, who is also guided by complexity principles in her work, and is mentioned in Curt Lindberg's alchemist story. She has formalized mistakes as learning experiences. She holds a weekly meeting called "Lessons Learned." It began with her telling her staff a story about a mistake she had made and what she learned from it, which set the ground for others to tell their stories. It continues today as a place where people learn from each other—freely critiquing each other, collaborating to find new solutions, collectively persistent in asking, "What is it that can be changed that can make things better?" Speaking to her and her staff, what engulfed us was the palpable connection between people—lots of joking, teasing, and playfulness, eye contact deep with meaning, an acute attention and sensitivity to each other. Here people talked about *their* hospital, *their* patients, *their* practice.

The paradox of allowing: direction without directives; freedom with guidance; authority without control.

Accessible

Be accessible physically
Paradoxical leaders make themselves visible in their organization and accessible to a broad range of people. For Hatim Tyabji this was being accessible to everyone in VeriFone through e-mail and accessible to his customers by trav-

eling 500,000 miles a year. Dick Knowles was accessible face-to-face, evident in leather worn off his shoes from walking the plant floor. Tony Morgan had an open-door policy. For owner Vic Babel, talking to customers was a priority, not a distraction. These leaders spent a lot of time talking to their people, their customers, and they recognized that time spent on developing relationships strengthens connections and makes for a more robust system.

Be accessible emotionally
At the core of paradoxical leaders is care. And when leaders care, they become emotionally accessible. They are not limited to rational thinking but speak from the heart and felt emotion as well. They are accessible to being moved by others, and don't hide it. Remember Tony Morgan "losing it" in front of the organization, Dick Knowles "losing it" in front of the community, Hatim Tyabji saying firing people wouldn't have been so traumatic if he didn't care, John Kopicki upset as he told the staff they would have a freeze in wages and how terrific they were and the group applauding him in the end?

Paradoxical leaders also make themselves accessible by opening themselves to people in the organization, in order to see more clearly what people really need. Remember Tony Morgan standing terrified on the platform when he realized he wasn't addressing what people needed and wanted at that time, and openly recognizing and admitting it? Or Dick Knowles realizing he was part of the problem at DuPont and opening himself to criticism and listening to what people really thought of him?

When a leader has access to his feelings, not just his thoughts, we saw in these stories the power leaders have to move their organization by speaking from the heart.

The paradox of accessibility: visible and invisible, mutual but not equal. Visible, as available when needed; invisible when not needed; visible, as mutual and one of the people; and yet as a leader not mutual and invisible as one of them.

Attuned

A paradoxical leader has a finger on the pulse of the organization, and he or she does this, as we said previously, in two ways: by having a sense of the organization as a whole and making choices in the interest of the whole, which departs from a reductionistic and a "parts" approach to the organization; and by recognizing the importance of being aware of the interactive level of the organization, that is, attuned to the quality of interactions between people in the organization. As Peter Senge pointed out, "the problems originate in basic ways of thinking and interacting, more than in peculiarities of organization structure and policy."[7] For example, one CEO of a large plastics company was interested in how complexity could help his organization. The owner and senior management were all young MBAs working in executive offices that were separated by a big wall from their factory. It turned out they were sitting on top of an organization they knew little about; they discovered they were running a sweatshop. Before they could think about more sophisticated approaches to their business, they needed to get their company up to minimal standards. They exemplify a lack of attunement. To be attuned, leaders learn to:

Empathize

Leaders must be able to put themselves in their employees' shoes and imagine what work might be like for them or how they might experience changes occurring in the organization; and also able to be in customers' shoes, like Mary Anne Keyes imagining herself as a patient, or Vic Babel imagining what the customer's aesthetic needs are. As Hatim Tyabji put it, it's not a dichotomy between touchy-feely or deliver the numbers—both can and do coexist and inform each other.

Listen and Respond

As Tony Morgan said, the best thing you can do is "shut up and listen." *How* you listen can change people. When you listen with your whole being, people know it. We also heard in these stories that listening, but not responding, is no better than not listening, and can be worse. Listening for issues and responding to them becomes the guide to organizational change rather than imposing change efforts.

Intuit

Leaders can't make decisions on facts alone, because they'll never have all the facts; it's too complex. There's no perfect answer. And even if you did have one, things are changing. By the time you plan it out and execute it, the answer is outdated. Where once decisions could be made in years, now you have months. Rational thinking is not enough—the wisdom of the unconscious needs to be engaged. Instead, trust your gut and listen to your intuition, instinct, and impulse, without being impulsive. It was Hatim's gut feeling that eventually led VeriFone to electronic commerce. The paradox here is holding rational goals while allowing irrational and unexpected connections; holding fact and possibility simultaneously.

Discriminate

Having a sense of the whole and the interactive dimension of the organization guides the leader to know what the culture needs. The leaders in these stories were careful in who they included in the organization, not necessarily the technically best people, but rather the right people—those who were not only qualified for the work but were the best fit for the culture of the organization. Leaders also discriminate by pointing out avenues of exploration.

Deliberate

Leaders are attuned to the undercurrents of their organization. They speak the unspeakable; they ask tough questions; they give the collective a voice. They keep the system open by providing fresh leadership so the organization doesn't fall back into old ways.

Faith and trust

Leaders have trust in the process and take leaps of faith in the intelligence and capabilities of their people.

   The paradox of attunement: knowing and not knowing. Knowing through hunches, intuition, senses and not knowing all the facts.

Soft Is Hard

When leaders can learn to recognize, contain, and live with paradoxes, their leadership can lead the way to a culture of change in their organization, where people have opportunities to grow and self-efficacy can develop. It may be tough but it's not impossible, as Carol Hassan, CEO of Watford City Council in England, told us:

"I had a lot of trouble at the beginning unlocking adopted positions, intractable situations, and getting them to rethink things. I tried to break down the rigidities. I didn't do this deliberately, but I think I created a lot of uncertainty. What they expected was, 'Well the former CEO is gone, now you tell us what to do.' What I did, and didn't realize at the time, was I let a structure emerge, let a new organization emerge out of the issues at hand. They were used to having six-hour corporate management meetings where the chief exec would sit at the top and talk bilaterally to the people, and they would respond when he spoke to them. I would go in with my flip chart and ask, 'What kind of meeting should we have?' They looked at me fearfully; it was palpable in the room. They thought that I already had in my head what was going to go on the flip chart. I had to fight this thing in their head that I was just totally disorganized.

"There were a whole series of meetings like that. They were standoffs really. They thought I had an agenda when I didn't. I'd be analyzing the problems openly and they were almost in shock the first time. But I kept putting it back to them. Once I asked, 'Why do you think the city councilors have lost confidence in the management team?' They just looked at me as if nobody ever said that. But they knew it. It was quite tricky because they were very threatened. They thought I had a list of who was going to go. So it was speaking the unspoken.

"They're beginning to see that my putting it back on them is about making honest choices about what they wanted to do, about the way they wanted to work."

As we said, paradoxical leadership may be one of the toughest things you do, but once you get a hang of it, leaders say there's no going back. Bob Shapiro sums up his ride as a paradoxical leader in this way:

"In the first year I was CEO, I really thought I ran the place. . . . By midway into my second year, I realized I wasn't running it, that we had the right people, at least in a lot of places, and *they* were doing it, not me. I understood what they were doing, I understood where we were going. I understood what they were trying to accomplish, and I liked it. It felt good. By my third year, I didn't even understand it. And it felt wonderful. As is perfectly appropriate, it felt as if the place was outgrowing me."

And the people say "we did it ourselves."

Chapter 16

Emergent Teams

Only those who attempt the absurd will achieve the impossible.

Albert Einstein

Many of us have already seen or been part of emergent teams—usually during times of crisis. That crisis could be relatively confined, such as when the water supply was cut off in a hospital, as we heard in Curt Lindberg's alchemist story. Or it could be more extensive, like the hurricane in Miami, when Veri-Fone people quickly rallied to help out fellow VeriFoners.

In emergent teams, everyone jumps into action; everyone intuitively knows what needs to be done; different people guide the collective action at different times, depending on the current needs and who has the requisite skills to match; the right people turn up at the right time; and it's all done in the spirit of goodwill and care. And the results are often beyond the imagined. A hospital is able to function without a main water supply through a surge of creative solutions and, according to the medical director, functions better than it ever had. And, as we heard in the anecdotes about a former CEO of Monsanto Company, people remember responding to crises at work as their most rewarding work experience, because it gets them out of the box. This capacity in people, and in teams, to do what is necessary in stressful situations by breaking through the normal day-to-day bureaucratic structures is the soul at work. Gaining access to this same potential in noncrisis times is a fervent desire of management strategists.

Modern Western culture has traditionally emphasized and admired individual accomplishment, and, as Jon Katzenbach and Douglas Smith have written, this "makes us uncomfortable trusting our career aspirations to outcomes dependent on the performance of others. . . . Even the thought of shifting emphasis from individual accountability to team accountability makes us uneasy."[1]

Equally, as Peter Drucker has pointed out, "In corporations, you are often dealing with prima donnas, yet it is a team where people often don't perceive that they have to work together."[2] Nevertheless, Drucker has been proselytizing about the productive and innovative potential of teams for more than half a century. General Motors ignored his advice in the 1940s, but came to see its validity the painful way—through the example of Japanese automakers in the 1970s. These days, gallons of printers' ink are spilled annually in the name of lauding the value of teams in the workplace (for a sampler, see *The Work of Teams*[3]). And there are plenty of data that show that not only do people feel more fulfilled when they are part of self-managed teams, but also that this translates to a stronger traditional bottom line for businesses that promote the model.[4]

For instance, Honeywell's defense avionics plant points to the implementation of self-managed teams as the source of dramatically improved on-time delivery, from 40 percent in the 1980s to 99 percent in 1996.[5] In one Bell telephone operating company, self-managed teams led to higher customer service and increased monthly sales revenues.[6] And the management philosophy of Whole Foods Markets, a natural foods grocery chain whose sales grew by 864 percent between 1991 and 1996, with an increase in net income of 438 percent, is predicated strongly on the power of self-managed teams. "We invest in and believe in the collective wisdom of our Team Members," the company's 1995 annual report states. "The stores are organized into self-managing work teams that are responsible and accountable for their own performance." Jack Welch, CEO of General Electric, attributes his company's stellar economic performance to the value of teams. He said rhetorically, "If you can't operate as a team player, no matter how valuable you've been, you don't really belong at GE."[7] Finally, a business survey has shown that more than three quarters of people in traditional work groups say they would volunteer for teams if they had that opportunity; and less than 10 percent of people who are members of teams would prefer to revert to traditional supervision.[8]

These success stories of self-managed, or self-directed, teams should be sufficient to encourage every organization to harness their power for greater success, but many fail, for reasons we set out below. Before we do so, it is worth making a distinction between emergent teams and traditional self-managed teams, as we saw in the organizations we worked with. Once formed, emergent teams do indeed self-manage. The key difference is that members of emergent teams are also *self-selected:* people choose to come together around a problem/challenge that one or more of them has identified. They come together because they care about the collective goal, and want to take responsibility for moving collectively toward that goal. They are not simply assembled as a group by a manager, and then given free rein to work together as they choose. Emergent teams self-select and self-manage, and are a key manifestation of organizations operating creatively as complex adaptive systems. In the corporations we worked with, we saw that they were the source of much of what made their organizations adaptable and successful in traditional business terms.

Barriers to Genuine Teams

As Drucker has pointed out, people in organizations have always in effect been part of a team, but "until now the emphasis has been on the individual worker and not on the team."[9] With that switch in emphasis, we find that our organizations are now littered with teams of many kinds: work teams, task force teams, problem-solving teams, cross-functional teams, and so on. There are front-line teams, and teams up the line, top teams. The formation of teams has wisely become a major tactic of organizations as they seek ways to respond to the demands of the modern, fast-changing business environment. And there is no doubt that genuine, self-directed teams are among the most creative and adaptable units with which companies can thrive in a fast-changing economy. In fact, it's too complex for solutions to come from one person anymore.

The emphasis here is on *genuine,* because, the above examples notwithstanding, teams too often are teams in name only, the creation of what Drucker calls "fashion-conscious" managers who have learned that teams are a Good Thing, but have not sufficiently understood the concept or have not taken the necessary time or commitment. "Companies are rushing into [creating teams] and expecting immediate results," he said in an interview in *Fortune* magazine in the fall of 1998. "In most cases, teams don't even work."[10] Stephen Covey, founder and chairman of the Covey Leadership Center, makes a similar point, saying that although managers profess to embrace team building and all that that implies in terms of giving power to their people, "the old benevolent-authoritarian paradigm has stayed the same."[11]

The problem is that many attempts to access the creative capacity of genuine teams are often shallow and superficial. Too many companies literally or metaphorically put people together in a room, and then call them a team, leaving the creation of an effective team entirely to chance. Or, just as futile, people's behavior may be tightly orchestrated, so that they go through the motions of teamwork, but without being a genuine team. Furthermore, it is well documented that after the experience of downsizing, people often feel less loyal to their employers, and superficial attempts at creating teams only embitter people more, as we heard in Lily's and Laura's alchemy stories about team initiatives.

Creating process teams in reengineering projects was an attempt at nudging creative capacity in people: managers empowered people to decide how and when the work was done, gave authority to make decisions, and an ability to create their own slots. And yet, reengineering projects failed 60 to 70 percent of the time. So why did people frequently not feel empowered? And why did the experience not engage the soul? Process teams concentrated on efficiency and optimization, but too often ignored the human factors. People knew that process teams were not initiated for their well-being, in the spirit of encouraging them to learn and grow, or as an opportunity for them to influence the direction of the organization. Workers recognized that it was yet another strategy to get more out of them, to extract better economic performance in order to meet the numbers. The contradiction of developing teams while managers often ruthlessly pursued bottom-line profits and huge remuneration was not lost on employees. Workers recognized the difference between a situation where they needed to fit into a plan rather than being afforded an opportunity to discover how they best fit in the organization. It was all upside down. Managers of process teams overlooked the fact that if people thrive, so will the organization, and that the chances are good that the numbers would flow from that.

The same thing happened with the empowerment movement. As business professor and consultant Chris Argyris states, "Managers love empowerment in theory, but the command-and-control model is what they trust and know best."[12] The duplicitous empowerment message was, "Yes, do it your way, but it better be what I want." And, yes, we, like Drucker, dislike the word "empowerment," a word that in its essence is hierarchical, where a so-called empowered one gives power to the so-called disempowered. The act may be magnanimous but the structure hasn't changed.

The problem with creating teams in this way is that teams were *imposed* onto the people, which made it no different from the traditional work groups with a single leader and a set agenda, except that these groups were, at least, honestly autocratic. Deception has hardened workers, who were already cynical from downsizing, who sarcastically asked what flavor-of-the-month application they would be subjected to next.

More strategies, more financial incentives, higher compensation, corporate status climbing—all this was aimed to motivate people, and it works, but only to a point. What these approaches continue to eschew and leave untapped is the source of productivity and innovation—the deep well of ingenuity in people, their limitless potential, their desire to create, contribute, and participate. Many team efforts fail because of these reasons—imposition of teams; teams not allowed to participate in the process of setting the course of action for the organization; and people not having a potential to influence the organization. In other words, imposing teams on people doesn't work because they aren't genuine teams. As Jon Katzenbach and Douglas Smith state in their important book *The Wisdom of Teams,* "Despite the attention teams have been receiving, the true high-performance team . . . is rare."[13] This is true for front-line teams, but most particularly for so-called top teams, because strong CEOs in the traditional sense are not natural team leaders, still less team members.

The Power of Intent

The difference between, for instance, process teams and emergent teams can be summed up in one word—intent. It's not a question of making money but rather *how* one makes it. The intent behind emergent teams is to cultivate people's competencies so they can be as good as they can be, and to create diverse opportunities for them to participate in and contribute to organizational goals. People in emergent teams have an opportunity to influence opinion and actions, to actively participate in shaping the task that might impact the entire organization. The belief here is that when people are connected to their work and to the organization, people flourish, and so then will the organization. The human factor is not a side issue in emergent teams—it's central.

The intent behind creating emergent teams is not a strategy for achieving a planned linear goal, but rather to engage nonlinear processes in the organization. Simple problems can be dealt with in a more linear sequential approach, solving one thing at a time. And, certainly, a linear approach is necessary for complicated problems. We wouldn't want a medical team approaching a routine surgical operation in a nonlinear, experimental way.

On the other hand, complex business problems require a lot of interactive components, that is, a lot of experimentation—trying different things simultaneously, in different parts of the organization—all done in the spirit of seeking those unpredictable nonlinear results. Emergent teams exist at the edge, and keep the organization adaptable. They become a way for the organization to find what might or might not work, and become a source for leaders to assess what's new, different, and changing in an organization. John Kopicki assessed the adaptability of his organization by gauging what Muhlenberg Medical Center was doing differently from one year to the next.

Value is placed on inquiry rather than on plans. The intent here is that emergent teams are opportunity-seeking rather than just problem-solving. Remember the slogan at Muhlenberg Medical Center: "Just try it." Like the buttercup, emergent teams are a way of putting out feelers, searching for where the fertile ground is, for what takes root and grows and what doesn't. Emergent teams are potentially the creators of small changes that can have an enormous effect on the whole organization.

Like process teams, emergent teams are allowed initiatives without prior authorization, are allowed to run with the problem. But unlike process teams, they are also more likely to be given the support and guidance they need. We saw that managers of emergent teams work hard at following through with their word to nourish the entrepreneurial collective spirit rather than try to direct it or interfere with it. Giving teams authority to pursue inquiries effectively distributes authority in the organization. In nature, distributed control makes for a quicker response time to changes in the environment. The same applies to organizations. In an unstable environment, such as today's rapidly changing business environment, the emergent team is a way to learn as you go.

The businesses in this book were highly innovative, and this could be attributed in part to their frequently allowing teams to emerge rather than always imposing them. What do these teams look like? Usually emergent teams were small, less than a dozen people, which made them agile. They were the gazelles of the organization, able to respond and move quickly. Their strategies and goals were negotiated and renegotiated among the members on the team, generating emergent strategies; that is, a general but strong direction rather than having to follow a specific plan. And most of all, as we said, they were experimental. They adapted to new information, which made them flexible, permeable, and fluctuating.

Emergent teams transformed a linear process, where people had their own territory and protected it, to a nonlinear one, where people came together on the common ground of a central task, be it a project, a client, a problem. With different expertise and understandings present in the team, everyone had an equal say because everyone had something to contribute. Breaking down hierarchy and linear processes, solutions came very quickly, as was the case with St. Luke's and Muhlenberg Medical Center. Rather than people limiting themselves to doing their own task, everyone talked together. At DuPont's Belle plant, emergent teams effected the installation of a new control system in half the time for half the money the company typically paid.

We also heard that working in an environment that encourages emergent teams can be difficult. Some people found it hard to take the responsibility of putting forward an idea, and being accountable for it. Others felt uneasy about volunteering to join an emergent team, because they were used to being assigned to teams. Remember Sue McGraw's comments about her early weeks at St. Luke's: "That was very difficult to begin with, because in my previous organization, in most organizations really, you're usually told what to do." But once people feel they had a genuine opportunity to initiate projects and make them happen, as we heard at the Industrial Society and Monsanto, people are full of ideas as to what might lead the company down innovative paths and they work hard to execute them, inviting others to join them.

Conditions for Emergent Teams

We said earlier that in times of crisis, teams emerge, prove to be highly effective, and people experience fulfilling work. Certainly, during times of crisis in organizations we see the power of emergent teams as people take action. Given that people can't work at a crisis pitch continuously, how then can we engage this innate ability to form genuine, effective, and innovative teams? If we take a look at times of crisis, we can see that certain elements come into alignment that spark people into action. Let's take the example of Jim Dixon, the former CEO of Cellular One in San Francisco, during the 1995 earthquake. In response to the breakdown of communications, he distributed three thousand cell phones free of charge to anyone who needed one. There was no hesitation in the team about what had to be done or how to organize it. People just did it, jumping into action because they had a *shared purpose* and there was a sense of *urgency*. As Jim told us, "It was both humanitarian and good business. It was the realization that our product is socially valuable and, under many circumstances, it's critical." There was also a sense of *mutuality* in that everyone had something to contribute to the cause and people saw that in each other. And, finally, it was driven by a sense of *care:* they cared about helping people out and cared about getting the job done. At the end of the crisis, that care manifested in the fact that Jim got all but ninety phones back, the others being lost. "Because our effort was generous," said Jim, "we had nothing to worry about." For the team members themselves it was a new awareness of their capabilities. "They had a chance to see a certain caliber in themselves," Jim told us. "They now know they are more and can do more than they thought they could."

These same crisis elements—*shared purpose, urgency, mutuality,* and *care*— were more or less aligned in the businesses you read about here, which created conditions for teams to emerge in varying degrees in these organizations, and tapped into previously untapped potential. People in these organizations had a clear sense of purpose; a sense of urgency helped focus them to be more attentive and present; mutuality was manifested as respect where people affected and were affected by one another; they cared about their projects, and cared enough to want their organization to be a better, growing organization. If those conditions exist in your organization, then your organization is ripe for emergent teams, too. But if those conditions don't exist, they can be cultivated. The organizations you read about actively cultivated conditions for teams to emerge.

Cultivators

Emergent teams reframe management's task. From a complexity science perspective, managers are not managers, but cultivators. Cultivators don't manage people; in fact, they rely heavily on people managing themselves. They cultivate people. They don't streamline processes, but instead connect people to each other to create new pathways and fluid communication, and then the processes streamline themselves. They replenish people by creating new opportunities for participation, and enrich interactions by forging new connections to resources and people. They support teams by giving them what they need to succeed.

Rather than controlling people with defensive strategies, such as not listening to people, projecting a veneer of self-importance, hoarding and withholding information, and inflexible rigor; rather than treating people like pieces on a chessboard, a doing "to" people, the cultivator works to get all the people in the system to be, as the *Wall Street Journal* columnist Tom Petzinger put it, the eyes, ears, and brains of change in the organization. In other words, cultivators work hard to bring out people's strengths by giving them lots of responsibility and freedom and support, and then getting out of the way. In this manner, genuine teams can emerge, where people can learn and contribute, so that the collective learns and the organization thrives.

The effect of the cultivator approach manifested itself as a palpable connection that we saw and felt as we met various teams and cultivators—a deep respect, regardless of status or position in the organization, and an ease with themselves and each other. What emerged from these teams was often more than anyone could have imagined, and sometimes results came short of a miracle—outcomes that no one person intended, expected, or foresaw. Remember the Industrial Society reaching impossible financial goals, and the dramatic increase in productivity, reduction of emissions, and increase in safety at DuPont's Belle plant? Dick Knowles did this by enriching the nonlinear processes in the complex adaptive system, that is, the chemical plant.

We do not mean to create the illusion of ideal worlds in these organizations, with managers happily and with ease assuming the mantle of cultivator, and their people wholeheartedly and always seeking ways to contribute to the whole and be collectively creative in emergent teams. What we describe are *possibilities,* the *potential* that *can* be unleashed when people are able to embrace this way of being and working. Yes, the Industrial Society *did* achieve some impossible financial goals, but not all of them. Yes, productivity, emissions, and safety *did* improve at DuPont's Belle plant, but there were still occasional clashes between management and workers. Yes, St. Luke's *did* become highly creative and successful as an advertising agency, but the workplace was by no means free of bickering and jealousy. We also heard that when day-to-day pressures were high, and when uncertainty swelled, managers were often tempted to revert to the "safety" of being traditional managers, not cultivators (see Dick Knowles's and Bob Shapiro's stories, for example), and workers yearned for more traditional, structured ways of working (see St. Luke's and the Babels, for example). What we saw, then, were not ideal worlds, but worlds in which for much of the time unusual levels of creativity and community were engendered when managers were able to act as cultivators and workers felt the freedom and confidence to coalesce as emergent teams.

We found that, when they were able, managers as cultivators in these organizations focused their efforts and attention on *inclusive diversity, openness, fertilizing connections,* and *holding the space,* which cultivated conditions for teams to emerge and people to self-organize. By focusing on these dimensions of the workplace, they created a feedback loop from which a shared purpose, a sense of urgency, mutuality, and care emerged. We'll talk about these behaviors separately, but they are in fact dynamically interconnected, as is the nature of complex adaptive systems.

Inclusive Diversity

We know from complexity science that complex adaptive systems thrive on diversity—the ingredient that spices up the "critical mess"—and will self-organize and naturally move toward the zone of creativity and adaptability. These cultivators placed a lot of value on diversity, knowing that the more variety in perspectives, the greater the likelihood of arriving someplace very new—as long as the perspectives are not so divergent that there is no common ground. Having too much diversity can be as bad as having too little.

Diversity has always been present in modern organizations; it is only recently that businesses have come to value and see the benefits of diversity—that it enhances adaptability because there are fewer restrictions on what people are willing and can do. Diversity provides an opportunity to expand the realm of possibilities while seeking a common ground of understanding, vision, or purpose. With diversity comes a greater expansion of new ideas, methods, and approaches.

However, it is not enough just to value diversity. It has to be actively included. In other words, diversity serves no good if there aren't opportunities afforded for these differences to interact, for these differences to be included. Inclusive diversity keeps the buffet table of perspectives full because it allows for all ideas to be worth listening to, such as the Babels wanting the driver's opinion as well as the decorator's.

Inclusive diversity takes many shapes and forms in the workplace. Of course, diversity in gender, race, and age brings a richness of perspectives. For example, when was the last time a senior person in your organization exchanged ideas with a Generation X person? Siemens, of Germany, for example, put together mentoring teams, hooking new, young, and bright employees with more experienced, older senior staff. The immediate assumption is that the mentoring goes from senior to junior level. In this case, it was the younger staff who were the mentors, bringing the senior staff up to speed on using computer technology, information systems, and the Internet.

Cross-department teams, a practice at VeriFone and Muhlenberg, provide an opportunity to share information, catch redundancies, and increase the potential for creative and efficient solutions. We saw the benefits of this clearly at St. Luke's in their effectiveness and creativity as an advertising agency. We also saw this at DuPont's Belle plant, where mechanics and operators worked with engineers to quickly install a new control system. BMW exemplifies how cross-department emergent teams can lead the way to markets of the future. As

Peter Foster, who initiated a diversity approach on his team of BMW engineers, told us:

"They were trained to defend their functional territory; they weren't trained to go out of their territory and find common solutions. We were still creating technically refined cars, but we saw our limits and that's why we tried this approach—to train our people so they look for common problem solving together in other functions, not just for themselves. There was a lot of competition among them, yet there was a lot of interaction and cooperation. It was actually quite unique to see the closeness develop. And it was extraordinary what we achieved." What they achieved was the BMW 500 series.

Inclusive diversity begins with hiring people, such as at 3M, which began hiring liberal art graduates into their Information Technology division. But bringing diversity into an organization that has a long tradition of a certain type of culture is not easy, as Monsanto's Bob Shapiro told us: "The tendency is for people to want to surround themselves with people who make them comfortable, and the people who make you comfortable often are people a lot like you." As a cultivator, attaining the diversity you want to achieve requires a constant struggle. When a strong practice of inclusive diversity has been achieved within the organization, however, it can extend outside, to include the suppliers, customers, complementors, the community, and even competitors, as a way to combine efforts in joint problem solving, as we saw in the Babels' story.

But inclusive diversity is not an easy balance to achieve. Too much diversity can bog a team down; not enough creates teams where everyone thinks alike. And of course, businesses are often confronted with restrictions for creating diverse emergent teams, such as trade unions and difficult people. Global projects add another layer of complexity, where more effort is needed to come to a mutual understanding and acceptance among different cultures. VeriFone managed global diversity in their worldwide offices by including different practices within branches in different countries. When it works, inclusive diversity breaks down barriers, as Dick Knowles put it, between "us" and "them," that can lead to a "we."

Openness

Cultivators create a sense of openness in an organization by creating opportunities for people to learn, to participate, and contribute, and they do this by opening up projects to self-selection. They are also open with information and resources—the oxygen of organizations—which nourishes the collective intelligence, making for an interactively robust and wiser system.

Opening Up Projects, and Self-Selection

As we said earlier, emergent teams are self-selected. Cultivators invite new voices into the processes that influence the organization that too often are limited to a select few. That means not only allowing but encouraging anyone, and especially those who are overlooked, who want to participate in a project to do so. We saw the benefits of opening projects to $8 per hour secretaries at Muhlenberg Medical Center, how it was a general practice at the Industrial Society, DuPont's Belle plant, VeriFone, and at St. Luke's. These projects were initiated by the leaders, such as Jeanne Babel opening up a customer service task force, or by staff, as in the Industrial Society and Monsanto. Whatever the case, anyone who was interested in a project was invited to become part of that project.

Behind self-selection lies the wisdom that people who are "in" the problem probably have a lot to contribute to finding a way "out" of it. As people move up in organizations, their tasks become more and more distanced from day-to-day operations. Front-line people, on the other hand, are immersed in the problems—delivery, producing, reliability—and are a tremendous source of information about the customer, the market, and the daily operations. Often their wealth of knowledge and experience remains unrealized, because no one higher up in the organization ever asked them what they thought. And if management ever did, they often didn't act on it, as Rhonda Owens at Muhlenberg Medical Center so succinctly pointed out.

Also, self-selection keeps people engaged. As we said earlier, if people aren't climbing a hierarchical ladder, then they need learning and experiential goals to keep them involved.

Open with Resources and Information

In complex adaptive systems, the better the flow of information, the more connections people make and see, the greater the possibilities for adaptability. Limiting information limits the system. When information rests in a few hands, those who have it feel a need to hold on to it for personal power, and use it to dictate their own agendas. It limits what is possible; it shuts others out. Instead, cultivators treat information, "not as gold bars you put in the vault of a bank, but as a world of abundant information," as Bob Shapiro pointed out. Protecting information slows things down, and in fast-changing times, that hinders adaptability. Cultivators believe in throwing information into the common pot of knowledge, knowing that they can also take things out. They watch the flow of information in their area of jurisdiction, synthesizing disparate pieces of information, watching for new patterns in situations, recognizing patterns that apply to new situations, informing the internal organization of external realities.

When management opens access to resources and information, it flattens out the hierarchical relationships. We saw the power of this in the VeriFone e-mail culture. E-mail in general is a great equalizer that breaks down hierarchical barriers to information. Openness with information eases paranoia and anxiety in organizations. People, more often, would rather know the realities than be left in the dark to speculate, which often leads to suspicions, rumors, and worst-case scenarios. When people are informed and know the challenges, they will reorganize themselves so that they are better able to address them, as Dick Knowles pointed out.

A democratic access to information and resources predisposes people to get what they need to thrive, cultivates people's ability to get a sense of complex problems, arouses curiosity, creates a context for discovering better-informed solutions, which ultimately gives organizations what they need to deal with changing times.

Fertilizing Connections

Fertilizing connections demands strong interpersonal skills from the cultivator. These skills include supporting people in their work—by connecting people who might benefit from each other's experience; by encouraging people to learn to deal with, rather than avoid, difficult people and situations; by guiding them to move through difficulties rather than just cope with them; by generating constant conversation—discussions, sense making, brainstorming, and even storytelling. For instance, Linda Rusch, vice president for patient care at Hunterdon Medical Center, New Jersey (see Curt Lindberg's alchemist story in Chapter 13), recently set up a newsletter that gathers stories of people's work experience so that others could learn from them. Fertilizing connections with people is to work with them from *where* they are rather than from where you would like them to be or from where they think they should be. Cultivators help people frame problems and don't rush in to solve them. They work *with* people, helping them through their fears, their limitations, their doubts. As Hatim Tyabji said, "Try to do your best to understand what their insecurities may be, and then work with them. When you reach out to them, they will reach right back."

Cultivators fertilize people's *ideas* by seeing their potential and nurture those nascent seedlings of innovation; they develop competencies and encourage people to stretch beyond their comfort zone. Like Tony Morgan, cultivators invite people to come up with "crazy ideas." Similarly, Jack Welch invites his people to "stretch," to be led by dreams rather than by plans, even though they have no idea how to reach them. And Lawrence Bossidy, CEO of AlliedSignal, says, "Senior managers should be less worried about getting off-the-wall suggestions and more concerned about failing to unearth ideas."[14] When ideas are released, people, as Dick Knowles pointed out, "discover meaning in their work. . . . It's the difference between doing what you have to do to keep from being fired, and being fired up and doing the max." And as we saw in these stories, cultivators respond to new ideas and follow up on them and they instill a practice that even though an idea may be yours, it doesn't belong to you—it belongs to everyone.

Cultivators fertilize connections by attending to the health of the collective. This includes pruning those people who drain and take away energy from the whole, those who create toxic connections, those who are misplaced and don't fit. They are what John Kopicki calls "culture casualties." And cultivators attend to the whole by eliciting information, seeking the important questions, and carefully listening to opinions and ideas as to what is needed to make things better collectively.

Holding the Space

Cultivators have an enormous faith in people's ability to do what they need to do if they are given a safe space to pursue their goals. The cultivator holds the space by making it a safe space for expressing opinions and ideas. As Chrissie Wright, of the Industrial Society, stated, this encourages risk taking: "I was willing to take that risk because it felt safe. . . . What Tony did was create a context for risk, by legitimizing it and saying it was valid, rather than a mad thing to do. It was very liberating."

Cultivators hold the space by "being there" by attending to the nonquantifiable factors in the environment, such as learning, discontent, enthusiasm, and are not there looking over people's shoulders. Cultivators recognize palpable experience—they can *feel* the excitement of possibilities, the heightened level of energy, as well as the obverse. They sense when a team is growing and attracting interest and when it isn't. They are there working to get people excited about their work. Because they are in there with their people and close to the situation, they can nurture adaptability rather than manage change.

Mostly, cultivators hold the emotional space. Because emergent teams are on the roller-coaster edge, there are lots of ups and downs, and these teams are often cauldrons of emotional fluctuation. Cultivators recognize that feelings such as confusion, uncertainty, anxiety, incompetence, frustration, wanting to "fix it" and not knowing how, are indicators that the team is on the edge of creative adaptability. Rather than trying to alleviate this tension, cultivators hold it, by reassuring people and having enormous faith that they can find their way. Bob Shapiro did this when he pushed Monsanto into chaos as a path to reinventing the company; as did Andy Law, during the first difficult year of creating St. Luke's; and so did Dick Knowles, when he invited his people to help him save the Belle plant, even though there was tremendous uncertainty about how it would turn out. This is difficult work because many managers have a hard time with emotions—their own as well as others'.

And finally, cultivators hold the space by *embodying* the conditions for emergence. They themselves strive to be open and available, to demonstrate an appreciation for diverse perspectives, to encourage and support, to turn thoughts into action, and are themselves in constant interaction. Consequently they are well connected to the people they work with. And most of all, they don't coach, but let the people do it for themselves. They are too busy to direct others because they are diligently cultivating conditions in their garden.

These conditions, which value the uniqueness of individuals, which value fulfilling people by nurturing and stimulating their capabilities, lead to an environment that gives people a potential to deal with times of uncertainty, armed with what they need, what they know, and what they need to find out: an environment of unusual creative potential during noncrisis times.

Patience and Paradox

We've talked about how to create conditions for genuine teams to emerge and coalesce. When that happens, how do you cultivate creative emergence within a team? One condition that cultivates the emergent team is *patience*. Unlike times of crisis, when the purpose is very clear and there isn't time to get to know people, emergent teams in normal times take longer to develop. It takes patience to get everyone on board to what the problem is and what the task is. It takes patience for emergent strategies to unfold from the negotiating, renegotiating processes. It takes patience to build a critical mess from which a common purpose and a clarity of direction will emerge. It takes patience for people to personally connect to the project and to each other. It takes patience to go from what is known to what is becoming. It takes patience to get cooking.

But once it takes, it can take quickly. Like water, it heats and heats, then enters a phase transition, and suddenly it changes. Once it reaches a boil it doesn't take long for it to roar. Emergent teams simmer and stew, but they, too, go through a phase transition, and, once engaged, the work goes swiftly. This is what the people of St. Luke's experienced during their first year of experimenting with new ways of working. Another way of putting it is that it's the Chinese cooking style of teamwork. Most of the time in Chinese cooking is spent on preparing to cook—chopping vegetables, making sauces, marinading. But once it's done, the cooking itself goes quickly.

Even though slow at first, in the end, however, this way of working is more efficient. Time isn't wasted on restating why things are being done in a certain way, of going back to square one because choices were made prematurely. In emergent teams people know the "what" and the "why," whether they fully agree with it or not. Traditional teams follow a more mechanistic pattern, which consultant Jim Highsmith names as the "plan-design-build" pattern. Emergent teams follow another pattern, what he calls "the iterative life cycle: speculate-collaborate-learn."[15] In other words, the end point for an emergent team is "not the *implementation* of the project, but the *acceptance* of the project," as Muhlenberg's Mary Anne Keyes put it to us. Emergent teams require patience because you can't push the river. Solutions, innovations can't be accessed before their time. That means giving them a chance, as Jeanne Babel noted, "to bloom or wither."

The paradox of emergent teams, which is a characteristic of the creative zone, is potential contained within parameters. Constraints of a few simple guidelines by the cultivator and by the team itself work to guide the potential. Guidelines specified by the cultivator are often minimal, which allows the team to bring complexity to the situation. Jim Taylor, president and CEO of University of Louisville Hospital, gave his interdepartmental team of nurses one guideline: "meet weekly." Peter Foster of BMW gave his team one guideline: "Approach me when you have a problem. I'm here to try to sort it out with you." Janet Biedron's at Muhlenberg was "make me look good." Jeanne Babel's guidelines were "show up mentally as well as physically; serve the customer; keep the place stocked and clean." From a few simple guidelines, complex behavior, rich with adaptation and creativity, can rise.

Collective Steering

We found there were common practices of interaction within emergent teams, not unlike the rules that guided the boids model we described in Chapter 2. Boids, as you may recall, is a computer model that simulates the complex behavior of flocking guided by a few simple rules. Like birds and boids, emergent teams engage in a similar behavior—collective steering. *Collective* in that no one person gets credit for the achievements of the group, nor the blame. At St. Luke's, that manifested in their refusal to enter for industry awards because typically they are given to an individual rather than a team. *Steering* in that all members of a team have an influence on the direction of the project and a responsibility within the given direction.

The following three practices, translated from boids to human terms—mutuality, fluctuating authority, resilience—are a vortex of progression: from mutuality, fluctuating authority emerges, from which resilience emerges, and all together from these interactions emerges collective steering.

No. 1: Stay Close—Mutuality

Mutuality keeps people close to one another. We saw mutual *respect* in these teams, as we said before, a recognition in each other as each having something unique to contribute to the cause, regardless of power differences. People felt that they had at least a chance to *influence* the direction and action of the team.

They were mutual in that they held themselves *accountable*—that the onus belonged to each and every one, a melding of individual and mutual accountability. They were mutual in their efforts to *learn* as a team; a range of knowledge was mutually valued and a lack of it handled. And they were willing to learn from each other.

When a sense of mutuality develops in a team, members assume the best, that actions of others on the team—even though they might sometimes seem obscure—have an intent of goodwill. Mutuality transforms "you and me" to an emerging "us." If you're not part of the problem, you are the problem.

No. 2: Keep Up—Fluctuating Authority

As in a flock of birds, where each takes a turn at the head of a flock, emergent teams have no one leader, but many. Authority of each team member surfaces at different times depending on who has the experience and knowledge relevant to the issue. As one manager told us, "If someone outside of a team asks who the leader is, then that person has never been on a good team."

No. 3: Don't Bump into Anything—Resilience

Emergent teams don't get stopped by obstacles, because they care about the project and each other. As we heard in many stories, people on emergent teams were resilient because they didn't want to let the other members down. Like birds, they often found their way around obstacles—the unexpected, the surprises—by being improvisational and resourceful. They would pool all their resources, choosing what was needed for the moment. One of the more common obstacles that people bump into is not enough information sharing among team members. One simple rule that Liz Rykert, a consultant and group facilitator, uses to circumvent this obstacle is: "If I have more information than you, I have an obligation to share it. If I have less information than you, I have an obligation to ask." Working around obstacles makes the team resilient.

Two Paths

When teams fail at collective steering and creative adaptation, it can usually be traced back to a failure to establish a practice of mutuality, which permeates and poisons the other practices. If there isn't time to establish a familiarity and mutuality among team members, and they fail to respect and be influenced by one another, be accountable, and learn, then credibility and faith in others is undermined. It devolves into a sense of people being on their own and resorting to every person for her- or himself. In this context, people will cling to their roles and draw authority from their status or lack of it. People stop paying attention to each other, some dominate, while others retreat and don't bear their share of responsibility. When people become alienated, fluctuating authority collapses. If, in the face of surprises, there is insufficiently clear communication, there will emerge a failure to understand; and if this failure is met with a lack of effort to understand, resilience collapses into confusion.

With confusion, collective steering becomes disoriented; why and where we are going comes into doubt, and a different critical mess gathers. Small unrelated inaccuracies, misunderstandings, misinterpretations interact, and a primordial pool percolates until it tips, and what emerges is not collective steering, but rather chaos and dissipation, where teams disintegrate and members cease to be members, where people may be *doing* teamwork but are not *being* a team.

On the other hand, when these three practices of mutuality, fluctuating authority, and resilience come into play, practice becomes play, and play becomes possibilities, and possibilities become your future. As Stephen Covey has said, most managers acknowledge that "the vast majority of the workforce . . . possess more talent, more creativity, more initiative and more resourcefulness than their present jobs require or even allow them to use."[16] As we've seen, these dormant resources are tapped into during crises, and emergent teams is a way of tapping into these same resources under noncrisis conditions. As Bob Shapiro said, "It works because this is what people really want."

Chapter 17

Relational Practice

Spirit is not in the I but between I and You. . . . It is not like the blood that circulates in you but like the air in which you breathe. . . . It is solely by virtue of his power to relate that man is able to live in the spirit.

Martin Buber, *I and Thou*

Jeff (a pseudonym), a technically brilliant chief information officer, worked for a large telecommunications company, and was considered to be among the best in the world. He frequently received major job offers—$1 million a year was a typical lure. Because he was so revered, people from all around the world would come to work with him, attracted intellectually to the technological challenges they would face with him, and also wanting to develop their skills under his guidance.

Jeff put together a technically skilled team for a major project—a dream team in anyone's estimation—and quickly got everyone working.

A year and a half later, all the members of Jeff's team resigned.

Jeff assembled another team, and the same thing happened again. He would lose several people and bring new ones on until he basically had a brand-new team. It happened again and again. Jeff became confused about being a leader.

What was the problem here?

If we focus on relationships, the mystery resolves itself.

Knowing intellectually that relationship building is widely said to be valuable, Jeff tried to develop team-building skills. But he applied these skills in a very mechanical way, like tricks he pulled out of a magic bag. He had strategies for talking to people, engaging them, providing opportunities. But he wasn't really there; he was only going through the motions to reach certain ends. He didn't see *genuine* relationships as being very important or having much value—it was more an obligation and something he did initially for team building, because it was the thing to do.

Initially his strategies and skills worked. But as soon as he got a team spirit going, he would think, "Great. We've done the relationship, connection, feedback stuff. Don't need to do it for another year or so. Now we can get to the real work." Been there, done that, he blew it off. He, in a sense, devalued relationships by making nonrelational activities more important, by separating relationships from real work.

Since he didn't value relationships in and of themselves, he was unwilling to give up something valuable in order to develop them—time. He thought developing genuine relationships was a waste of time. This was due partly to the fact that he wasn't really interested in people personally. His agenda at meetings rarely included people as people, such as asking "How are you doing?" "How is the team getting along together?" and all those things that can build a sense of connection. When he did ask someone how they were doing, it wasn't a personal question. He was asking them to tell him how business was. By not being interested in people for themselves, Jeff disconnected himself from the team.

After a year, the team asked Jeff if he even knew where their offices were. He didn't. Their response was straightforward: "Then you wouldn't be able to find us, would you?" Jeff not only couldn't find them physically, he couldn't, nor cared to, find them as people was the message he was giving.

Because there were no relationships holding the team together, when they encountered a particularly stressful period—a multimillion-dollar, short-deadline project—they had nothing to fall back on, nothing to hold on to. And the team fell apart.

Jeff's team, having come from all over the world, expected to find a community of relationships. That's not unreasonable given they were spending seventy hours a week with each other and were sacrificing a balance in their lives—with their families, their communities, their other involvements. If they didn't have a community of relationships at work, it was absent in their lives. If it was absent in their lives, then a significant portion of what made them human beings, what makes people feel good about themselves, was gone. When all else is the same, and people don't have the work relationships they want, it becomes a priority, and so they left.

Strategic Paradox

It's not that Jeff himself may not have longed for connection and relationships—we all do; it's our nature. It's how we grow and thrive. For whatever reasons, Jeff had lost connection to that need in himself, and as a result had developed a *strategic paradox.* He tried to develop team relationships without *being* truly present. Strategic paradoxes are interpersonal strategies people develop that prevent from occurring the very thing that the person needs in order to be successful and wants to have as a human being. These strategies paradoxically prevent genuine connections and relationships; that is, they maintain disconnected and superficial business-based relationships.

Some people maintain disconnected relationships for the sake of keeping a job, for the sake of keeping a customer, for the sake of getting a job done—all of which sounds laudable. But these strategies work only for the short term. They do not work in the interest of sustainability of work relationships with customers and co-workers, because connections are weak, as we saw in Jeff's case. When push comes to shove, people move on rather than move together to take on the challenges. Within an organization, weak connections make for a poor flow of information. Unwittingly these strategies perpetuate a dysfunctional, disconnected, maladaptive system. Inadvertently these strategies, from front-line to executive levels, collude to preserve existing hierarchies, inequalities, and isolation, limiting feedback loops and thus adaptability. Strategic paradox is like comedian Steve Wright put it—suffering from amnesia and déjà vu at the same time; that is, a feeling that you are forgetting the same thing over and over again—the need for connected and caring relationships.

A Need for Affiliation:
Caring and Connected Relationships

Jeff's story illustrates what is common in the world of business: that is, many people tend not to place value on relationships. When we overdevelop our human need of ambition at work—that is, achievement, power, and success—we lose balance in our organizations. We lose sight of the obvious: that business in its most fundamental sense is an exchange between two people in a mutually benefitting *relationship.* If we bring only a mind of ambition to our work relationships, we are in danger of disregarding people as we strive toward self-serving goals, which can dehumanize our organizations. In the process of reinventing Perot Systems, CEO Mort Meyerson recognized the consequences of such single-minded ambition: "The emphasis on profit-and-loss to the exclusion of other values was creating a culture of destructive contention. . . . We risked becoming a company where the best people in the industry wouldn't want to work." And he adds, "There's a much larger calling in business today than was allowed by the old definition of winning and losing."[1]

That larger calling needs a balanced mind and a balanced organization. We can achieve that balance by recognizing and developing our human need for *affiliation* in our work relationships; that is, we can counterbalance striving for power and success with our need for care and connection, our desire to be engaged as a member of our organization. It's affiliation that creates rich connections in an organization from which a community of care and shared purpose can emerge—the staying power for organizations during times of change. Visa's Dee Hock expressed this sentiment this way: "When an organization loses its shared vision and principles, its sense of community, it is already in a process of decay and dissolution even though it may linger with the outward appearance of success for some time."[2] Professor Henry Mintzberg, in his no-mincing-words manner, observed the same: "Lean *is* mean and doesn't even improve long-term profits. . . . Organizations need continuous care, not interventionist cures. . . . Great organizations have souls; any word with a *de* or a *re* in front of it is likely to destroy those souls."[3] True affiliation is a way to engage people and bring the balance needed to generate robust, adaptive, and healthy emergence in too ambitious organizations.

Addressing needs for affiliation brings no small benefit to the organization. As we discussed earlier, there have been many studies showing that organizations who pay attention to people, that is the relational world, were more financially successful. When people experience caring connections, they become motivated. Caring and connected relationships motivate people because, through connections with others, people feel able to do more and be more, and have a revitalized ability to act. When the workplace becomes a web of connection, people feel safer, real, satisfied.

We've written about paradoxical leadership and cultivating emergent teams, but they don't work in and of themselves. Although Jeff had strategies for building teams and a style of leadership that worked for a while, it crumbled, because it was lacking in a deep simplicity. At the source, beneath paradoxical leadership and emergent teams, are caring and connected relationships that meet our human need for affiliation.

As GE's Jack Welch puts it, "If managers don't get out and care about their people, the people won't do things for them. You have to constantly care. The only thing that makes our company is the fact that our people are in the game."[4] Bob Shapiro says something similar about Monsanto: "If we get authenticity and if we get caring in the workplace, then we've got something very important. The rest will fall into place." VeriFone's Hatim Tyabji, in his retirement message, characterized care as the core of him as a leader: "I have one character trait that runs to excess—it is my sense of caring. I care deeply for VeriFone and its mission. I care deeply for our customers and partners. And above all, I care deeply for each of you." And Alex, the greeter at the River Café, told us that the staff felt a very personal care from the owners, Ruth Rogers and Rose Gray, and how powerful that was in building a committed work community, which in the restaurant business usually consists of a transient population. In fact, care is a constant in all these organizations, not only on a professional level but also personal, which leads to a greater sense of community.

How then do we begin to generate caring and connected relationships at work? We begin with awareness. We begin by being aware of the world of relationships and by paying as much attention to these micro dynamics in organizations—how they influence social processes and psychological health of individuals—as we currently do to macro issues, such as economic performance and strategies.

We begin by recognizing that caring, connected relationships are not things you have, not static entities, objects that you hold, lose, forget, ignore, replace, and, most of all, take for granted. They are not a given. Rather, they are moving and dynamic, like an improvisational dance, constructed and reconstructed, transforming, and in constant motion. And most of all they are open-ended, uncertain, and mysterious. They are another garden to cultivate.

Just as emergent team members see difference in others through diversity, relationships are a place where we see similarity—we are more alike than we are different. As alchemist Curt Lindberg put it, "You are me." It's being aware that we all struggle to *be*—to be seen, to be cared about, to grow at work. And this is a global reality. As Katherine Beall of VeriFone stated, it's "recognizing people for just being people." At the core, people are gentle creatures, wishing to be seen for themselves and valued for who they are and what they can bring to the table. These important dimensions can't be seen with the eye, but rather require a fine vision for seeing where our own hearts and the hearts of others are and finding a way to engage them.

Stories, Conversations, Trust

The affiliative self is engaged by the narrative rather than the analytic mind. That means to develop caring and connected relationships is to become genuinely interested in others and to invite conversations and engage people's stories. In a fast-changing world inundated with information, we are also in an accelerated rate of disconnection and loss of meaning. Conversations become a way of connecting to each other, for assimilating information and discovering meaning, that is, it is through our conversations that change happens. Conversations generate interaction in the system and a potential for strong connections. And we know that strong connections in a complex adaptive system make for a robust and creative system.

Increasingly, the edge for business success is through the reality of the conversation between you and your customer and colleagues, as our world becomes ever more complex. For instance, technology no longer delivers the edge it used to, because everyone can have access to good technology. The edge is the service, and that means developing a relationship and engaging in an ongoing conversation to know your customer—who they are as people, their interests, their needs. For VeriFone, this means having teams right next to their customers for this very purpose.

The organizations you read about took cultivating relationships seriously and recognized the importance of developing conversations. They recognized that informal, nonlinear conversations, unlike agendas, are a pathway to unexpected nonlinear results. At St. Luke's, they created a physical space that encouraged conversations among the staff, believing that at a game of table soccer or over a cup of coffee in the chill-out space some of the best ideas could come up. Similarly, managers at Siemens' power transmission and distribution plant in North Carolina removed the time clock, expanded the cafeteria, and added flip charts to encourage lingering lunch breaks and nonlinear learning, seeing the wealth of thinking that comes from the informal conversation.

It was clearly visible that these organizations took cultivating conversations seriously by the mere fact of the *time spent on relationships*. Remember how the entire staff of St. Luke's go away every year for a week to reinvent itself? And how VeriFone senior staff meet for a week, every six to eight weeks? And how the Industrial Society took the whole organization away for a three-day retreat and plan to do it again? The point here is that spending time in conversation with others which develops constructive relationships is not wasting time;

it's essential to the health and growth of the organization, for creating what former Royal Dutch/Shell executive Arie de Geus calls a "living company."

Engaging people's stories deepens the conversation and is a way to instigate the delicate work of building trust in an organization. Knowing people's stories—their hopes and fears, expectations and disappointments, their insights and insecurities, aspirations and avoidances strengthens the connection, enriches the relationship, and generates care because we get right into people's personal experience. People's stories illuminate the diversity of their experience, challenge the plausibility of perspectives, and capture the flow of changing realities. Remember how Vic Babel spent a half-hour getting to personally know a customer, even though there would be no sale? At Monsanto, we saw time spent in getting to know people's stories—what they could and wanted to contribute to the whole.

Mark Levine, a physician and director of the family practice residency program of Hamot Health in Pennsylvania, who has been learning about complexity, commented to us, "Two years ago I would never have dreamt that I would be thinking about relationships, but I am now!" It's not that he didn't care about his people before; it's just that he didn't think to show it. He started talking more personally to staff, asking how their lives were going, and he saw a dramatic shift in the ambience of his workplace and a more collaborative spirit developing.

Being able to engage people's stories is an indicator that we are building trust and a sense of community. People have to have a degree of trust to tell their story to others and when they do and people begin to know each other's stories, it creates a sense of connection and belonging, and trusting relationships. But this is delicate work.

As Jack Welch put it, "What we are building is fragile. It's built on trust. The process can be set back in a heartbeat by people at any level who see leadership as a process of intimidation, whose own lack of esteem makes them unable to trust and let go."[5] His message here is that *every* aspect of the business, including making budgets, running meetings, organizing projects, has to embrace certain values and ways of being in relationships in order to nurture trust. It also means that to develop trust you have to begin to trust, as former CEO Jim Dixon of Cellular One in San Francisco told us: "What I recognized with my partners is they can't distrust me if I trust them."

Trust makes business transactions—large and small—go more quickly, more efficiently, and be more sustainable. Hewlett-Packard's acquisition of

VeriFone went at lightning speed and with conditions congenial to both sides because, we were told, of the trust that developed at a personal level between the two companies' leaders.

We found in the companies we worked with that there were patterns in their values that guided their conversations and engaged their stories, which, when realized, made for positive connections and caring relationships. These ways of being were evident at all levels in the organizations—from CEO to receptionist. These ways of being were how they were with each other in the organization, and outside the organization with suppliers, customers, the community. Of course, not everyone; not all the time. But enough to make a difference. It was the very same buttercup. And it was this way of relating to each other that created a web of interdependent relationships that provided continuity for people in times of rapid change and fragmentation. And it's a practice every person in the organization can engage in as a way of making changes in the workplace. We call those values and behaviors a *relational practice.*

A Relational Practice:
The Value of Small Actions

Relational practice starts with you and how you interact. It begins with committing to cultivating and sustaining constructive relationships. It's committing to developing relational skills by attending to the *quality* of your exchange with people. Too often people in business feel they can't afford to spend time on relationships. Given what you know about the role of relationships in human complex systems, that they are the deep simplicity from which all else emerges, can you afford *not* to? It doesn't take a lot more time. You already spend time interacting; it's a question of *how* you spend that time and the quality of your exchange. Isn't it worth taking just a little bit longer to find out someone's point of view you don't understand, rather than summarily dismissing it as being off target?

It's a practice of developing personal awareness through *reflection and action*—an awareness of our impact on others and their effect on us, and being aware of the quality of the relationship itself and taking responsibility for "it." If "it" doesn't feel right, it needs to be addressed. It's seeing what you bring to relationships, what others bring, and being clear in representing yourself. It's avoiding knee-jerk reactions, and allowing time for reflection before action;

that is, responding, which engages rather than alienates. There aren't many things we can control in life, but we do have some control, some choices in our own behavior. As Visa's Dee Hock puts it, "The first and paramount responsibility is to manage one's self. One's own integrity, character, wisdom, knowledge, time, temperament, words and acts."[6] Change toward a more adaptive and humane workplace starts with each person willing to take an honest look at themselves and act accordingly.

A relational practice is a practice of small actions—the small things we say and do in our interactions that can engage or alienate, nourish or deplete. We may strive for great things, but life consists of small things. We may want to change the world, but it's our being that we can change. It's the small ways we are with people that can make a huge difference in the workplace, that can give us access to our own soul and the soul of others at work. It's the small things we say and do that determine whether we leave a trail of goodwill behind us or not.

The four A's of relational practice—be *authentic, acknowledge others,* be *accountable*, and be *attentive*—are about a way of being in these conversations that can generate positive connections and rewarding relationships. It's not about "building relationships," because relationships aren't structures that can be built and completed, and then left on their own. You heard some leaders in our stories talking about building relationships, which for them reflects the tension between a mechanistic language and a more moving, organic reality. Rather, like complex systems, relationships start with a connection that happens when people share a mutual interest in each other, and then they unfold and may develop, often in unexpected ways.

Cultivating relationships is a daily practice, like the other practices, to strive toward, to pay attention to. It's not about being this all the time, although that would be great, but *most* of the time, which sets the foundation for, and places value on, another way of *being* in the workplace, that nurtures trust, affiliations, and constructive conversations. It is a zen of relationship, beginning again and again.

Be Authentic

Authenticity is not a static state located in a moment of time. It flows from being truthful and open in the relationship, a constant practice of being more fully ourselves. Only when we take the risk to be authentic in how we represent ourselves and how we respond to others can we truly connect with each other and truly be present. Being authentically connected to others rather than disconnected is the only way to take on the challenges of the twenty-first century. As Andy Law told us, "Being honest with the public is not just the best way to work, but the only way to work in the future." Remember the comment of David Page, owner of the restaurant Home, about the plastic grin and tinny greeting with which wait staff all too often greet their customers. "It's just not genuine, and customers know it," he told us. "We try to teach our staff to be real, and the best way to do that is to be real yourself. It has to come from you." In a complex world, inauthenticity only complicates things and slows things down.

Being authentic is not always easy, because we may know what we think, but may be fearful of saying it out loud. We may find ourselves, as a result, disconnected from others who are not being authentic, because connection comes with mutuality. We may find ourselves in a contentious relationship, as poet and consultant David Whyte found himself in and challenged by saying, "Hey, you can't walk away. I'm angry with you and that means we have a relationship." But we also may find those stimulating connections that help us see more clearly, that enliven us, that join us to others. We also may find that saying the very thing we fear will alienate us, surprisingly connects us, when others listen to what we say and respond in a spirit of openness and trust. We may find by telling a dark secret about our work situation to another that they, too, hold the same secret, or are very sympathetic to it. All these unexpected and uncontrollable outcomes in relationships are part of the practice of authenticity.

Authenticity is a practice of reflection and action that builds trust because people in your organization, in other businesses, in your community know where you are really coming from. It's about learning to live deeply in your own truth. There are three starting points for developing authenticity in the workplace: listening to your language; a process of uncovering; and recognizing inauthenticity.

Starting Point 1: Listening to the Language

Capital Holding Corporation's Direct Response Group (DRG) took on reengineering. In telling their story, senior vice president Pamela Godwin said, "We're building a flexible system in modular parts. If one part becomes irrelevant in a year, we can throw it away."[7] Implicit in this statement is a view of the organization as an object with movable parts that can be replaced and even thrown away. But what is the system? Is it not a collection of people? And these modular parts—do they not consist of people, too?

Listening to the words, images, phrases, and metaphors we use in our conversations about the workplace reveals whether we are perpetuating a mechanistic, dehumanizing context, whether we are forging human connections or forging disconnections. Certainly, there is a problem with language, or a lack of language, to describe the relational world in a linear and reductionistic world of nondynamic words that assume stability, balance, and equilibrium. But the language we use does give us access to hearing the mechanistic mind. For instance, instead of engaging in the intricacies and complexities of human experience, do you demand simple solutions? Rather than appreciating the qualities in people, do you measure them? Does everything have to be quantified, calculated, categorized for it to exist? Do you stay on a linear path of control, and overlook the side effects of such an approach, which in fact are not on the side, but integral to the whole? Do you insist on reducing reality into models, and disregard metaphors? Do you minimize the human dimension in business, thus rendering people irrelevant? Listen for the omission of people in business talk.

Another example. In a small company of seventy-five people, a manager and co-director simultaneously resigned; events that would likely create some turmoil. A consultant was asked to assess the stability of the organization. His concern was with what measure he should use to determine if this was a significant change. Can you measure the emotional flux of insecurity and anxiety? Is it too simple a solution to consider talking to the people in the organization and providing a safe context for them to talk things through with each other as a way of determining the effects of the change?

In his discussion of the changing role of CEOs as coaches, AlliedSignal's CEO, Lawrence Bossidy, amplifies many aspects of complexity, such as a focus on interactions, a leader as empathic and connected to others. But he, too, slips into a mechanistic mind when he says that leaders "have a responsibility to make people as good as you can make them." Although altruistic, you don't make people—you make things. You create conditions which help people create themselves.

Similarly, Chris Argyris, in dispelling the myth of empowerment, says, "Clearly, if it is internal commitment that provides the kind of outcomes that CEO's say they want, then they must be realistic and judicious in their demands for it."[8] You can't demand commitment, just as you can't demand respect—it's not an object to extract and be given to you. Listen for objectification of people.

These are not personal criticisms, because we, in writing this book, struggle with it all the time. A mechanistic way of thinking and speaking has permeated all our minds, existing in all of us in varying degrees—the unacknowledged, unaware tendency to remove ourselves from the messiness of humanity. But rather, these examples can help us recognize the tension in our own thinking, the psychological struggle that we all face as we embrace a view of the business world that is a dynamic, changing, and organic one. To be authentic is to come to terms with our own tendencies.

Paying attention to how we speak is important, as the psychologist Jerome Bruner writes: "[Language] imposes a point of view not only about the world to which it refers but toward the use of mind in respect of this world. Language necessarily imposes a perspective in which things are viewed and a stance toward what we view."[9] Language shapes reality, and reality shapes language—a feedback loop. Listening to our language, hearing it in ourselves, gives us a choice to think differently, to consider other words, a chance to remember that businesses are human.

A language that speaks to care and connection, of relationship, is more suitable than the language of mechanistic efficiency and separateness when we are speaking of organizations that are concerned with reliability and adaptability. Are we looking for "tools" to fix problems rather than to better understand them? Are we seeking that "killer app," rather than engaging in the existing processes? Are we "applying" complexity, rather than recognizing that organizations are already complex systems? Are we asking how we get more productivity and creativity *out* of people, rather than cultivating their innate ingenuity? Are customers users? As Henry Mintzberg says, tongue-in-cheek, in his criticism of an article in *Fortune* magazine: "It's simple to calculate net present value. . . . The sum of years one-through-n is how much your customer is worth. . . . Just a few easier steps to a happier customer."[10] Listen to the language.

Starting Point 2: Uncovering the Secret Story

To engage in a process of uncovering is to speak the unspeakable, what British business professor Ralph Stacey calls the "undiscussables," and Canadian business professor Brenda Zimmerman calls the "wicked questions," in an effort to clear the deck and come clean. This inquiry reveals the "cover story"—what is espoused in the workplace, and the "secret story"—what is actually happening but not discussed. It's uncovering the "secret story" of failures and mistakes that already exist; the lack of trust; uncovering the need to be heard; uncovering where people feel excluded, disconnected, and resistant; uncovering repressed feelings, uncovering resonance and tension. Being authentic about what is really going on, which can be tough, is the only way businesses can have a chance at success because dealing with the real problems at hand, rather than soft-pedaling illusions, is the only way of resolving them. The process of uncovering is not about "coping" with difficulties, but rather "moving through" them, to stimulate and engage the process of unfolding through honest and direct discussion, as in John Kopicki insisting on people being straight rather than keeping secrets.

This is not an easy journey—"very painful" is how many in senior management described it at the Industrial Society, and as we saw for Dick Knowles when he was confronted by his team. But it is a necessary passage for real change in an organization.

It's asking yourself and challenging yourself with "Do I *dare* to say what I really see, think, and feel?"

Starting Point 3: Recognizing Inauthenticity

Authenticity is not a tactic for maneuvering for personal power, because, by its nature, you can't fake it. Instead it's tracking when you are being disingenuous. As Tony Morgan said, "It's about being observant of yourself when you're inauthentic," which can lead to more positive rather than negative outcomes. It's being aware of when you slip back into the old role, as Tony would catch himself doing. It's dropping the mask, as DuPont's Belle plant did when Dick Knowles invited the community to visit the plant and see what they were doing—the "protective shell was gone," he said, and instead a "permeable membrane where information flowed through both ways" was created.

Inauthenticity leads you to playing games, and as Dick Knowles said, "If you go back to playing games, you go right back to the hierarchy." But more than that, it's a waste of energy. Focusing on how you appear and looking good rather than connecting with who you are and to others are behaviors driven by insecurity, which diminishes rather than enhances people. People become preoccupied—busy covering for themselves, being on guard, trying to impress, dancing around issues. "Inauthenticity," Bob Shapiro said, "diverts energy and makes us tired at the end of the day, so it's an efficiency as well as a mental health issue." Being real rather than trying to look good is a lot simpler, makes life easier, and takes a lot less energy. When being authentic becomes a collective norm, there's a lot less destructive politicking going on and work relationships are a lot simpler and take a lot less energy. We heard many times in the companies we worked with that people experienced far less politicking than they faced in other companies they had worked for.

It's not only tracking inauthenticity in yourself but also listening for it in others. And beware of those who are inauthentic. At an information technology conference we attended, we were stunned by the audience's response to a speaker. Information systems people, by their own admission, are known to be next to the bottom on social skills in a wide range of professions, just above forest rangers, as they put it; and so, it appears, in their ability to recognize inauthenticity in others.

The presenter they absolutely loved, who had presented many times before and had an obvious rapport with the audience, was guiding them in social skills. One of his examples was that if they wanted a certain something, and the person they were with wanted something else, what they should say, he suggested, was "I just want you to be happy." The punch line? Saying it this way increases your chance of getting what you want, because the person you're with would think you were being considerate. In fact, the audience was being instructed on how to be manipulative and calculating. The message was that self-serving, inauthentic, manipulative behavior pays off. Wrong message for developing richly connected organizations and sustainable economic webs.

Acknowledge Others

Loyalty and commitment are closely associated to people's experience of being recognized as a person by the people they work with and for. We saw this with Janet Biedron at Muhlenberg Medical Center, who said of her manager, "She sees I'm an honest player," and who in turn was fiercely loyal to her and gave 200 percent. Rhonda Owens, whom Janet managed, felt the same way about Janet—it just spreads.

It's important to make visible a job well done, as we saw with Tony Morgan in proclaiming his heroes, but also, as we saw at the Industrial Society, appreciating noble attempts, even when they fail. Loyalty and commitment were also engendered when people were recognized for their altruistic attempts and community efforts, as we saw at VeriFone, such as the VeriGift program, where people donated vacation time for others with personal crises. In other words, recognizing others is not just about money.

Money is effective as a motivator, but it has its limits. The soul's need for affiliation and connection with others can't be met with pecuniary benefits; rather, it is met with acknowledgment. If people feel devalued, invisible, not supported, they aren't going to give you their best, no matter how much money you throw at them—they'll do enough to get by. Acknowledging people for their intrinsic value as human beings with lives, in addition to their functional contributions, is a small change that doesn't cost anything, takes so little, and can make a big difference. But it has to be authentic.

Acknowledging people is expressing appreciation; it's being able to empathize and put yourself in other people's shoes; it's that small "thank you"; that small "well done"; and that small offering of "what can I do to help" that has an amazing impact on people. Acknowledging people means you know their story enough that you can see their impact on the organization and genuinely appreciate it. And it's good business, as John Kopicki pointed out: "People hunger for recognition and when they receive it they are extremely motivated."

When we consider people as part of complex adaptive systems, different kinds of behaviors take on value. Behaviors that facilitate the web of connections are important because connections enhance the organization's effectiveness in traditional business terms. It's recognizing and acknowledging the relational work done in organizations that is not part of the job description and is often invisible.

It's acknowledging and valuing the following behaviors:

Conduits—the ones who spread news within the organization, the good things people have done, the concerns that need to be dealt with, keeping people informed, and so enriching and fueling a positive work atmosphere.

Coordinators—people who on their own organize things that benefit the whole and the greater good.

Connectors—those who generously connect people to each other, helping them get what they need.

Coherers—those who keep things together and running smoothly by dealing with all the messy details so others can move forward.

It's acknowledging these behaviors that are already there but often not validated and, too often, taken for granted.

As authenticity serves in the interest of trust, acknowledging others serves in the interest of justice. Who have you appreciated today?

Be Accountable

Accountability is moving out of the blame/victim mode. Do you admit to mistakes? Can you be wrong? Do you own up to failures? Or do you point to others, try to sneak away, dance around the issue, rationalize, make excuses?

Accountability is admitting what you don't know. As we saw at DuPont's Belle plant, it's far more efficient for managers to say to the front-line people, "We don't know how to do this." And as we saw at VeriFone, people were supported in getting help, but it was up to the person to ask.

Accountability is striving to keep your word, as we saw at the Industrial Society, to be as good as your word, and when you mess up, it's taking responsibility for it. Claiming rather than denying human vulnerability builds inner strength and is more forgivable than denying it. It's caring enough to meet your commitments and taking responsibility for them—to customers, co-workers, and with the community at large. And when people are members of teams, accountability, as we said, fluctuates between the individual and collective levels.

Accountability serves in the interest of integrity. To what degree will you take responsibility?

Be Attentive

Being attentive is a total commitment of looking, listening, sensing, feeling, intuiting, being. It's coming back to your senses to gain common sense.

Being attentive to others is as Hatim Tyabji pointed out "to take a deep interest in people." At VeriFone, this interest and care is even institutionalized in their many programs for VeriFoners. It is, as Hatim says, "being sensitive to the people in the organization—that's what really makes the organization tick."

To be attentive is to be curious about a person's story, because we all have one. It's Mary Anne Keyes at Muhlenberg sitting down with an employee whose child was having problems, and knowing those three hours spent hearing her story would come back fourfold. Or as Will Pape at VeriFone said in regard to global partners, "How can I see it their way?" It's Sheridan McGuire at the Industrial Society asking people how they want to shape their work.

Being attentive is most of all listening. People often ask for tools for listening—it's your ear. It's listening with a human ear—whether you listen empathically, whether you listen for resonance, whether you listen for what people need, yearn, desire. Theoretical, technical, technological solutions divorced from human listening are useless. We saw how attentive VeriFone was to their customers; we saw how attentive the Babels were to customers, by developing seminars that responded to their customers' needs, and to their community; we saw how David Page and Barbara Shinn were genuinely attentive to the needs of their customers and their staff at Home restaurant. But listening is not enough—it's responding and acting on what you hear and, as we saw in VeriFone and Muhlenberg Medical Center and others, with immediacy. Being attentive serves to enhance your presence as well as others' and gives access to awakening the collective soul at work.

● ● ●

And finally, a relational practice is a path of listening to and speaking from the heart, not just the mind. It can shift an atmosphere of fear and uncertainty to one of positive energy that is palpable, felt, and coherent, which would characterize all these organizations—a place where people can take pride and joy in their work, support each other and grow and learn within a web of relationships. These relational practices are a pathway to *amplify* and *bring into being* the positive dynamics of organizations as complex adaptive systems, which leads to a positive feedback loop, to business success and to a more humane and lively workplace.

Chapter 18

Care-nections and the Soul at Work

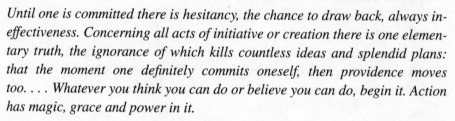

Until one is committed there is hesitancy, the chance to draw back, always ineffectiveness. Concerning all acts of initiative or creation there is one elementary truth, the ignorance of which kills countless ideas and splendid plans: that the moment one definitely commits oneself, then providence moves too. . . . Whatever you think you can do or believe you can do, begin it. Action has magic, grace and power in it.

Goethe

Prediction is difficult, as Niels Bohr said, especially about the future. But of one thing we can be certain: as we enter the twenty-first century, business organizations, and society as a whole, will be riding the tsunami of Great Change. How business leaders as *individuals* navigate these uncertain waters will determine which organizations will survive and thrive, and which will sink. How business leaders *collectively* navigate these waters will determine whether society will survive and thrive, or drift into a maelstrom of unimaginable human catastrophe, if the natural environment, already under great strain, is pushed into collapse. The future is fraught with peril, for individuals, for institutions and business organizations, and for human civilization. Business is now the most potent force for social transformation in the world, and with that power comes responsibility to act for the collective good. We therefore also face a time of great opportunity, for those with eyes that are open to seeing a different way of being in the world, and heart enough to commit to it.

Changing Lives, Recasting Landscapes

The revolution in communications technology—and it is a revolution, in terms of new channels and falling costs—already affects us all, in ways small and large. We can shop for groceries on the Internet, for instance; we can download data from libraries, museums, and other institutions around the world, perhaps for a work project or a hobby, effectively visiting these remote places, in mind if not in body; and we can seek out like-minded individuals or groups, forming communities in cyberspace; and individuals no longer have to be in an urban setting to be an integral part of the world of commerce, but can conduct business locally, nationally, or even globally from remote locations; all without leaving our home or office. Our daily lives as individuals have already changed.

And our lives as members of organizations have already changed, too, as the same technology begins to recast the landscape of business. In the connected economy, driven as it is by the communications revolution, companies find themselves as players in a fluid, constantly vacillating economic web, where their fate is affected by the behavior of other members to a degree unprecedented in the world of business as we knew it. The pace of innovation and of forming and re-forming alliances among companies creates an environment of urgency in the workplace that is also unprecedented in the world of business as we knew it.

With this urgency comes exhilaration, certainly; but also stress and uncertainty about the future. Stress for everyone in the organization, not just for CEOs and senior executives, who traditionally have shouldered the burden of steering a safe course for their companies; but stress also for middle management, supervisors, and front-line people, who don't know what their job will be tomorrow, or even if they will have a job at all. And as the pace of innovation and vibrancy in the web picks up—even escalates, as it surely will—urgency, exhilaration, stress, and uncertainty will inevitably increase, too.

Our central argument has been that, because business organizations are complex adaptive systems, not the mechanistic entities that traditional business thinking has assumed, the new science of complexity offers a new way of thinking for people at all levels of business in this new environment. It offers leaders a new way of thinking about their company at two levels: first, the company as a whole, as a living entity in itself, and as a member of an economic web, which we will discuss here under the heading "The Connected

Economy"; and second, the company as a collective manifestation of its peo-ple and how they work together, which has been our principal concern in this book, and is addressed here as "The Care-nected Organization."

The Connected Economy

As we said in an earlier chapter, economic webs have always existed, but they were limited in the number of connections within the web, limited in their geographic extent, and limited in their pace of change. In the connected econ-omy, all that shifts, big-time: there are, and will be, many more connections in each company's web; webs are, and increasingly will be, more geographically extensive, and often global; and they are changing, and will continue to change, at a vastly greater and accelerating rate, in terms of who is a member and who is not, and in the nature of the interactions, when competitors become collaborators, and collaborators become competitors, or perhaps are both at the same time.

In the connected economy of the twenty-first century, the future will not be a continuation of the past, so that you cannot figure out how to operate in the fu-ture by looking to what you were doing yesterday or even today. Leaders who embrace web thinking need to find ways of seeing the company's strengths and weaknesses—its future potential—as manifested in its adaptive landscape, which maps what the company *can* do against what it *needs* to do in the pre-vailing business environment; leaders need to find ways of seeing opportunities and potential dangers in their interactions with competitors, collaborators, and complementors; and they need to embrace the uncomfortably high degree of uncertainty and unpredictability that is inherent in life in the web.

As we've said many times, the shift in thinking that is required to work in the way the world *really is,* not as it has been or as many still fervently *wish it would be,* is hard, even for those who acknowledge that it is inescapable, if survival is the goal. It is much easier for leaders to talk about the new organi-zational structures that are appropriate for success in the connected economy than it is to take on the personal challenge of letting go of the illusion of con-trol and a predictable, ordered world. Recognizing limited control feels hard in the most settled of times, and it might seem impossible—or even irrespon-sible—when you don't know what will take its place. But it is essential for continued survival. We want to stress very clearly, however, that the new style of management is *not* simply doing nothing and waiting for good—or bad—things to happen. And it is *not* about concentrating only on change, because the business must accomplish day-to-day goals, too. As we saw in the stories, the new style of management is more about creating conditions for the organization to be successful in the new environment. These leaders seek ways to *influence* their organizations rather than control them, recognize that diversity is not fragmentation, that economic dynamism is not deterioration, perspectives which lead to a greater capacity to adapt and evolve. And it is still an experiment in progress, and probably always will be.

In the connected economy of the twenty-first century, the successful companies will be those that are highly adaptable and agile, and probably small. In 1965, Fortune 500 companies accounted for one fifth of jobs in the United States; that figure has halved, to one tenth, and continues to fall. *Small is now big,* and will get bigger. In the United States, small companies currently innovate at twice the rate of large ones, and account for 80 percent of exports, because small companies can more easily be adaptable and agile in a fast-changing business environment. This trend to increasing ascendancy of the small over the big will continue. In the connected economy of the twenty-first century, the business landscape will be dominated by dynamic economic webs of small companies, constantly changing, constantly innovating. The mega-mergers of the 1990s will probably be seen in retrospect as more an expression of a mechanistic mind-set that was retreating to the familiar ground of hierarchy and control in *reaction against* the uncertainties of the business environment of today and tomorrow, rather than an appropriate, creative *response to* it. And the difficulties that many of these mergers face might be attributed to the ineffectiveness of a mechanistic perspective in dynamic times—that businesses are not merging with a static entity, but rather with a living organism of which they will and should engage in a dynamic feedback loop.

We said that prediction is hard, perilous even, but here is one. In the connected economy of the twenty-first century, women leaders will not only be a greater force than they are now, as the barriers of gender bias continue to erode, but they also will become a major force. In the United States, women own more than 40 percent of businesses and are starting new businesses at twice the rate for men, according to the Small Business Administration. More to the point here, however, is that the style of management practice that most effectively enhances the business success of companies as complex adaptive systems includes close attention to genuine relationships and to recognizing and creating webs of interdependence. In the Western world, this feminine talent is much more developed in women than in men. Although we saw it expressed in the male leaders we worked with, most women quite naturally find it easier to work that way than do most men. Male leaders who want to be successful in the new economy will need to put away the traditional macho mask of leader as lone ranger, and find this more feminine faculty in themselves; or, probably in many instances, simply uncover what they feel they have had to hide. Life in economic webs is hard for everyone; and, remember, in the world of spiders the females dominate, often having the males for supper!

Beyond Complexity Science As Science

In our work, we were led to look at organizations as complex adaptive systems, those that structurally were flat, and encouraged rich, open communication. What we found within these organizations was a dynamic vortex of five levels of relationships: 1, between individuals; 2, among teams; 3, to the CEO, or, more particularly, the organization's purpose. Further, 4, the organizations had relationships with other organizations and to the community. Last of all, and most tenuously developed in most companies as of yet, 5, there is a relationship to the natural environment. This nested set of relationships represents a new view of organizational dynamics, within and without the organization. Understanding these dynamics identifies the source of creativity and adaptability in business and leads to different behaviors. In short, it is a new theory of business. It is a theory, rather than a collection of actions with desired outcomes, because it flows from a new understanding of what organizations are and how they work, informed by the science of complexity.

We don't have to bring complexity to the business world, because businesses are and always have been complex adaptive systems. The secret of success in the new business environment is simply to recognize that fact, and then work appropriately with the principles of such systems in a human context, as we describe in this section. Recognizing that businesses are complex adaptive systems means understanding that they fluctuate between different states, from static to chaotic, with the zone of creativity in between. Different states are appropriate for different times, as we explained earlier: a static state, when the environment is little changing and certain; and a chaotic state, when old patterns need to be broken through, to be replaced by something new, but as yet unknown; and the zone of creative adaptability, when innovation is necessary. Complexity-guided management doesn't just toss out traditional mechanistic management models, but rather encompasses and expands them.

One of the most powerful of human abilities, which, however, is too often undervalued, is intuition. It is therefore not surprising that many astute business leaders have already intuited what we have made explicit, that is, a way of working with organizations as complex adaptive systems, and have had success: Intel and Hewlett-Packard are prominent examples. Others can learn those ways, and profit by doing so, both in the realm of human fulfillment and traditional business success.

Many aspects of management practice guided by the principles of complexity science are already alive and well in some organizations, either through people's intuitions of what seems right, or as parts of business theories, particularly in human relations management and Peter Drucker's work. What we have done is identify an intellectual framework for these behaviors collectively, and have formed them into a coherent whole based on a scientific understanding of the dynamics of business organizations. We can see that these behaviors—such as authenticity, respecting others for who they are, tapping into the intelligence and wish to contribute in everyone in the organization—are efficacious in the business environment, not because being "nice" to people is a good and human thing to do, which, of course, it is; but because we are engaging the dynamics of the complex adaptive system, and moving the system to the zone of creative adaptability. This is what we saw in the companies we worked with, and we know that there are many pockets of people exploring the same avenues in other businesses. Complexity science validates these behaviors, if you like, and brings them all together under an umbrella of this new theory of business.

If you have been pursuing this style of management—either in part or whole—you no longer have to defend being "soft," because now you know *why* it works, not just that it *does* work. And, of course, you know that far from being soft, it is very hard, and requires strong interpersonal skills. But it is worthwhile, if you are seeking business success as well as creating a supportive, congenial work environment. If you have not been pursuing this style of management, we hope that you will be persuaded of the logic of doing so. In the connected economy of the twenty-first century you cannot afford to try to succeed with management methods that were developed in a different age and for a different type of business environment. You might succeed for a while, but ultimately you will falter.

We said that the principles of complexity science led us to a deeper understanding of the true dynamics of business organizations, because they share those dynamics with other systems that the science is studying. It has been important to have the science behind us, because simply following intuitive impulses might lead to a decent way of working—for a while; but it would have no foundation. Having said that, however, we would argue that the experience of working with organizations as complex adaptive systems has advanced the science in a way, too; that is, in the human dimension.

Science, by tradition anyway, needs to be analytical, needs to be able to define its terms and conditions, which is why scientists often choose to work with simple systems, such as, in the complexity realm, computer models: they are amenable to these needs. Human social systems—including the business environment—are far more complex than computer models are at present and probably will be for a very long time, and perhaps for all time. The science has done its job: it has brought us to a position of seeing organizations through new eyes. It might, through further advances, illuminate organizations in ways we don't yet see. But businesspeople no longer need constantly to seek the validation of the science for each new way we might feel—through intuition—is right to work with organizations as complex adaptive systems. We cannot describe organizational behavior with the rigor that complexity scientists—or any scientists—would recognize as scientific, and we might never be able to do so. But we can now claim to have a deeper sense of organizations as complex adaptive systems than even the most prescient manager did previously. We can claim the emergent understanding of our organizations as our own.

Sustainability and the Fifth Relationship

We said that the least developed of the five levels of relationship that a complexity science view of business has given us is organizations' relationship to the natural environment, which is a complex adaptive system on the largest of scales. Each of us, by nature, has a connection with nature: biophilia is part of the deep being of *Homo sapiens*. And yet each of us as individuals is part of a collective enterprise that is putting tremendous strain on the natural systems upon which our continued existence as a species depends.

The press of producing more food for a population of six billion, and growing rapidly, and the press of building new cities, infrastructure, and harvesting raw materials, is causing species to become extinct at an alarming rate, a rate that is rapidly approaching the extent of the extinction that put an end to the long reign of the dinosaurs sixty-five million years ago. That event was the fifth such massive collapse of life in earth history, the fifth so-called mass extinction. If the world's economic machine continues to operate in the future as it has in the past in relationship to the natural environment, we risk precipitating another mass extinction, the sixth in earth history, in which we would not only be its cause but also likely one of its victims.[1] Polls in the United States and in Europe show that threats to environmental health are a rising public concern, for good reason. In the twenty-first century, that concern will grow even sharper.

As Monsanto's CEO Bob Shapiro expressed so cogently, business must urgently turn its huge talents to finding ways of operating that produce the goods and services—particularly food—we want, while doing no further damage to the environment, if business wants to stay in business. Only by paying more attention—serious attention—to its relation to the natural environment, its impact on the environment, and ways to ameliorate and reverse it, can business lead to a sustainable economy. The demands—known and unknown—of the connected economy are not the only challenge businesspeople at all levels face in the twenty-first century. Our continued existence as a species—or at least a level of civilization that Western society currently enjoys—also depends on new business thinking, through addressing the fifth relationship in an innovative and responsible manner. But herein lies an opportunity as well—an economic boom for those companies who deal with environmental issues. Those who work on avoiding ecological calamity will drive a new economy based on renewable resources.

The twenty-first century will be a time when business generally can exercise its enormous potential for social change and good in a realm where traditionally, and for most companies at any rate, its impact has been for the worse. It can begin one company at a time, slowly building a critical mass of collective awareness and responsibility. But the ultimate challenge for our business leaders is to find a way to join together, as secretary general of the United Nations Kofi A. Annan stated recently, "in a global compact of shared values and principles that can give a human face to the global market." This is in the areas, he goes on to say, "of human rights, labor standards, and environmental practice."[2] The connected economy is a fact of life, but without the private sector's active commitment and support in enacting a set of core values, a connected economy is more vulnerable to being a collapsed economy. As Kofi Annan concludes, "If we want to maintain the global markets and multilateral trading systems, all of us have to make the right choices now."

The Care-nected Organization

We said earlier that, in addition to giving leaders a holistic view of their companies as members of an economic web in the connected economy, a complexity perspective gives a new way of thinking about organizations as the collective manifestation of its people and how they work together. Again, the three relationships within the organization are: relationship between people; among teams; and to the organization's purpose. The key action—as in true, *felt* action—that strengthens connections, enriches relationships, and leads the organization as a whole to business success is care, hence the care-nected organization. Care may not sound like the typical business power word, but as we saw in these stories, it is indeed a power action.

Getting There from Here

So how do we get *there,* the new business environment of the twenty-first century, from *here,* from the way things work now? We said that business is and will be the most potent force for social transformation in the world. That social transformation begins at home. We know the centrality of relationships for change and business success from the science of complexity. And we know the importance of mutuality as the foundation of these relationships, in spite of the power differences that may exist between people. We get *there* from *here* by recognizing that the greatest, and largely untapped, resource of the business community is the power of caring and connected relationships for creating constructive change—adaptability, innovation, and productivity. It's also caring, connected relationships that make stressful situations tolerable. Recognizing this reframes our business concerns to the level that all work is relationship. The work of relationships, acting from care with an intent to connect, taps into what has been dormant and is still waiting in our organizations—people's desire to be fully engaged as human beings in the workplace. It's seeing what has always been there.

Businesses that take the relational dimension seriously will be the successful businesses of the future, because that's where good people want to work and where people will give their best. Because *there,* relationship is humanship and humanship engages the soul at work. We saw how engaging the soul at work releases enormous potential for change and engages processes where the system can heal itself. Engaging our need for human affiliation, our tribal instinct, brings *there* into being and another way of working.

That "being" is guided by a different shared purpose. A machine has a *sole* purpose; a human organization has a *soul* purpose. The soul purpose is not about money; it's about actualizing dreams of a higher purpose that serve the greater good. That might be eliminating paper from the business world, as those at VeriFone are working to do, which helps businesses, like banks, spend less time and money on paper, and which also adds benefit to the environment. It may be bringing beauty to homes, as the Babels do. Or it may be a lofty goal like Monsanto's, dealing with feeding the world. The most humble products can and do contribute to the whole—it's identifying *how* it contributes that engages us. When a collective understanding of values and purpose is realized, questions of motivation and productivity become irrelevant—people know what to do, and do it. Engaged in work, bonded by a common and larger purpose, aware of belonging, the soul purpose emerges and generates the spirit of the organization, team spirit, and community spirit.

To get *there,* where the soul is at work, is not just a step-by-step adaptation, but rather about big leaps. Leaping into newness and unexplored territory with an open and alert mind and heart. Entering a different reality can feel very unreal—it's disorienting at first being *there* when you're used to being *here,* especially when *there* is and will always be changing. It's doing exactly what we fear: stepping into the unknown.

Breaking the Silence Barrier

We know that people want to love to go to work, want to love their work, and want to feel a camaraderie and a bond with the people that they work with.

They want dignity in their work. Although many long for this goal, it seems only a lucky few experience it. One of the greatest barriers to actualizing this reality in our organizations, for creating an environment of high adaptability and creativity, is not control, but fear. What drives controlling behavior is fear of the unknown. As odd as it may sound, holding on to something familiar, even if it's misery, is often more comfortable than stepping into the uncontrollable, the unforeseen, and the unexpected. We may feel unhappy with our jobs, but all too soon it feels like too much work to do anything about it; we get tired, and just go on with our old ways. Even when we may make that leap into the unfamiliar and try something different in our organizations, daily stresses make it easy to regress to old ways of being and doing. We saw, with many leaders in our stories, that powerful pull back to the old.

Facing the unknown is difficult because we feel vulnerable when we don't know. Not knowing in the business world can feel dangerous—we fear we might seem foolish or be diminished by others. The pace of work helps us to run away from our fears, but we can't continue the current pace that distances us from our humanity and humanness, where we sacrifice personal and family lives.

Although the unknowns that come with change are largely uncontrollable, we do have some control in how we face them. We do have control in how we think about the unknown, and this is important, because how we *think* about things leads us to *feel* certain ways. When we face the unknown, what we come nose-to-nose with is uncertainty. But most of us don't really allow uncertainty in its fullest meaning. Being uncertain means it can go either way, for better or worse, or nowhere. What we often tend to do is think the worst. When we think the worst, we feel anxious and fearful; then we try to get control. What if we allowed ourselves to be genuinely uncertain; that is, allowing the paradox of good and bad outcomes to coexist? We know that paradoxes are a gateway to the zone of creative adaptability. What if we influenced the dynamics in this zone with positive thinking? What if we faced the unknown with *curiosity,* wanting to find out? What if we allowed ourselves to be open to surprising unfoldings, to the mysterious processes at work, that complexity science is uncovering? What if we had *faith* in those processes? When these processes are being influenced by caring connections rather than by indifference and disconnection, we can have faith in them. We can at least have control in how we engage in this unknown journey—with humility, and whether we leave a trail of goodwill behind us or not.

Silencing fears, not allowing them to be expressed, creates an invisible barrier to information flows in organizations. What if we broke the barrier of silence about our fears and uncertainties and talked to each other about them and collectively addressed them? We saw as in the case of the Industrial Society what a powerful move it was on Tony Morgan's part to address the fears that lurked and immobilized his people. Addressing fears is also a powerful way of discovering who your true allies are, who is really there with you. In truth, silent fears carry a magnitude that spoken fears don't. Once said, listened to, and addressed, fears have a way of shrinking in power.

Personal Deep Work: Passion

Getting *there,* to a new way of being and working for business success, starts with *deep work,* personally and collectively. Personally, deep work means developing a caring and connected relationship to yourself in terms of your work, that is, to reflect on what you are doing and why you are doing it. It's listening to your heart's desire, to what you really care about. Each and every person is responsible for finding *your* work, for discovering what engages *your* soul, whether it is at the workplace or elsewhere. Obviously, if you are reading this book, engaging your soul at work matters to you. Then take it seriously. Ask yourself, whether you work in a hospital, restaurant, publishing house, construction, retail, or whatever, "What am I passionate about; what is my passion?" It's asking it until you know, and then acting on it. It's not waiting around for someone else to see it in you. When we connect to our passion, then work becomes love.

We saw the plausibility of work as love in our stories. Certainly, it's easier at Monsanto, where people can instantly respond to, and care about issues like world hunger. But even at the Babels' paint and decorating store, Jeanne Babel saw "a potential in everyone to get excited about what they do at work." Cultivating people's passion and getting people on board with the soul purpose is, she says, "fundamental to creating an innovative environment." In the Industrial Society, the metaphor "jelly in the box" holds true for these organizations in their overall effort to accommodate the way people are in the world more— from Hatim Tyabji, who personally found more challenging work for an employee of VeriFone who was about to leave, to a careless worker at DuPont's

Belle plant who became enthusiastic and excited when he found work there that he could be passionate about at the same plant. "When people begin to discover meaning in their work," as Dick Knowles said, "you develop a real community that way." And we saw that when passion is engaged, people can be more and can do more, as in how people responded to Tony Morgan's question "What more can you do?" To connect to your passion is a different and deeper approach to work than the traditional way of fitting into a job description. It's deeper than just doing whatever happens to fall in your lap; it's deeper than working for power and its benefits, because it's taking yourself, your life, your work seriously.

Finding our passion is a personal journey into *dream time,* awakening our imagination of what might be possible, of reclaiming or newly discovering our dreams, of learning to listen to the longings in the soul—what touches us, moves us, compels us, reverberates in us in our world of work. It's seeking those caring, connected relationships that will guide us. We saw in our stories that the leaders cultivated distributed leadership throughout their organizations, and that unlikely people often became trailblazers into the future. We saw that many people found themselves in unexpected and unimaginable places in terms of their work—that's the nature of being in complex systems. It's recognizing that more is possible than we can imagine. We *are* much more, and can *do* much more, than we now think, as is evident during times of crisis. Our future businesses will need much more from people, both in leadership and support positions, in order to deal with the future problems, many of enormous magnitude, that will beset us. We need everyone on board with themselves.

To inquire about your passion places the responsibility of your work life squarely in your lap. This inquiry may lead to recognizing that the organization you're in is not right for you, if what is dear to your heart is not possible. It means seriously considering whether you can continue work which doesn't express your care. It might mean finding organizations that are more aligned with who you are; it's finding your pack.

Each and every one of you has to believe, if you do not already know, that you have something to contribute. We all have a calling, if we will take time to listen. Connecting with our individual purpose will make us more whole as people, and benefits the whole—no matter how small, or humble, or grand that offering might be. Every offering, from a cup of coffee served with kindness, to forging global alliances, is needed for the health of the whole. It's taking pride in your work, ennobling it with care, no matter what it is. It's also being grateful for all the many offerings that come our way, that serve the whole, such as the invisible people who come and clean our offices every night. Not many organizations have the courage to go as far as St. Luke's did in expressing collective recognition through sharing out the company's equity equally among all, from chairman to housekeeper. But think of the power of that. This is good work. And needless to say, it is very difficult work. It takes a strength of character that some might say is in limited supply in the workplace today. But, we would argue, it is waiting to be awakened in many.

When people are aligned to their purpose, when the gap between values and behaviors closes, what people experience is a stream of *ease,* because they are finally in their element. That's not to say there aren't challenges and hardships; that, too, is equally a vital process of the soul at work. But recognizing when the ease comes is to bring into being what has always been there and waiting to be engaged—our innate resourcefulness, intelligence, creativity.

Collective Deep Work

Future success for organizations is collectively doing *deep work* now. People collectively in an organization asking themselves what they care about, what they need, and what they can give to the soul purpose can be a way of reorganizing an organization to be more effective, because people aligned with their passion are fully engaged, fully involved people and they're more effective.

We said in the beginning of this chapter that organizations will need to consider how they can benefit the greater good. You can't serve others well if your own organization is dysfunctional. Deep work places the work of reevaluating operating policies, business goals, a learning environment within a context where authentic, connected, caring relationships are also being cultivated. It's doing work not in boxes but with people. That is to say, cultivating honest conversations about business concerns that include our uncertainties and anxieties, our not knowing. Only through these kinds of conversations, which are supported by the quality of relationships between people, can a true reality and a real assessment of the organization emerge and with it an opportunity to address what really is. Only by addressing what really is can an organization genuinely evolve, adapt, learn, and be sustainable, as we saw with the Industrial Society and Muhlenberg Medical Center, for example.

Organizations that undertake deep work, we also saw, can be expressive in their care and don't have to worry so much about sexual harassment suits because, underpinning these expressions, which is missing in harassment cases, is a connected relationship between people.

Deep work also includes actively addressing our collective interdependence, within the organization, between organizations, with nature. When we commit to an action of care in terms of our interdependence, then supporting each other in our individual and collective endeavors is the way to go. The point here is about keeping a tension of a multiplicity of values alive, that is, the tension between making choices for the collective or for the individual. If we act only from self-interest and choose only in terms of the individual rather than also making choices that benefit others and the whole, the entire system is affected. We don't rise alone and we don't fall alone. As we saw in the Industrial Society, people supported each other because they came to see that your problem is my problem. We may evolve on our own, but that's limiting; we co-evolve in our organizations only to the extent that we mutually support each other.

Again, deep work is hard work. These kinds of work relationships demand the best in us—a generosity of spirit. And this generosity of spirit is not easily accessible when jobs are being cut, people are being fired, cultures are changing with mergers. But when we can remember what's important to us, what we need to do and our work, especially during difficult times, it can be a way of weathering those storms.

The successful organizations of the twenty-first century are care-full organizations. They cultivate people, encourage participation, and work toward creating a fulfilling work environment. Able to engage people's stories and dreams, and patient and diligent with the unfolding of the soul purpose, these organizations listen, respond, intuit. They find their unique way guided by a deep simplicity—a place within each of us that cares and desires a sense of connection with others. It starts with a commitment and a small action. As writer Anaïs Nin put it, "We don't see things as they are, we see them as we are." And we are and can be more than we think we are.

Notes

Chapter 1: Relationships: The New Bottom Line in Business

1. A. S. Grove, *Only the Paranoid Survive,* Doubleday Currency, 1996, page 123.
2. J. Micklethwait and A. Wooldridge, *The Witch Doctors,* Times Books, 1996, page 14.
3. Ibid.
4. "The Anti-Management Guru," *The Economist,* April 5, 1997, page 64.
5. T. S. Kuhn, *The Structure of Scientific Revolutions,* 3rd edition, University of Chicago Press, 1996.
6. T. Morris, *If Aristotle Ran General Motors,* Henry Holt, 1997, page ix.
7. Ibid., page 7.
8. P. Senge, Foreword to A. de Geus, *The Living Company,* Harvard Business School Press, 1997, page x.
9. A. Briskin, *The Stirring of the Soul in the Workplace,* Berrett-Koehler, 1998, page x.
10. J. B. White, "Re-Engineering Gurus Take Steps to Remodel Their Stalling Vehicles," *Wall Street Journal,* November 26, 1996, page 1.
11. G. Koretz, "The Downside of Downsizing," *Business Week,* April 28, 1997, page 26.
12. A. de Geus, "The Living Company," *Harvard Business Review,* March-April 1997, page 58.
13. Ibid., page 52.
14. Morris, *If Aristotle Ran General Motors,* page xiii.
15. Senge, Foreword to A. de Geus, page xi.
16. J. Bruner, *Actual Minds, Possible Worlds,* Harvard University Press, 1986, page 11.
17. Ibid., page 16.
18. J. Gleick, cited in T. Burlando, "Chaos and Risk Management," *Risk Management,* April 1994, page 60.

Chapter 2: The Vernal Pool

1. M. Pollan, "Dream Pond: Just Add Water. Then Add More," *New York Times,* January 22, 1998, page F1.

2. C. Crook, "Strategic Planning in the Contemporary World," *American Programmer,* March 1996, page 10.

3. G. Hamel, "Strategy Innovation and the Quest for Value," *Sloan Management Review,* Winter 1998, page 11.

4. J. Seely Brown, *Seeing Differently,* Harvard Business School Press, 1997, pages ix, x.

5. B. Goodwin, *How the Leopard Changed Its Spots,* Charles Scribner's Sons, 1994.

6. E. O. Wilson, *Consilience,* Alfred A. Knopf, 1998, page 70.

7. See, for example, J. H. Holland, *Emergence: From Chaos to Order,* Helix Books, 1998.

8. Interview with the authors, Cambridge, Massachusetts, August 1, 1998.

9. R. Lewin, *Complexity: Life at the Edge of Chaos,* Macmillan, 1992, pages 106–29.

10. S. Kauffman, *At Home in the Universe,* Oxford University Press, 1995.

11. A term coined by J. H. Holland, a pioneer of complexity science, at the University of Michigan, Ann Arbor.

12. See, for example, P. Senge, *The Fifth Discipline,* Doubleday Currency, 1994.

13. J. Gleick, *Chaos: Making a New Science,* Viking Press, 1987.

14. See, for instance, G. Morgan, *Images of Organization,* Sage Publications, 1997.

15. S. Overell, "Big Game Theory in the Workplace," *Financial Times,* August 8, 1997.

Chapter 3: Management in Wonderland

1. D. H. Freedman, "Is Management Still a Science?" *Harvard Business Review,* November-December 1992, page 27.

2. Cited in ibid.

3. Ibid.

4. Ibid.

5. M. F. Guillén, *Models of Management,* University of Chicago Press, 1994, page 12.

6. J. Pfeffer, *The Human Equation,* Harvard Business School Press, 1998, page xv.

7. R. Lewin, *Complexity: Life at the Edge of Chaos,* Macmillan, 1992, pages 172–96.

8. Guillén, *Models of Management,* pages 7–15.

9. P. F. Drucker, Introduction to *Mary Parker Follett: Prophet of Management,* P. Graham, ed., Harvard Business School Press, 1995, pages 1–9.

10. "The Powerful IT Organization," organized by CIO Communications, Orlando, Florida, April 26–29, 1998.

11. T. Peters, *Thriving on Chaos,* Harper Perennial, 1991, page 635.

12. D. Hock, cited in S. Caulkin, "Chaos Inc.," *Across the Board,* July-August 1995, page 36.

13. C. Crook, "Strategic Planning in the Contemporary World," *American Programmer,* March 1996, page 10.

14. S. L. Brown and K. M. Eisenhardt, *Competing on the Edge,* Harvard Business School Press, 1998, page 3.

15. Grove, *Only the Paranoid Survive,* page 130.

16. A. L. Goldberger, "Non-linear Dynamics for Clinicians: Chaos Theory, Fractals, and Complexity at the Bedside," *Lancet,* Vol. 347, 1996, pages 1312–14.

Chapter 4: The Consequences of Connections

1. A. M. Brandenburger and B. J. Nalebuff, "The Right Game: Use Game Theory to Shape Strategy," *Harvard Business Review,* July-August 1995, page 57.

2. J. F. Moore, *The Death of Competition,* Harper Business Press, 1996, page 10.

3. J. Baden, *Wall Street Journal,* August 19, 1991.

4. All the quotations by Stuart Pimm are from an interview with the authors, May 1, 1998.

5. W. B. Arthur, "Increasing Returns and the New World of Business," *Harvard Business Review,* July-August 1996, page 105.

6. All the quotations from Stuart Kauffman are from an interview with the authors, Cambridge, Massachusetts, May 1, 1997.

7. Kauffman, *At Home in the Universe;* U. Merry, "Organizational Strategy on Different Landscapes," www.edgeplace.com, Dr. Uri Merry's Web site.

8. J. Hagel III, "Spider Versus Spider," *McKinsey Quarterly,* No. 1, 1996, page 6.

9. Ibid., page 15.

10. A. Brandenburger and B. Nalebuff, *Co-opetition,* Doubleday Currency, 1996.

11. Hagel III, "Spider Versus Spider," page 6.

12. Arthur, "Increasing Returns," page 100.

13. Interview with the authors, Cambridge, Massachusetts, July 10, 1997.

Preamble: Complexity and Narratives

1. J. Bruner, "Life As Narrative," *Social Research,* Vol. 54, No. 1, Spring 1987, page 12.

2. J. Bruner, *Actual Minds, Possible Worlds,* Harvard University Press, 1986, page 5.

Chapter 6: St. Luke's: The Ox That Took Flight

1. "Precocious St. Luke's Is Adland's Wimbledon FC," *Campaign,* January 9, 1998, page 1.

2. Ibid., page 21.

3. A. R. Sorkin, "Gospel According to St Luke's," *New York Times,* February 12, 1998, page D1.

Chapter 8: Cornelia Street and River Café: Food for the Soul

1. "The Talk of the Town," *The New Yorker,* July 22, 1996, page 25.
2. J. Walsh, "The Ruth and Rose Experience," *The Independent Long Weekend,* April 26, 1997, page 3.

Chapter 9: DuPont: Down on the Plant

1. Interview with the authors, Sundance, Utah, October 28 and 29, 1997.
2. J. Gleick, *Chaos: Making a New Science,* Viking Press, 1987.
3. M. J. Wheatley, *Leadership and the New Science,* Berrett-Koehler, 1992.
4. J. Holusha, "Bracing for the Worst in Chemicals," *New York Times,* June 4, 1994, page A35.

Chapter 11: The Industrial Society: Free to Achieve

1. C. Mailer, P. Musgrave, and G. Demons, *History of the Industrial Society,* Industrial Society, 1986, page 20.

Chapter 12: Monsanto: Transformation of a Chemical Giant

1. R. Shapiro, in Monsanto Company's 1997 annual report, page 2.
2. Based on interview with the authors, Chicago, August 31, 1998.
3. M. M. Waldrop, *Complexity: The Emerging Science at the Edge of Order and Chaos,* Simon & Schuster, 1992.
4. J. Jacobs, *Death and Life of Great American Cities,* Vintage Books, 1993.

Chapter 13: Alchemists: Changing of the Guardian

1. C. Fishman, "Change," *Fast Company,* April-May 1997, page 64.
2. M. Bates and D.W. Keirsey, *Please Understand Me,* Prometheus Nemesis, 1984.
3. Senge, *The Fifth Discipline,* page 58.
4. Cited in Fishman, "Change," page 66.
5. Ibid., page 72.
6. Ibid.

7. Based on interview with the authors, May 10, 1997.
8. Based on interview with the authors, April 12, 1997.
9. Based on interviews with the authors, June 27, 1997, and September 9, 1998.
10. www.edgeplace.com

Chapter 14: The Buttercup Effect

1. H. Bortoft, *The Wholeness of Nature,* Lindisfarne Press, 1996, page 256.
2. This metaphor has been adapted for literary consistency from Gareth Morgan and Ric Irving's metaphor, "Farmers don't grow crops, they create conditions in which crops grow."

Chapter 15: Paradoxical Leadership

1. R. Greenleaf, *Servant Leadership,* Paulist Press, 1977.
2. R. Connors, T. Smith, and C. Hickman, *The Oz Principle,* Prentice Hall, 1994.
3. A. Bryant, *New York Times,* November 1, 1997, page 6.
4. N. Tichy and R. Charan, "The CEO As Coach: An Interview with AlliedSignal's Lawrence A. Bossidy," *Harvard Business Review,* March-April 1995, page 72.
5. H. Mintzberg, "Musings on Management," *Harvard Business Review,* July-August 1996, page 8.
6. Cited in D. Freeman, "Corps Values," *Inc.,* April 1998, page 100.
7. Senge, *The Fifth Discipline,* page 27.

Chapter 16: Emergent Teams

1. J. R. Katzenbach and D. K. Smith, *The Wisdom of Teams,* HarperBusiness, 1994, page 4.
2. P. F. Drucker, *Managing in a Time of Great Change,* Dutton, 1995, page 346.
3. J. R. Katzenbach et al., eds., *The Work of Teams,* Harvard Business School Press, 1998.
4. R. Batt, "Outcomes of Self-Directed Work Groups in Telecommunications Services," in P. B. Voos, ed., *Proceedings of the Forty-Eighth Annual Meeting of the Industrial Relations Research Association,* Industrial Relations Research Association, 1996, page 340.
5. "Work Week," *Wall Street Journal,* May 28, 1996, page A1.
6. Batt, "Outcomes," page 344.
7. J. Lowe, *Jack Welch Speaks,* John Wiley and Sons, 1998, page 103.
8. Batt, "Outcomes," page 346.

9. Drucker, *Managing in a Time of Great Change,* page 240.

10. B. Schlender, "Peter Drucker Takes the Long View," *Fortune,* September 28, 1998, page 168.

11. S. Covey, "Putting Principles First," in R. Gibson, ed., *Rethinking the Future,* Nicholas Brealey Publishing, page 38.

12. C. Argyris, "Empowerment: The Emperor's New Clothes," *Harvard Business Review,* May-June 1998, page 98.

13. Katzenbach and Smith, *Wisdom of Teams,* page 4.

14. Tichy and Charan, "The CEO As Coach," page 82.

15. J. Highsmith, "Messy, Exciting, and Anxiety-Ridden: Adaptive Software Development," *American Programmer,* April 1997, pages 23–29.

16. Covey, "Putting Principles First," page 38.

Chapter 17: Relational Practice

1. M. Meyerson, "Everything I Thought I Knew About Leaders Is Wrong," *Supplement to Fast Company: New Rules of Business,* page 6.

2. D. Hock, "Institutions in the Age of Mindcrafting" presented at Bionomic Annual Conference, San Francisco, October 22, 1994.

3. Mintzberg, "Musings on Management," page 6.

4. Lowe, *Jack Welch Speaks,* page 5.

5. Ibid., page 89.

6. Hock, "Institutions in the Age of Mindcrafting."

7. M. Hammer and J. Champy, *Reengineering,* HarperBusiness, 1994, page 191.

8. Argyris, "Empowerment," page 100.

9. Bruner, *Actual Minds, Possible Worlds,* page 121.

10. Mintzberg, "Musings on Management," page 8.

Chapter 18: Care-nections and the Soul at Work

1. R. Leakey and R. Lewin, *The Sixth Extinction: Patterns of Life and the Future of Humankind,* Doubleday, 1995.

2. K. A. Annan, *Boston Globe,* February 2, 1999, page A15.